MASTERING

NAVIGATION

AT SEA

Twenty years from now you will be more disappointed by the things you didn't do than by the ones you did. So throw off the bowlines. Sail away from the safe harbour. Catch the Tradewinds in your sails. Explore. Dream. Discover.

Mark Twain

Other books in the series

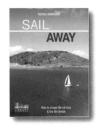

SKIPPER'S LIBRARY

MASTERING

NAVIGATION

AT SEA

DE-MYSTIFYING NAVIGATION FOR THE CRUISING SKIPPER

PAUL BOISSIER

FERNHURST
BOOKS

Published in 2020 by Fernhurst Books Limited.
The Windmill, Mill Lane, Harbury, Leamington Spa, Warwickshire. CV33 9HP, UK
Tel: +44 (0) 1926 337488 | www.fernhurstbooks.com

A catalogue record for this book is available from the British Library
ISBN 9781912621095

Front cover photograph © IM_photo / shutterstock.com
Back cover photography: Susie Boissier at the helm

All other photographs / illustrations © Paul Boissier execpt where indicated.
All charts © UKHO except where indicated.

Designed by Daniel Stephen
Printed in Malta by Melita Press

CONTENTS

PAUL BOISSIER
PROFESSIONAL NAVIGATOR

Paul Boissier has spent much of his professional career working on the sea, or in support of the people who go to sea, and in his leisure time he is an avid yachtsman.

In the Navy he commanded and navigated warships and submarines in many parts of the world, ending his career as a senior Admiral. He then spent 10 years as Chief Executive of the Royal National Lifeboat Institution, the charity that saves lives at sea and operates over 340 lifeboats around the UK and Republic of Ireland.

As a cruising yachtsman Paul has sailed his own boat around the UK, northern Europe and in the Mediterranean. He has also spent time afloat in other parts of the world as far apart as western Canada, South America and Australia.

This lifetime's experience has given him a unique perspective on navigation, from the bridge of a warship, to the cockpit of a cruising yacht and the control room of a submarine. And, of course, at the RNLI, his work often involved dealing with the consequences of navigational miscalculations by other water users.

Paul brings the subject to life in this book that is designed to help yachtsmen refresh their knowledge of, and their enthusiasm for, the timeless skills of navigation.

He loves the sea and has had a lifelong fascination with charts and navigation, as illustrated by his other two books written for Fernhurst Books:

Learn the Nautical Rules of the Road

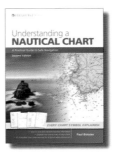

Understanding a Nautical Chart

INTRODUCTION

You only have to look at a globe, or a map of the world, to realise just how much of the surface of this planet is covered by water, and it doesn't take much thought to recognise the importance the oceans have to our everyday life and well-being. As sources of food, in the way they dictate our weather, their role as global trade highways, for their mineral deposits, recreation and the almost unbelievable diversity of life that they support

There's an extraordinary world out there, which sadly very few of us are lucky enough to witness at first hand. The sea is the world's last great wilderness: wild, untamed and more powerful than you can possibly imagine. There are no roads crossing it, and even today we actually understand very little about it. In 2018 the US National Oceanography and Atmospheric Administration (NOAA), estimated that:

"Currently, less than ten percent of the global ocean is mapped using modern sonar technology."

So, when you set out on a sea voyage, you really are going into the unknown. And you have to be prepared, because, for all its beauty, the sea doesn't even notice that you're there, and it's completely unforgiving of any weakness that it finds, in you or your vessel.

One of the greatest skills of seafaring is, and always has been, the art of navigation. Finding your way across a featureless seascape by day and by night is not simple, and it can be quite daunting until you build up a bit of experience.

I remember looking out at the sea when I first joined the Navy, wondering how on earth I was supposed to navigate a ship across that great, empty expanse. But in the end it's worth all those long hours of study – at home, and at sea – learning the timeless skills of navigation, because navigation unlocks the potential to explore the seas, and seafaring has a deep, visceral attraction for many of us.

We are fortunate today because, as navigators, we stand on the shoulders of the giants who went before us, and we have at our disposal the great array of skills, instruments and techniques that they developed. It wasn't always this simple. Two thousand years ago, seafaring generally meant adopting the 'point and shoot' method of navigation: head towards the setting sun, and with luck America will eventually appear in front of you. This was an imprecise and risky form of navigation, but it got the Vikings across the Atlantic and it allowed the Romans and the Phoenicians to open up the seas around Europe for maritime trade and travel.

Then came the astonishing invention of the magnetic compass, first used by the Chinese for maritime navigation about a thousand years ago, which allowed seafarers to steer a moderately accurate and consistent course across the water without relying on daymarks, luck or heavenly bodies. It didn't tell seafarers where they were, but it did make for more accurate voyages.

From the 15th century onwards, maritime charts became more accurate and more widespread, and people started to systematically record the position of heavenly bodies. This led, in the 16th-18th centuries, to a succession of increasingly accurate navigation instruments, all designed to measure the altitude of a celestial body – most commonly the sun or the pole star – which gave mariners the opportunity to calculate their latitude with a fair degree of accuracy. These instruments – backstaff, quadrant, octant and finally sextant – supplemented the simple directional reference provided by the compass and, with increasingly accurate charts, gave mariners the ability to estimate their position when out of sight of land. Returning to the English Channel from the Cape of Good Hope, you would go a good distance west into the South Atlantic, then head north, checking the midday altitude of the sun, and turn right when the sun told you that you had reached 50° of northern latitude. With a fair wind, clear skies and a little luck, the Lizard Lighthouse on the south coast of Cornwall would suddenly pop up over the horizon one day. That was the theory, although the history of shipwrecks around the Cornish peninsula shows that this was, quite literally, a hit-and-miss operation.

A sextant can give you a very accurate read-out of latitude, but to use it for longitude, you must take account of the earth's rotation – and for that you need an accurate time reference. In 1714, the growth of an increasingly ambitious global navy led the British parliament to offer a massive prize of £20,000[1] to anyone who could find a reliable way to determine longitude at sea. This famously encouraged John Harrison, the English clockmaker and carpenter, to develop a series of accurate maritime chronometers that allowed mariners, using some relatively simple spherical geometry[2], to get an accurate position, both latitude and longitude, from the observation of heavenly bodies.

Until recently, astronavigation was the main way of fixing a ship's position during long sea voyages. It's only in the last few decades that the introduction of long-range radio navigation aids – Loran, Decca, the Transit satellite navigation system and now GNSS[3] – have given everyone access to their precise location.

Even so, it would be a mistake to think of GPS as infallible. It's good seamanship to ask yourself what you would do if you suddenly lost access to your satellite navigation system? Would you know where you are, and would you be able to complete the voyage safely? Or would you join that august band of navigators who have, at some point in their career, found themselves 'temporarily uncertain of their position'?

There have certainly been times in my life when I would have found it difficult to say precisely where we were. And when this happens, you suddenly realise just how lonely the oceans are. That's when you need all of the knowledge and experience that you have accumulated over the years to slowly re-establish an accurate position.

I once navigated a dived nuclear submarine back from the Atlantic into the North Channel, the small gap between Northern Ireland and Scotland, at night in a growing westerly gale. This was before satnav became widely available. The

---

[1] This was a staggering sum of money – equivalent to over £3m in 2020 currency.

[2] The words 'simple' and 'spherical geometry' may, to some, be something of an oxymoron. I agree wholeheartedly!

[3] GNSS, or Global Navigation Satellite System, encompasses all the global satellite positioning systems. Most of us use the US Global Positioning System (GPS). Because it's the most commonly used system, I will refer to GPS in this book.

conditions were hideous; I hadn't plotted a fix for 12 hours and we weren't picking up any useful signals from the radio navigation aids. The echo sounder wasn't telling me much either. I was on the point of thinking that it was just getting too difficult and that we would have to wait until daybreak when, like a tiny beacon of hope, I caught a glimpse of the loom of the Malin Head Lighthouse on the north coast of Ireland, and I took a bearing. Over the next hour or so I was able to plot a series of running fixes (Chapter 6) that got us home safely.

Good navigation is meticulous, but in all honesty it's not that difficult, and it is a skill that improves with practice. Like so many things in life, you start to enjoy it more as you get better at it…. And that's what this book is about: trying to de-mystify navigation and make it easier for people to understand and to practise, so that you are better able to enjoy your time on the water, in safety.

As a navigator, you should have the skills to:

- Know where you are at any given time and understand how accurate your position is
- Plan your voyage in a way that will keep your vessel and her crew safe at all times
- Predict and understand the present and future movement of the water around you
- Calculate the course to steer to get to your destination
- Estimate when you will arrive
- And be honest with yourself when things don't feel right

You must be able to do all this, reliably, at any time of the day or night, and in any visibility, recognising that the water around you is constantly moving, and that the depth of water in coastal areas can vary by over 10 metres in a 6-hour period. You're doing it, moreover, while you, your boat and chart table are being thrown around randomly by elements. That's quite a tall order, but people have been navigating for thousands of years and there is a tremendous bank of well-tried knowledge, best practice and data to draw on.

If I leave you with just one message from this book, the single most important thing that you can do as a navigator is to prepare thoroughly in advance, for even the simplest passages. The better prepared you are, the easier you will find it to concentrate on where you are going, to anticipate problems, avoid obstacles and, most important of all, to keep your crew and your boat safe.

I'm not a natural worrier, but as both navigator and captain of big ships, submarines, and yachts, I've always paid close attention to the vessel's navigation before leaving harbour, and all the time that we're at sea.

This attention to detail will give precision to your navigation and, if your brain is anything like mine, it brings enormous satisfaction as well. The satisfaction of using your skill, your knowledge and your learning to get safely from A to B is a great feeling, whether you're crossing the Atlantic or the Solent; whether you're navigating a nuclear-powered submarine or a small yacht. And when you arrive at the other end, find the time to enjoy the landfall, because passage making is one of the great arts of seamanship, as old and mysterious as seafaring itself.

My first offshore voyage as a newly promoted submarine Captain was a surface passage from Rosyth, just outside Edinburgh, all the way round the top of Scotland to the naval base at Faslane, on the River Clyde. By any standards, this was not a complicated trip for a warship – and for the first 90 minutes it all went incredibly well. It was when we got to the mouth of the Firth of Forth that I started thinking that something was not quite right. I walked back to the control room where the chart table was situated and took a quick look at the chart. The officer of the watch, who was very inexperienced, had completely forgotten to turn left and head up the Scottish coast... so we were happily heading across the North Sea towards Denmark. The problem was quickly resolved, and we turned north with no harm done – but it taught me a valuable lesson about being a Captain, and the importance of worrying, and of acting on your instinct when something doesn't feel quite right.

This is not a textbook to get you through the RYA Yachtmaster® syllabus. There are already a lot of very impressive books around to do that. I have written this book for people who are already sailors, people who may own their own boat, or charter regularly. It's written as a sort of aide-memoire to help you navigate with confidence, because navigation can be daunting. There's a lot to think about, and a lot that can go wrong. As someone said to me when I was training to become a submarine Captain:

"One day, when it all starts to go wrong, you'll find everyone silently looking at you, wondering how you'll get them out of this mess. It's your job to do exactly that."

The book consists of three parts:

- The **first** part talks about the tools that you have at your disposal as a navigator – the instruments, the information and the techniques that are available to you, and how to use them
- The **second** addresses the different types of navigation, from pilotage near the coast to offshore navigation
- And in the **third** I describe a simple passage from Lymington to St Peter Port

in the Channel Islands in a small yacht, showing how I would plan and make the passage

The book ends with a single chapter in which I have described some of the times when I, or others, haven't got it right, with some thoughts on what we can learn from these incidents. I have done this to show that we all make mistakes: there's no shame in it, and the best thing we can do afterwards is to learn from the lessons and avoid finding ourselves in the same situation sometime in the future. For that reason, if you have a cautionary tale to tell, send it to me at **fernhurst@fernhurstbooks.com** and I will include a selection of the most valuable in subsequent editions of this book.

Throughout the book I have tried to describe the 'right' way to do things, but there are places where I have gone a little off-piste in demonstrating practical alternatives to the orthodox methods. These are practices and techniques that may or may not be in the textbooks, but which I have learnt to use and to rely on over the years. I've shared them in this book so that you can try them out for yourself.

At the end of the day, navigation is something very special. It's half science and half art, with a dash of excitement thrown in by the unexpected... because something unusual always happens on a sea voyage. For me, navigation is a challenging, timeless and absorbing discipline that is endlessly rewarding – it's a ticket to explore the other side of the horizon, and plot your own course over the sea – which is a freedom like no other.

I hope that this book will give you the confidence to consider yourself a navigator, and to enjoy this great art.

Paul Boissier
September 2020

1

THE WORLD, & HOW IT'S PORTRAYED

Life would be so much easier if the world was flat.

And even if we accept that it isn't flat, it would be quite a lot easier if it was a perfect sphere. In either case, you could create a beautiful mathematical model for charting the world which would be both simple and accurate.

But life's not like that.

The earth is very nearly a sphere... but not quite. It's properly described as an 'oblate spheroid', a fact that is handy if you're ever setting the questions in a pub quiz, but otherwise almost entirely useless.

4.543 billion years of constant rotation has given the earth a bit of a middle-aged spread: it's rather shorter than a proper sphere, and broader round the equator – to the extent that the diameter across the equator is about 42.7 kilometres greater than the diameter through the poles.

CHART PROJECTIONS

The job of the chart makers is to find a way to accurately represent this irregular, almost-but-not-quite spherical object on a 2-dimensional piece of paper (or screen). And they have done well. There are getting on for 100 different 'chart projections'[4] listed in Wikipedia, and doubtless many more that have not been listed there. But there are just 3 of these, which are used extensively for maritime navigation, that you and I should be aware of:

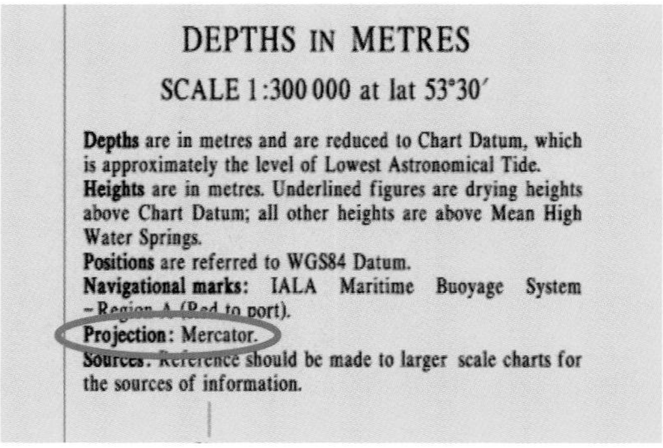

DEPTHS IN METRES

SCALE 1:300 000 at lat 53°30'

Depths are in metres and are reduced to Chart Datum, which is approximately the level of Lowest Astronomical Tide.
Heights are in metres. Underlined figures are drying heights above Chart Datum; all other heights are above Mean High Water Springs.
Positions are referred to WGS84 Datum.
Navigational marks: IALA Maritime Buoyage System – Region A (Red to port).
Projection: Mercator.
Sources: Reference should be made to larger scale charts for the sources of information.

Chart title showing the projection used

---

[4] 'Chart projections' is the term for these 2D representations of the earth used to draw charts and maps.

- Mercator Projection
- Transverse Mercator Projection
- Gnomonic Projection

The projection in use is always marked in the title block of the chart. In the above case a chart of the southern North Sea has been drawn using the Mercator Projection.

MERCATOR PROJECTION

In many ways it's quite impressive that the most common chart projection in use today was developed almost 450 years ago, by a Flemish cartographer called Gerardus Mercator.

Imagine the world floating in space. And imagine wrapping an enormous cylinder of white chart paper round it, touching the surface of the earth only at the equator.

Then, if this is not pushing your imagination too far, imagine a big light in the centre of the earth shining outwards, and projecting the shadow of the land masses onto this cylinder of paper. That's the idea behind the Mercator Projection.

As you can imagine, at the equator there is very little difference between the size

The Mercator Projection

and shape of the land and its portrayal on the paper. But the charted scale of latitude extends as you get closer to the poles, and the north-south distortion increases. The poles don't appear on the paper at all. You end up with a chart of the world that looks something like this.

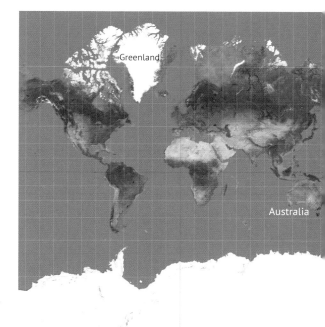

Flat map of the world showing huge distortion near the poles (Daniel R. Strebe, 2011)

You can see the extent of the distortion that occurs towards the poles by comparing the images of Greenland and Australia on the chart. It is perhaps surprising to realise that, in terms of land area, Greenland is actually just 28% of the size of Australia – which is not how it looks on this map.

There are nevertheless a number of attributes of the Mercator Projection that are incredibly valuable to the navigator:

- All lines of latitude and longitude cross at right angles
- Angles on the earth's surface are the same as the equivalent angles on a chart
- Lines of longitude are straight, and evenly spaced across the chart
- Lines of latitude are also straight, but have variable spacing, becoming less compressed as they move away from the equator
- And finally, a straight line on the chart from, say, Plymouth to Barbados will cross all lines of latitude and longitude

at the same angle, giving you a constant bearing to steer from departure to destination – this 'rhumb line', as it is called, may not be the shortest distance between the two points on a big trans-Atlantic voyage[5], but it is incredibly convenient for shorter journeys

As a navigator, the great majority of the charts that are used for everyday navigation are drawn with the Mercator Projection, or its younger brother, the **Transverse Mercator Projection** (see below).

BUT – and this is an important but – there is one big thing which you must bear in mind when using a Mercator chart. The latitude scale – and hence your reference

for distance (see Chapter 3) – varies from the top of the chart to the bottom, so that when you measure distance using the latitude scale on the chart, you must use the scale adjacent to the part of the chart that you are working on.

Take a look at this relatively small scale, high latitude chart: the chart of Tierra del Fuego[6] at the southern tip of South America. This is a Mercator chart.

If, on this chart, you set your dividers to measure 30nm (or 30 minutes of latitude) at Cape Horn (about 56°S), and then move them to the top of the chart (about 51°S), the distance covered by the dividers at this latitude is actually closer to 34nm.

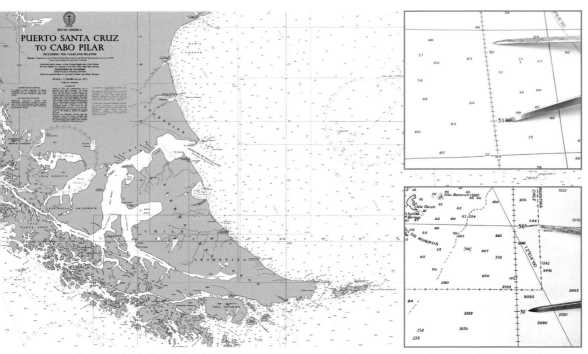

Small scale, high latitude chart of Tierra del Fuego

Dividers measuring 30nm at Cape Horn (bottom) measure 34nm at the top of the chart (top)

---

[5] The shortest distance between 2 points on the earth's surface is a great circle track (see Gnomonic Projections below).

[6] This chart, *No. 539*, which is a current chart first published in 1966, has been drawn in black and white rather than colour. This indicates that it is a fathoms and feet chart rather than a metric chart (Chapter 2).

This effect is more noticeable at high latitudes, and on small scale (large area) charts.

And that's why you must always measure distance using the latitude scale closest to the part of the chart you're working on.

TRANSVERSE MERCATOR PROJECTION

Even at high latitudes, you can work perfectly happily on a Mercator chart as long as you are in open water. But it's understandably quite difficult working in pilotage or restricted waters if the difference in latitude and longitude scales gives you too much distortion. As a result, the chart maker often uses a Transverse Mercator Projection for mapping small harbours and bays around the coast.

The Transverse Mercator Projection is quite an ingenious extension of the simple Mercator Projection. Instead of wrapping the cylinder of white paper around the equator, why not wrap it around the poles, touching the surface of the earth along the line of longitude that you are particularly interested in?

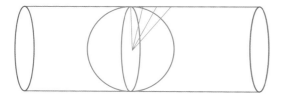

Transverse Mercator Projection

That way, no matter what your latitude, so long as you're working close to this line of contact, there will be little or no distortion.

In practice, Transverse Mercator Projections are only ever used on large

scale (small area)[7] charts because, as you move away from the line of contact, the increasing distortion would make the chart incredibly confusing.

You can see the result of this extreme distortion on this chart of the world, drawn with the Transverse Mercator Projection. There is next-to-no distortion along the two meridians, which pass through the UK, France and Spain. But I really would not like to use the chart for a passage from the UK to the Caribbean.

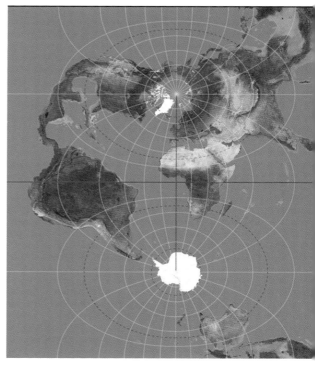

Transverse Mercator chart (Peter Mercator, 2010)

This is clearly not a projection to use over large sea areas, but it is perfect for small charts and plans. As long as you're working in a small area, a Transverse Mercator chart will look and feel exactly the same

---

[7] If you're confused by the terms 'large scale' and 'small scale' charts (and you wouldn't be the only person who is), it's useful to remember that large scale charts cover a small area, and small scale charts cover a large area.

as its older brother, the tried-and-tested Mercator Projection.

AND ANCHORAGES IN THE EAST SOLENT AREA

DEPTHS IN METRES

Depths are in metres and are reduced to Chart Datum, which is approximately the level of Lowest Astronomical Tide.
Heights are in metres. Underlined figures are drying heights above Chart Datum. Vertical clearance heights are above Highest Astronomical Tide. All other heights are above Mean High Water Springs.
Positions are referred to the WGS 84 compatible datum, European Terrestrial Reference System 1989 Datum.
Navigational marks: IALA Maritime Buoyage System – Region A (Red to port).
Projection: Transverse Mercator
Sources: See Source Diagram. See the Mariner's Handbook for information on Source and Zones of Confidence (ZOCs) Diagrams. The topography is derived chiefly from Ordnance Survey maps and aerial photography.

RIVER HAMBLE–REGULATIONS   CONTROL OF NAVIGATION   RADIO REPORT
choring is not permitted between No1 light   Navigation within the Dockyard Port of   Vessels 20 metres and ove
icon (50°50'·34N 1°18'·64W) and the M27   Portsmouth is subject to the provision made in   required to contact Hamble F

The UKHO's Plans of Harbours and Creeks in The East Solent Area are all drawn using the Transverse Mercator Projection: they provide an accurate, distortion-free image of a small area, perfect for inshore navigation

GNOMONIC PROJECTION

Gnomonic charts (pronounced 'no-monic') are very different from Mercator charts in both construction and appearance. In this case, you have to imagine your big sheet of white chart paper resting flat on a single point of the earth's surface, with the shadows projected onto it from a single, very bright light at the centre of the earth.

So, for instance, if you lay the paper on the North Pole, all the lines of longitude will be shown as straight radial spokes running away from the pole, and the lines of latitude will be concentric circles, centred on the pole[8].

As you would expect, gnomonic charts produce increasing levels of distortion as you move away from the point of contact, but of course you can use any point on the surface of the earth as your reference point: you don't have to use the North Pole.

Gnomonic charts have three specific uses in navigation:

1. Like the Transverse Mercator Projection, Gnomonic charts have the ability to portray small, localised areas close to the point of contact with minimal distortion. So, you will sometimes see small harbour chartlets drawn using Gnomonic Projection.

2. Secondly, they are invaluable when you are working at very high latitudes, where Mercator charts start to lose their relevance. Nuclear submarines heading north under the ice cap often use Gnomonic charts for their navigation.

3. And thirdly, a straight line drawn on a Gnomonic chart shows the **Great Circle**[9], or the shortest route between

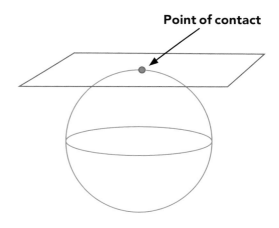

Point of contact

Gnomonic chart projection

---

[8] This projection has a passing resemblance to a sundial. Hence the name: a 'gnomon' is the raised part of a sundial which casts the shadow from which you can tell the time.

[9] A great circle is a line on the surface of the earth that cuts the earth exactly in half. This can be defined by just 2 points, in the case opposite, London and Vancouver. It is always the shortest geographic distance between those points. The equator and the meridians of longitude are also great circles.

the two points. These charts are therefore immensely useful for long-distance ocean route planning.

A quick glance at a gnomonic chart will explain why, when flying from London to Vancouver, two cities on almost exactly the same latitude, you end up passing over Reykjavik and central Greenland, both of them a good deal further north than the start and destination cities.

If you're ever planning a long ocean passage, it's worth buying one of the *Gnomonic Planning Charts* produced by the UKHO. On these charts, the great circle track between 2 points is represented by a straight line, so the shortest distance between the SW Approaches and Bermuda, for instance, starts off by going almost directly west, and ends up heading into Bermuda on a south-westerly course. Plotted on a Mercator chart, this route would appear to be a long, lazy curve and quite a divergence from the straight rhumb line.

Of course, in a small boat, or even a big ship, the shortest distance between 2

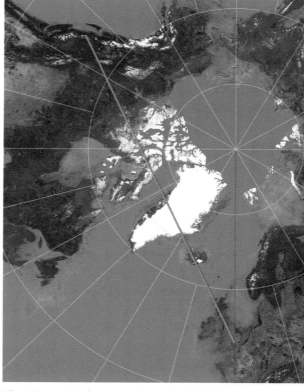

The Great Circle route between London and Vancouver (Daniel R. Strebe, 2011)

points may not always be the quickest, and you should also consult the *Admiralty Routing Charts*, which are produced for every month of the year, and which show the most likely winds and currents to expect on your voyage.

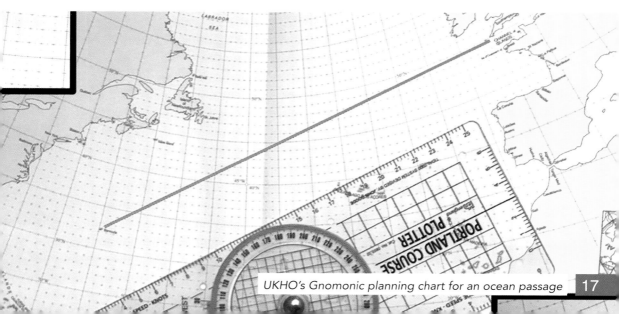

UKHO's Gnomonic planning chart for an ocean passage

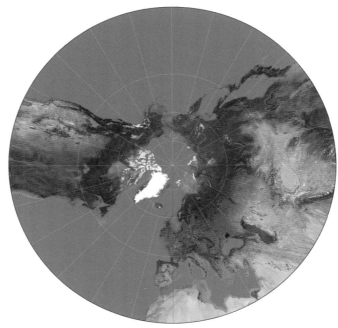

Map of North Pole using Gnomonic chart projection (Daniel R. Strebe, 2011)

HORIZONTAL DATUMS

Chart projections are the cartographer's way of portraying the 3-dimensional surface of the earth on a 2-dimensional sheet of paper (or screen), allowing us to make sense of the world, and navigate across its oceans. But they only solve one of the chart maker's problems. The other big problem is how to assign meaningful positions to places on the earth's surface when it is not exactly spherical.

This sounds like a slightly arcane problem, but increasingly you and I are asking our GPS sets and our phones to consistently navigate down to a few metres of accuracy on the irregular surface of an object that is roughly 7,900 miles in diameter. So, the way that the earth is modelled inside your GPS set or your mobile phone is critical to the accuracy of the system.

The models used to define position on the earth's surface are called Horizontal Datums.

A number of countries have defined their own horizontal datums, including:

- **OSGB36**: Ordnance Survey Datum, used for land mapping of the UK
- **ED50**: European Datum, developed after the Second World War to properly map international borders
- **GDA94**: Geodetic Datum of Australia[10]
- **NAD83**: North American Datum, which ensures consistency of position across the United States, Canada, Mexico and Central America

---

[10] When it was established in 1994, GDA94 was identical to WGS84. However, it recognises the continental drift of the Australian continent (approximately 6cm per year), and the 2 datums are steadily diverging. The difference in 2020 is estimated to be 1.8m.

Most of these are fairly localised datums, designed to provide consistency of position in a single country or a group of countries. WGS84, by contrast, or the World Geodetic System of 1984 to give it its snappy formal title, provides a common position reference for the whole world, using a very accurate virtual model of the earth's surface. WGS84 is used by the US Global Positioning System (GPS), and it's also used in most commercial GPS units.

Of course, each system models the world in slightly different ways. As a result, they can often assign different positions to particular objects. *The Mariner's Handbook* illustrates this by comparing the position of South Foreland Lighthouse, a few miles north-east of Dover, using 3 separate datums, as shown below.

The difference between these positions is not huge – less than 200 metres at most – but in some parts of the world the inter-datum errors can be a lot bigger. Where the differences between datums are of such a size that it is likely to have an impact on the safety of navigation, they are set out in the title block of the chart, and when you see this, you really do need to take account of the errors.

WGS84

It's worth spending a bit of time discussing WGS84 because, if you use GPS in your boat, it will in all probability use WGS84 as its horizontal datum.

An increasing number of maritime charts produced by the UK and US Hydrographers, and many other national charting agencies, are now drawn to be compatible with WGS84. In a nutshell, when you see the words '*WGS84 POSITIONS can be plotted directly on this chart*', similar wording, or just '*WGS84*', you can safely plot positions from the US GPS system directly onto your chart without correction.

Check for these words (or similar) before plotting GPS positions on your chart

There are still a number of charts, however, which are not drawn to the WGS84 datum, where you will have to correct the GPS position before plotting it on the chart. There is no 'WGS84' notation in the

3 CHART DATUMS FOR SOUTH FORELAND	
HORIZONTAL DATUM	**GEOGRAPHICAL POSITION**
Referred to OSGB36 datum (the Ordnance Survey Datum for the UK)	51° 08'.39N 001° 22'.37E
Referred to the European (1950) Datum (which is the continental datum)	51° 08'.47N 001° 22'.35E
Referred to the World Geodetic System 1984 (WGS84) Datum (the worldwide datum used by the GPS)	51° 08'.42N 001° 22'.27E

margins of these charts. Instead, you will find a small table of inter-datum corrections in the title block.

This chart, for instance, covers a part of the northwest coast of France. It has been drawn with reference to the European Datum (Circle 1), and it tells you (Circle 2) that you need to correct GPS positions before plotting them on the chart and tells you how to correct for this.

Always check the title block before you use a chart, because some of these corrections are quite significant. The largest known discrepancy between the charted position and the WGS84 position is a massive 7 nautical miles in the middle of the Pacific Ocean. Most electronic chart plotters automatically make any necessary

datum corrections for you, but it's worth checking to make sure.

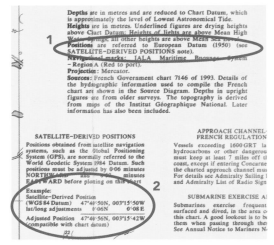

Chart drawn using European Datum

RECORDING & COMMUNICATING POSITIONS

Mariners generally define a position at sea in one of 2 ways:
- Range and bearing from a fixed object
- Latitude and longitude

RANGE & BEARING

If you're sitting at home, speaking to a friend on the phone, and you wanted to tell them where to park their car, you might say something like:

"Drive to the village pub, and the car park is about 200 metres down the High Street."

In other words, you give them a range and bearing from a conspicuous reference position. This is a simple way of defining a position on land, and its equally simple at sea where you could, for instance, describe your position as:

210° Portland Bill Lighthouse 13.2nm

Meaning that you are 210° from Portland Bill Lighthouse at a distance of 13.2 nautical miles. This is precise and unambiguous, and it's a widely used way of defining a position at sea. (The common convention at sea is to define a position as a range and bearing FROM a conspicuous point. Using the bearing of Portland Bill Light from you (030°) would cause great confusion!)

LATITUDE & LONGITUDE

The alternative is to use a pre-defined grid system, just like the road system in New York City, where you could say that the Empire State Building is on 5th Avenue and W 34th Street. That's it. No ifs, and no buts. No need to tell someone to take the third right after Tescos. Anyone can find their way there.

The maritime equivalent is latitude and longitude (always in that order). This too is completely unambiguous. So, using the WGS84 datum, the position of North

You can define the position of the Empire State Building using the grid of streets
(© TierneyMJ / shutterstock.com)

Foreland Light that we established earlier in this chapter is:

51° 08'.42N   001° 22'.27E

Note that when writing positions, the ° indicates degrees and a single apostrophe (') designates minutes, a minute being one 60th of a degree. For reasons lost in the mists of time, the apostrophe is always placed after the whole number of minutes, and before the decimal point. Sometimes, although less commonly, you will see a position described using seconds (") rather than decimals, a second being one 60th of a minute. So, the same position is also:

51° 08'25"N   001° 22'16"E

Importantly, one minute of latitude is one nautical mile in length[11], and one tenth of a minute of latitude (a little over 200 yards) is commonly referred to as a cable.

All positions, both latitude and longitude, are measured as angles from the centre of the earth.

LATITUDE

The North and South Poles – that is the True North Pole and the True South Pole – lie on the axis of the earth's rotation. Their positions are constant, and don't shift with time. The half-way point between the 2 poles is the equator, a great circle whose position is also fixed. The equator is defined as 0° north or south, and the poles are 90° north and south. The latitude of every intermediate position is simply measured from the centre of the earth as the angle between the equator and that point on the surface of the earth.

---

[11] A nautical mile is 6,076 feet, and a land mile is 5,280 feet, which is about 87% of a nautical mile.

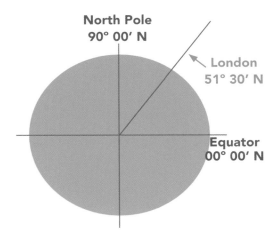

Latitude

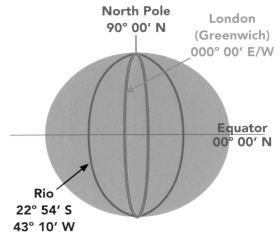

Longitude

LONGITUDE

Longitude is not quite so simple as latitude. It is defined by 'meridians', which are great circles passing through both North and South Poles, running down the surface of the earth from True North to True South.

The reference, or 'prime' meridian could have been placed anywhere, but for historical reasons, the location of the observatory at Greenwich in east London was chosen as the Prime Meridian, and the longitude of every position on earth is defined by the angle east or west of Greenwich, as measured from the centre of the earth[12].

Rather like the segments of an orange, the distance between meridians reduces as you move from the equator towards the poles. So, while 1 degree of longitude spans 60nm at the equator, the distance between the meridians steadily diminishes as you move north or south until you get to the North Pole, where submarine crews can stick a pole in the ice and complete a 'Round the World Race' in just a few paces.

MAGNETIC NORTH & SOUTH POLES

The True North and South Poles are defined by the rotation of the earth, and do not change. The Magnetic Poles, however, are defined by the earth's magnetic field which, is caused by the flux of molten material within the earth's core. And the magnetic poles do move, rather erratically, with the passage of time.

For the last 150 years the Magnetic North Pole has been drifting aimlessly around the islands of northern Canada. But recently it has sped up and started moving across the Arctic Ocean towards Russia. It is currently moving about 35 nautical miles each year.

In 2020, the North Pole was estimated[13] to be at about 86°N 163°E, while the Magnetic South Pole was located rather further from the pole, at about 64°S 136°E.

---

[12] Interestingly, the advent of WGS84 has revealed a slight inaccuracy in the position of the Prime Meridian in Greenwich. Keep it to yourself, but the actual Prime Meridian lies just over 100 metres to the east of the line engraved in the cobblestones at the Greenwich Observatory.

[13] Google offers a variety of different positions for the Magnetic North and South Poles. Any estimate of longitude is of course particularly sensitive in polar regions.

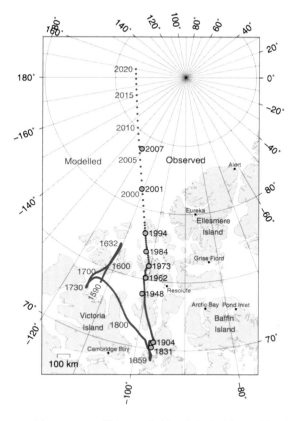

Movement of Magnetic North Pole (Cavit, 2016)

to use a single value for variation on a short passage, you should be prepared to recalculate variation from time to time if you are going a long way. To help with this, some small scale charts have sweeping magenta curves drawn across them which identify the points of equal magnetic variation.

These lines of equal variations are called **isogonals**, and when they appear on a chart, there is usually an accompanying note in the title block, explaining which year the readings are drawn up for, and how they should be used.

At the time of writing this book in early 2020, the variation around the UK south coast waters is about 1°W[14]. Variation this low is rare, and it's incredibly handy for the navigator of a small boat, because this is almost insignificant. But please don't be lulled into a false sense of security. In other parts of the world, the variation is much larger than this and, before long, it will start to increase around the UK as well, so you must know how to account for it.

VARIATION

There is almost always going to be a difference between True North (the direction of the True North Pole) and Magnetic North, as shown by your magnetic compass. And because of the movement of the Magnetic North Pole, that difference – which is called the **variation** – changes from year to year.

Most charts are referenced to True North. So, if you're relying on magnetic compasses for steering and fixing, you should always calculate the variation, and apply it to your compass bearing before plotting it on your chart (Chapter 3).

Variation changes as you travel across the surface of the earth, so, while it's OK

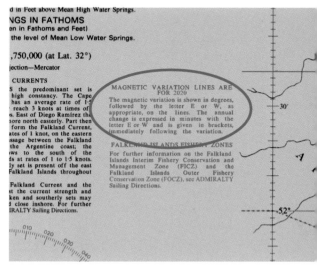

Explanation of date isogonals are drawn up for, and how they should be used

---

[14] That is to say that the direction of Magnetic North is 1° to the west of True North.

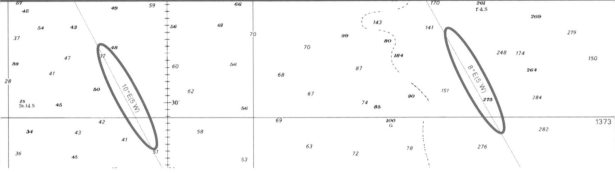

Chart showing isogonals – the figures in brackets indicate the annual change in variation from the date shown in the title block.

TIME

UNIVERSAL TIME (UT)

Over the last few decades, with the advent of atomic clocks and satellite navigations systems, there has been a need to define a time constant that is both accurate and universal. **Universal Time** does just that. It uses precise observations of celestial bodies to keep track of any small changes in the way that the earth moves in relation to the sun, and so defines the most accurate available time standard.

COORDINATED UNIVERSAL TIME (UTC)

There are about half a dozen versions of UT, but the most commonly used is the **Coordinated Universal Time**, or **UTC**. This has become the basis for civil time and time zones worldwide. Slightly awkwardly, UTC does not define time by celestial observation, but with an atomic clock – so it doesn't take account of the odd swerve or wobble that the earth occasionally indulges in after a good night out. So, from time to time, UTC drifts away from the other versions of UT and needs to be brought back by a series of small corrections, which are called 'leap seconds'. Using these leap seconds, UTC is always kept within 0.9 seconds of the other versions of UT.

GREENWICH MEAN TIME (GMT)

Greenwich Mean Time is a time zone, and it is the UK's legal time during the winter months, in common with a number of other West European and African countries on roughly the same longitude. It was traditionally defined by the time that the sun passes through the 0° meridian, as observed by the Royal Observatory in Greenwich, but is now aligned to the UTC.

DAYLIGHT SAVING TIME (DST)

Many countries shift the clocks by an hour to accommodate seasonal changes in the time of sunrise and sunset. In Europe and the UK, from mid-spring to mid-autumn the clocks are advanced by 1 hour to make life easier for the citizens (and more complicated for navigators). In the UK, Daylight Saving Time is sometimes referred to as British Summer Time (**BST**).

ABBREVIATIONS

I have used the abbreviations **UT** in this book when I'm referring to the time constant, and **GMT** or **BST** when I'm referring to specific time zones in the UK. Where I refer to Daylight Saving Time in other countries, I will spell it out in words.

THE EARTH'S ROTATION

LONGITUDE & TIME

The earth is spinning at quite a rate – one full rotation round its True North / True South axis every 24 hours. And, because of this, longitude is inextricably bound up with time.

The sun travels through 360° every day
That's 15° of longitude every hour
Or 1° of longitude every 4 minutes

Dublin lies at 6° 15'.6W, so in Dublin the sun will reach its zenith – the highest point of its daily travel – a fraction over 25 minutes later than it does in Greenwich (0° 0'.0W). And both sunset and sunrise will be commensurately later[15].

To accommodate the rotation of the earth, and to make sure that we all get up at more-or-less the same time of the day, the earth is divided into time zones, each roughly 15° of longitude (1 hour) in width.

The way in which longitude is measured in degrees east or west of Greenwich makes it all a little messy on the other side of the world. In mid-Pacific, at 180° East and West, lies the **International Date Line** – the point at which time changes not by one hour, but by a whole day.

If you decide to sail around the world from east to west, you will set your clocks back one hour with every 15° of longitude that you travel. But to make this work, there has to be somewhere in the world where you unwind all these changes and go back to square one. That place is the International Date Line. So, on your journey around the world from east to west, as you cross the International Date Line you advance your clocks by one day, resetting all the hourly changes that you have accumulated in crossing from one time zone to another.

THE TROPICS & THE ARCTIC AND ANTARCTIC CIRCLES

In the perfect universe, the axis of the earth's rotation would be at right-angles to the earth's movement around the sun. But in fact, the axis of the earth's rotation is displaced from the 'vertical' by about 23° 24'[16]. So, in the year that it takes for the earth to rotate around the sun, the sun appears to be north of the equator for 6 months, and south of the equator for the other 6 months. This gives us the seasons.

The limit of the sun's movement, north and south, is defined by the displacement of the earth's axis of rotation. So, if you were standing at a position 23° 24'N[17] on 21 June[18] the sun would be directly over your head at midday. The lines of latitude at 23° 24' North and South, which mark the limits of the sun's movement, are called the tropics: the Tropic of Cancer in the Northern Hemisphere, and the Tropic of Capricorn in the Southern Hemisphere.

This angular displacement has an effect at the poles as well. At 66° 36' North and South – that's 23° 24' from each pole – lie the Arctic and Antarctic Circles. These mark the limits of the regions where the sun never sets in the summer, and never rises in the winter.

---

[15] While the sun's passage through the zenith is purely a matter of longitude, the relative timings of sunrise and sunset are also affected by differences in latitude.

[16] The angle of the earth's displacement from the vertical varies between 22-24.5°. At present, it's slowly reducing.

[17] Somewhere like Havana, Cuba for instance.

[18] The Northern Hemisphere summer solstice can occur between 20 and 22 June.

2
CHARTS

In this book I refer to 'charts', and mainly reference Admiralty paper charts, even though I recognise that a growing number of mariners, both leisure and professional, are using digital charts as their principal navigation reference.

There is no inconsistency in this.

No matter what form of digital or paper chart you are using, the data and the fundamentals of navigation are the same – but do make sure that the information on your chart is reliable, that it comes from a trustworthy source, and that it is up to date.

DIGITAL CHARTS

There are 2 types of digital chart available for mariners: raster and vector.

Raster charts are digital copies of the paper chart, presented to the mariner on a digital navigation screen. They contain all the information that you are used to on a paper chart, in the same format. As a result, all the familiar symbology is there, just as it would be on a paper chart; the titles and source diagrams are available – so anyone used to working with paper charts would find a raster chart reassuringly familiar.

Vector charts are more flexible. The navigation data is portrayed in a series of short lines (or 'vectors') which make up the image on the screen. This can make the image quite spiky as you zoom in. The

vector system of joining up very short lines works well enough on the topography of the land and seabed, but it struggles with some of the more complex images that are needed for chart symbols. So additional information is often applied to the topographical backdrop by means of chart 'layers': navigation buoys, for instance, or sounding data, the radar display, AIS, light characteristics and many other features can all be selectively added or 'decluttered', depending on your needs at the time.

These data layers give vector charts great flexibility and widespread appeal. Moreover, since vector charts use so much less memory than raster charts, additional information can be added without substantial cost.

So, pictures, tidal data, port information and many other packets of information are often added to the data package without losing accuracy or utility. But with the ability to customise your chart display to such an extent, you must make sure that you don't inadvertently de-select important layers that you need for safe navigation.

Most small ship digital navigation systems are provided in vector format.

THE VALUE OF CARRYING PAPER CHARTS AS WELL AS DIGITAL NAVIGATION SYSTEMS

There is no hard-and-fast rule about whether you should carry paper charts or digital charts in your boat, or both. It's up to you. The International Maritime Organisation (IMO) is pretty relaxed about this too. It says this about pleasure vessel less than 150gt:

"Operators of small craft... should therefore have sufficient charts and published information on board to be able to plan the intended voyage and execute it safely."

In my yacht, I always have the appropriate paper chart out and open on the chart table, with a pencil track drawn on it, and I plot regular fixes on the chart from GPS, or other means. But I frequently refer to the chart plotter[19] to see the wider picture, and to keep an eye on the course and speed made good. This means that I am never wholly dependent on either paper or digital; if the chart blows overboard I will revert to electronic navigation, and if I suddenly lose power to the chart plotter I have the paper chart, with a recent fix, sitting on the chart table.

This system works well at the relatively slow speeds of a sailing boat, but if you're crossing the Channel at 25-30 knots in a big powerboat with a small crew, you may wish to rely more heavily on the chart plotter – although in this case I would always advocate carrying both a set of paper charts and a secondary hand-held GPS set as back-up.

CHART ACCURACY

Having spent most of my professional life working with Admiralty charts, I can vouch for the fact that the UK Hydrographic Office (UKHO) compiles its charts with extraordinary care and attention to detail, and they are, in my mind, about as good as you can expect a chart to be.

But even so, no chart is 100% accurate.

For years, as a junior watch-keeping officer in ships and submarines, I assumed that the information on a chart was a sort of holy grail of unshakeable truth. But when I started to look more closely at the charts, and spoke to some of the incredibly talented men and women who compile them, I realised how complex the job of charting the oceans actually is, and how little they know about the shape and the nature of the seabed. The UK Hydrographic Office readily admit this. In the *Mariner's Handbook*, they write:

"While the UK Hydrographic Office has made all reasonable efforts to ensure that the data supplied is accurate, it should be appreciated that the data

---

[19] I have always used a Raymarine chart plotter with Navionics Gold software, which provides a reliable and accurate vector chart.

may not always be complete, up to date or positioned to modern surveying standards and therefore no warranty can be given as to its accuracy. The mariner must be the final judge of the reliance he places on the information given, bearing in mind his particular circumstances, the need for safe and prudent navigation, local pilotage guidance and the judicious use of available navigation aids."

Note the start of the final sentence: *'the mariner must be the final judge of the reliance he places on the information given...'*. In other words, the UKHO will do its best to help you stay safe but, at the end of the day, you have to use your skill and experience to make a judgement about the reliability of any chart that you're using.

There are a lot of things that could detract from the reliability of your chart:

A SHIFTING SEABED

There are a number of places around the UK, like the Solway Firth near Carlisle on the border between England and Scotland (shown below) where the Hydrographer just doesn't bother to publish a survey because the seabed is so mobile. The people who navigate these waters, or places like the Wash in East Anglia, do so with great care, and a legacy of local knowledge. This is not a stretch of water that I would readily venture into.

OLD SURVEYS

Old surveys, conducted by lead line, or by single lines of soundings, have often left gaps between the survey lines where dangers can be lurking[20]. It is worth checking a chart's Source Data Diagram

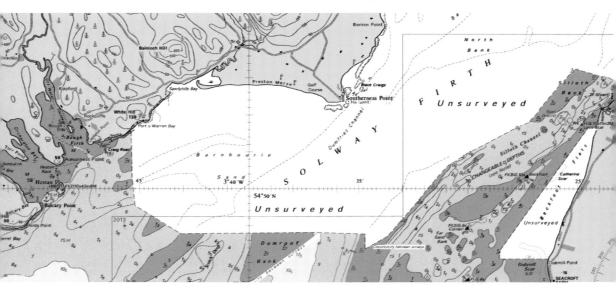

The Solway Firth where much of the area is not surveyed (shown in white)

---

[20] According to Dr Jon Copley of Southampton University, the entire ocean floor has now been mapped to about 5km resolution, which means that we can see most features larger than 5km across in these maps.... Multi-beam sonar systems aboard ships can map the ocean floor at about 100m resolution, but only in a track below the ship. These more detailed maps now cover about 10 to 15 percent of the oceans, which is an area roughly equivalent to Africa in size.

before use, to discover just how reliable the data actually is.

This chart, published in 2019, shows that 50% of UK waters have only ever been surveyed by lead line (red), or single beam soundings (amber).

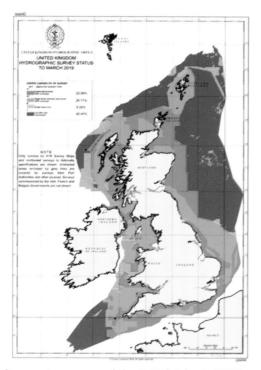

Survey status around the British Isles in 2019

DEVELOPMENT WORKS

Development works are constantly happening around the coast: new channels, mineral exploitation, wrecks, building works on the side of a navigation channel – all of these can affect the accuracy of your chart and the safety of your vessel. These changes are generally published as a *Notice to Mariners* when the UKHO learns about them.

STORM SURGES

Sea levels can be massively affected by storm surges, when a strong wind is blowing onshore, sometimes exacerbated by the 'suction effect' of abnormally low barometric pressure. This can artificially increase the depth of water by a number of metres. Equally, a strong offshore wind, coupled with high barometric pressure, can cause a negative storm surge which substantially reduces the depth of water (see p52).

SQUAT

If you're navigating at high speed in shallow water, you will often find that the stern of your vessel 'squats' down in the water as a result of the pressure wave around the hull. This can artificially increase your draught and reduce the expected under-keel clearance. Squat was a contributory factor to the grounding of the *QE2* off Martha's Vineyard in August 1992.

This is all pretty alarming stuff. But the good news is that the sea areas that are most heavily used also tend to be the best surveyed – and a lot of people have been there before you. So if you're sensible, plan well and use appropriate charts, you should be pretty safe.

WHAT A CHART TELLS YOU

A chart is essential to safe navigation. It should give you:

■ A distance scale, latitude and longitude
■ A north reference, both true and magnetic, together with one or more compass rose

■ The coastline in serious detail and the hinterland in rather less detail, focusing largely on the features most likely to be of interest to the navigator
■ Depth information with relevant contours and intelligently placed soundings

- Anchorages
- Underwater dangers, including rocks, wrecks, overfalls and obstructions
- Outline tidal height information
- Lights and navigation marks, sound signals, buoys, transits and shipping lanes
- Fishing areas, energy platforms, separation lanes, international boundaries
- Survey information showing the date and the thoroughness of surveys of each section of the chart

- A list of corrections that have been applied to the chart, and their dates
- And a lot more too…

And using the chart, you should be able to tell:
- Where you are
- What is around you, both under the water and on the coast
- Where your destination is in relation to your position
- And how to get there as safely as possible

BEFORE USING A CHART

Before you use a chart, it's worth spending 10 minutes just reading the information contained in the title block and the margins of the chart itself. There is an enormous amount of valuable information tucked away there, and it has been put there for a purpose – to help you use the chart safely. I would normally try to do this while planning the passage, when you have more time available, and the deck is not lurching around beneath your feet. Take a look, for instance, at *Chart 2845*, which covers Braye Harbour on the north coast of Alderney in the Channel Islands.

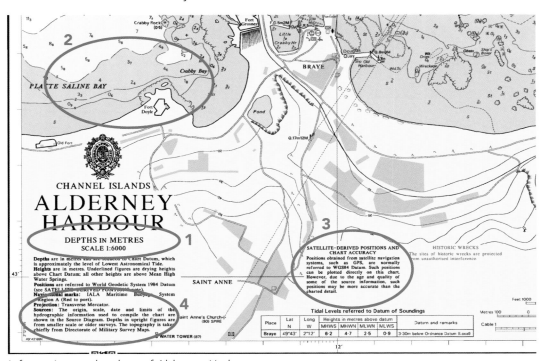

Information on the chart of Alderney Harbour

SCALE (CIRCLE 1)

The chart needs to be the right scale for your purposes. Pilotage, coastal and passage charts are all often drawn to different scales, and in general you need the largest available scale – but without having to endlessly change from one chart to another. The scale of a chart is shown in the title block. This one is drawn at a scale of 1:6,000, which makes it a pilotage chart designed for one purpose only: entry into, and departure from Braye Harbour.

COLOUR (CIRCLE 2)

The first thing that you will notice is that this chart has been printed in colour, with the land a sandy ochre colour, and the sea picked out in green, blue and white, depending on depth. That means that this is a metric chart (that is to say that depths and heights are shown in metres). The UKHO's imperial charts, with depths and heights in feet and fathoms, are drawn in black and white (see p14). These tend to be older editions, or charts which are not in great demand and so a low priority for modernisation.

TITLE BLOCK (CIRCLES 3 & 4)

The title block is just quietly ignored by many mariners, but it's always worth reading. Here, for instance, you can see that the chart is drawn to be compatible with the WGS84 datum, but the note titled 'SATELLITE-DERIVED POSITIONS AND CHART ACCURACY' (Circle 3) warns you that there may be some inaccuracies in the source data. This is borne out by the bottom left-hand note, titled 'Sources' (Circle 4). And, as if that's not enough, you can see that some of the sounding lines are broken (Circle 5), which tells you that the cartographer has only limited confidence in their accuracy.

WGS84 DATUM (CIRCLE 6)

This is important. Increasingly, charts are being published in a form that is compatible with the WGS84 datum and, where this is the case, you will see a note, printed in magenta.

If you can't find this written in the margin, look in the title block where it will tell you which datum has been used for this chart, and what corrections to make when plotting WGS84 satnav positions onto it (see p20).

SOURCE DIAGRAM (CIRCLE 7)

Always look at the Source Diagram of a chart before using it. You will immediately see that some parts of the island's coast were most recently surveyed in the mid-19th century by lead line; the approaches

Information on the chart of Alderney Harbour

to the harbour were last surveyed in 1959, and the harbour itself in the '80s and '90s.

It took me a long time to understand the meaning of the scale that is printed alongside the date of the survey, for instance: **1959   1:6000**

This tells you how wide the spacing was between survey lines. The assumption is that the surveyor will draw his survey lines on a working chart with a spacing of 5mm. So, a 1:6000 survey will be derived from survey work where the line spacing is 6,000 x 5mm = 30 metres – which is a pretty small gap. 1:15000, however, gives a line spacing of 75 metres, where it is possible for a wreck or a rocky pinnacle to hide undetected between the sounding lines,

and wider spacings make this more likely still.

The more recent surveys, carried out from about 2000 onwards, use multi-beam or swathe surveying techniques which quite simply do not leave any gaps at all.

CATZOC CATEGORIES

Increasingly you will find the areas delineated by a 'CATZOC' or 'Category of Zone of Confidence' rating which gives you a star rating for the quality of information in that area of your chart.

On paper and raster charts this appears on the Source Data diagram, and on a vector chart it should be available as a single layer overlay.

	CATZOC CATEGORIES			Stars on vector chart CATZOC overlay
ZOC	Position accuracy (m)	Depth accuracy (m)	Seafloor coverage	
A1	5	0.5 + 1% of depth	Full seafloor coverage. All significant features detected & depths measured.	6*
A2	20	1.0 + 2% of depth	Full seafloor coverage. All significant features detected & depths measured.	5*
B	50	1.0 + 2% of depth	Full seafloor coverage not achieved. Uncharted features, dangerous to surface navigation, not expected, may exist.	4*
C	500	2.0 + 5% of depth	Full seafloor coverage not achieved. Depth anomalies may be expected.	3*
D	Worse than Cat C	Worse than Cat C	Full seafloor coverage not achieved. Large depth anomalies may be expected.	2*
U	Unassessed			U

HOW TO LOOK AFTER YOUR CHARTS

Be kind to your charts. They have been drawn with quite extraordinary attention to detail, printed on distortion-free paper and you have spent hours lovingly correcting them over the winter months.

They deserve to be loved.

Only ever write with a soft 2B pencil. Anything harder, like a standard HB pencil, will leave a permanent mark.

Don't be tempted to put down your coffee cup, your wine glass, a bowl of spag bol, or an oily fuel filter on the chart. Chart paper will put up with a lot, but it was never designed for that.

When you have finished using a chart, rub out your workings, fold the chart back along the existing seams and stow it in a safe, dry horizontal stowage.

Always try to keep them dry. As a watch keeper on one of the Navy's last open-bridge minesweepers, I can remember trying to navigate down the coast of Yorkshire in a heavy autumnal storm. Water was breaking over the bridge, and the chart was like a sponge. It never lost its shape, which was a plus, but there was no way that we could use it for navigation or draw a fix on it.

CHART SYMBOLS & ABBREVIATIONS

Neither you nor I, nor anyone else for that matter, can possibly remember what all the chart symbols and abbreviations stand for. For instance, if you saw: cGR as a seabed description on a chart, would you instantly recognise that it stands for Coarse Gravel and Rock? I have to say that I wouldn't, and it's for that reason that I carry a copy of *Chart 5011* in my chart table bookshelf – or to give it the full name:

Chart 5011. Symbols and Abbreviations Used on Admiralty Paper Charts

This isn't a chart, of course; it's an A4 paperback booklet, but honestly, it's worth carrying a copy onboard. It's sold online and at most good chandleries. Apart from anything else, it shows how the symbols vary to give you precise information about a great variety of wrecks and rocks, showing that some may be safe to venture over, while others pose a genuine danger to shipping.

A complete copy of *Chart 5011* can also be found at the back of my book *Understanding a Nautical Chart*, also published by Fernhurst Books – and it costs less than *Chart 5011*!

Chart 5011

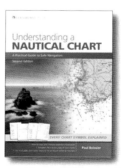

Understanding a Nautical Chart which also contains a complete copy of Chart 5011

DIFFERENT CHART PUBLISHERS

Admiralty paper charts are not cheap, but I like to use them in my yacht because I've used them all my professional and cruising life, and I trust them totally. But it's a matter of personal choice: there's no reason to restrict yourself to Admiralty charts and if you're cruising overseas you will almost certainly find yourself using locally produced charts and reference books.

I have often used Imray charts which are published and curated to a very high standard. They're easy to read and they have the great virtue of folding up much more tightly than Admiralty paper charts.

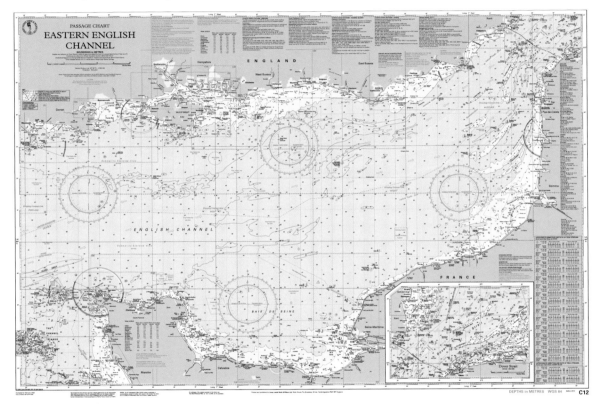

An Imray chart

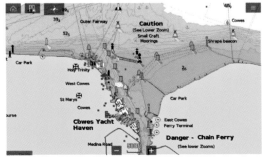

A Navionics chart

On my chart plotter I used Navionics digital chart software, which is very user-friendly, and have never found it to be inaccurate or inadequate for the task.

Choose a chart publisher that you feel comfortable with but do make sure that the charts can be regularly updated, and that they are produced and maintained to a high standard. After all, your safety and that of your crew depends on it.

CHART CORRECTIONS

CHART CORRECTION STATE

The correction state is one of the most important things to check before using a chart. It's easy to overlook, hidden away in the bottom left-hand corner of an Admiralty paper chart, but unless you know that your chart's up to date, you will have no idea how reliable it is. This shows the edition date (Circle 1) and the *Notices to Mariners* updates (Circle 2).

The correction state; try reading the QR code with your phone or tablet to get access to the chart correction webpage

HOW TO KEEP YOUR CHARTS UP TO DATE

I have yet to find anyone who really enjoys keeping their charts up to date. It's nothing like as enjoyable as getting out there on the water, but it's important – and I say this as someone who once nearly collided with an oil rig in the North Sea in poor visibility because I hadn't taken the trouble to update the chart before we left home. When, subsequently, I checked the *Notice to Mariners*, I found the oil rig's position was right there in my file – I just hadn't got round to inserting it.

In an ideal world, you would check each chart for the latest updates just before you use it. You may consider that life is too short for that sort of thing, but as a minimum I would suggest that you spend a few gentle evenings at home just before the sailing season starts, bringing your charts up to date. One day it will matter, and you'll be glad that you took the trouble.

I would also suggest that you update your chart plotter data card at least once per year – although with a subscription it's easy to update the data more frequently.

NOTICES TO MARINERS

Admiralty charts are updated using *Notices to Mariners* (NtM). These are published weekly by the UKHO, and they're free; you can pick them up from Admiralty Chart Agents around the world.

Or, more usefully, you can search for the latest updates by chart number, QR code (Circle 3), or date on **www.nmwebsearch. com**. This website also contains a hyperlink with instructions for keeping your chart up to date.

In practice, the simplest way to update a chart is to scan the QR code on the bottom left-hand corner. This will take you to a webpage showing the chart correction state, and you can insert any new corrections that you find there. Once you have inserted a correction, annotate the chart with the NtM number and date. It doesn't take long, and it's good to know that you're using a current chart.

For instance, when I scanned the QR Code on the bottom of the *Chart 2845* for Alderney Harbour, I was directed to the correction webpage for this specific chart. On the day that I visited this page, it contained 3 *Notices to Mariners*:

1562/2011, 4737/2012 and **5308/2015**. One of them, number **4737/2012**, contains a hyperlink to a cut-out-and-glue-in chartlet. The others are simple ink and pen corrections. All three were already recorded on the bottom left-hand corner of the chart (Circle 2) – so I knew that it was up to date for corrections.

UPDATING IMRAY CHARTS

It's just as simple to keep your Imray charts up to date. Visit the online Imray Correction page: **www.imray.com/ corrections/**

You put in the number of

The correction webpage from the QR code

the chart that you want to update, and this brings up a PDF with all the relevant updates to that chart. Check the bottom left-hand corner of the chart for its current correction state and apply any new corrections from the PDF. And don't forget to note the corrections that you have applied in the bottom left-hand corner.

LOCAL NOTICES TO MARINERS

Many local harbour authorities publish *Local Notices to Mariners*, which can be downloaded free online, and are often also pinned up in the harbour offices. If possible, it's worth checking these before you use a harbour, and they can change quite rapidly, so you need to keep an eye on them. By way of an example, I downloaded this document from the Poole Harbour website. Each line contains a link to a further page with information that may be relevant to users of the harbour.

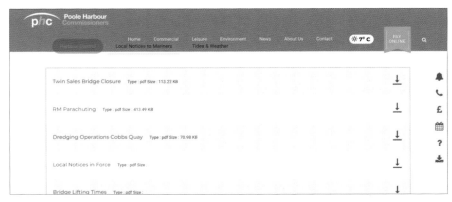

Poole Harbour's Local Notices to Mariners

3

POSITIONS, ANGLES, DISTANCE & SPEED

This chapter is all about how you use the chart to measure position, angles, distance and speed: the staple components of navigation.

EQUIPMENT

Navigating with a paper chart only really requires a few simple pieces of equipment:

- A 'proper' pair of **maritime dividers**. The best pair that I have found are the lovely big, tactile ones with a brass circle at the top and a wide span. They are robust, accurate and can be operated with one hand.
- An equally robust **drawing compass** with a spike at the end of one leg and a pencil attachment at the end of the other. This too should have a wide-enough span to cover a fair distance on your chart.
- A **2B pencil** – which is hard enough not to be inadvertently rubbed off when you run your hand over the chart, but soft enough to disappear when you rub it out. In my experience, the harder and more common HB pencils are rather too persistent.

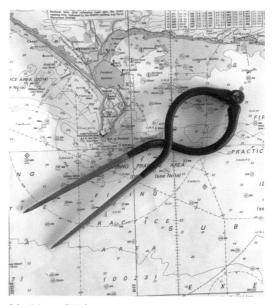

Maritime dividers

Drawing compass © Weems & Plath

- A good quality **soft eraser**.
- A **navigation notebook**. This is very much a matter of choice. I like the small lined A5 notepads with a spiral binding at the top. The book should be able to remain open at the right page for easy reference when you need it for navigation (an elastic band often helps with this), and it must be strong enough to stand up to life on a small boat.

2B pencil and good quality soft eraser

- And finally, you need a trusty **parallel ruler**. On naval ships and submarines, we were given heavy, brass parallel rulers to use, designed to survive a thermo-nuclear shock. In one particularly heavy storm off the Outer Hebrides, the parallel ruler flew off the chart table and gouged a 2-inch strip out of the lino flooring, narrowly missing the Engineer's leg on the way. On my yacht I have been quite happy to use a plastic Portland Course Plotter which is just as good at measuring angles but lacks the bloodthirsty personality disorders of its heavier cousin. There is also a more traditional design with 2 parallel rulers, bound together at each end, that you can walk across the chart. They all work perfectly well, and you only need to choose one that you feel comfortable with, that's completely reliable and strong enough to survive in a storm.

Navigation notebook – my choice is an A5 notepad

Over a lifetime of navigation, I have found that chart table equipment casts a strange, irresistible spell over otherwise entirely trustworthy members of your crew. Given half a chance they will either pinch them or use them for some dark purpose while you're not looking. I once found a submarine engineer using the point on my dividers to unclog a small and incredibly mucky oil pipe.

Guard your equipment and supplies ferociously (and make sure that you have an adequate supply of pencils, rubbers and notebooks to make up for the inevitable 'shrinkage' that will occur – even in a small yacht).

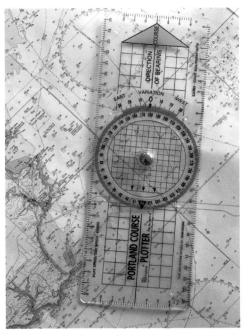

My preferred parallel ruler – a plastic Portland Course Plotter

POSITION

LATITUDE & LONGITUDE

Nowadays, getting your position is pretty easy – you just look at your GPS.

Alternatively, it's pretty simple to measure latitude and longitude on the chart:

- You set up a pair of nautical dividers to measure the 'vertical' distance to the nearest line of latitude
- Take the dividers to the latitude scale in the side margin and read off the latitude of the point that you're interested in
- And then you repeat the whole process 'horizontally' – to determine longitude against the scales on the top and the bottom of the chart

The graduations of latitude and longitude vary from chart to chart and I have mis-read the scales a few times, particularly when tired, or working close to the Greenwich Meridian, so it's worth double-checking to make sure that you've got the position right.

Of course, when working with a Mercator chart, remember that the latitude scale changes from the top to the bottom of the chart, so you have to measure the position at the same latitude as the distance you're measuring.

For example, on *Chart 2035 (Western Approaches to the Solent)*, you can use your dividers to measure the position of the Needles Lighthouse as:

50° 39'.73 N 001° 35'.50W

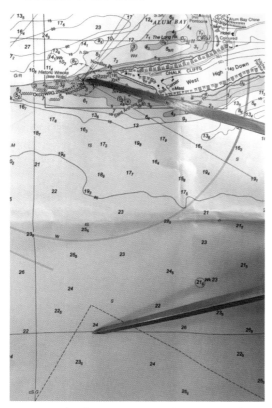
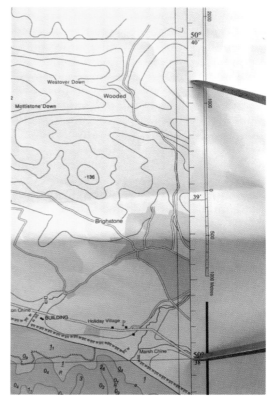

Use your dividers to measure the distance from the line of latitude (left) and read of the distance on the latitude scale at the same latitude (right)

ANGLES & BEARINGS

Angles and bearings are measured clockwise from True or Magnetic North, using the degree graduations around the edge of the compass rose. A full circle is divided into 360 degrees.

VARIATION

Standard UK Admiralty charts are always published with True North uppermost, and you will find a number of compass roses printed across the sea area, with True Bearings round the outside of the circle. This is incredibly useful in a big ship with a gyro compass permanently glued to True North, but most smaller vessels navigate by Magnetic North, using a magnetic steering compass, a magnetic flux-gate compass for the autopilot and chart plotter, and a hand-held magnetic compass for taking bearings. The difference in angle between True North and Magnetic North is called **variation**.

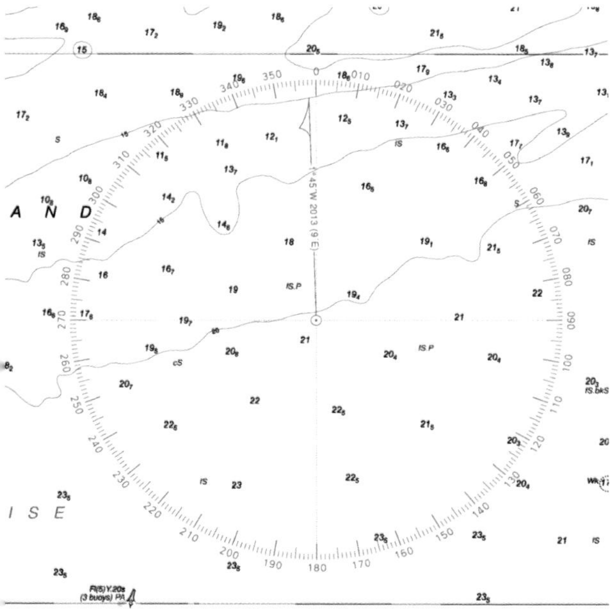

Compass rose on an Admiralty chart

The trouble is that the Magnetic North Pole moves around the Arctic Ocean in the same way as a bar of soap moves round your bath. So not only is it not in the same place as the True North Pole, but it's shifting, quite erratically, year by year (see p22-23). That means that the angular difference between True and Magnetic North – the variation – changes according to your location, and it also changes with time.

Normally, a single-sided Magnetic North arrow is printed within the chart's compass rose, with the variation, and the rate of change of variation printed along its shaft.

This compass rose is on *Chart 2035 (The Western Approaches to the Solent)*, and it shows that just to the southwest of the Needles:

**Variation in 2013 was 1° 45'W, shifting by 9'E (i.e. a reduction) every year
So, in 2020, the variation would be
9' x 7 = 63' or 1° 03' less
That makes the variation:
0° 42'W in 2020**

For the purposes of this book, I have used 1°W as the variation in the Solent, and the adjacent areas of the English Channel. You should, however, always check the variation when planning a passage, and recognise that this value may change across the length of your passage (see p23).

DEVIATION

Annoyingly, variation is not the only correction that you have to make to your magnetic compass. Magnetic compasses are also affected by ferrous metals in the boat's structure – like the engine, steel rigging wires and any other big lumps of metal, permanent or temporary, that happen to be nearby. Naturally enough the extent to which this interferes with your steering compass depends on the boat's heading. The resulting error is called **deviation**.

It's quite a simple procedure to produce a table of deviation against the ship's head by 'swinging your compass' – a splendid old nautical term for the process of steadying the ship on a variety of headings and measuring the compass error by taking bearings of a distant object.

You can either do this yourself (Chapter 9) or employ a professional Swinging Officer to do it for you. If I was swinging the compass out of idle curiosity, I would do it myself. If I needed a proper, certified Deviation Card for a long ocean passage, I would call in the professionals.

I have never known the skipper of a small fibreglass yacht go to the trouble of swinging its compass, because the magnetic signature of the boat is actually quite small – but even so, you should get it done if you're worried about the accuracy of your steering compass, or if you have a steel or ferro-cement boat. This will result in a Deviation Card from which it's quite easy to read off the deviation that you need to apply on any given heading.

CONVERTING BETWEEN TRUE, MAGNETIC & COMPASS BEARINGS

The ability to convert between True, Magnetic and Compass Bearings is an absolute core skill of navigation, and it all boils down to just 2 invaluable mnemonics.

There are 3 different bearings that you are interested in:

- **True Bearings**: The bearing of an object when related to True North – that is to say the axis of the earth's rotation. A gyro compass displays True Bearings.
- **Magnetic Bearings**: The bearing of an object when related to Magnetic North – that is to say the earth's shifting Magnetic North Pole. The difference between a Magnetic Bearing and a True Bearing is called variation.
- **Compass Bearings**: The bearing of an object when taken by the boat's magnetic compass (normally assumed to be the steering compass). The difference between Magnetic and Compass Bearings is called deviation.

Both variation and deviation are written down as degrees and minutes, followed by East or West to designate the direction in which they shift the compass. So, if variation is 10°W, the magnetic compass points 10° to the west of the true compass.

You can convert between these three bearings with the help of a couple of mnemonics.

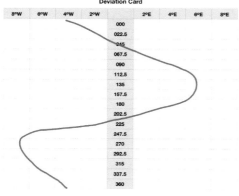

Deviation Card

C _ A _ D _ E _ T

That is to say:
Compass to True, ADd East

Which implies the corollary (sadly, there is no snappy mnemonic for this):
True to Compass, subtract East

> **Cadburys Dairy Milk Very Tasty[21]**
>
> And this gives you the order in which to make the adjustments:
>
> **COMPASS – Deviation – MAGNETIC – Variation – TRUE**

So, equipped with these 2 mnemonics, you can draw a small table (I have reversed the order of the second mnemonic).

Supposing that you want to steer a True Course of 125°T
Variation is 3°W
Deviation (taken from the Deviation Card above) 6°E
What would your Compass Course be?

TRUE	Variation	MAGNETIC	Deviation	COMPASS
	3°W		6°E	
125°T		128°M		122°C

Your Compass Course is 122°C

MEASURING ANGLES ON A CHART

For this you need a parallel ruler. If you wanted to measure the bearing of the Needles Fairway Buoy from the Needles Lighthouse (*Chart 2035*), draw a line from one to the

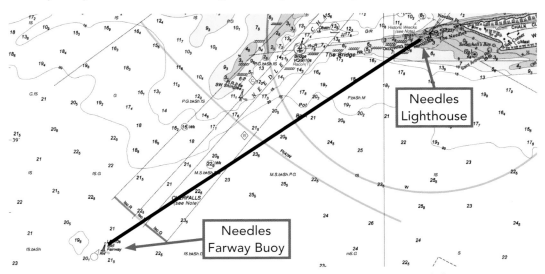

Draw a line from the Needles Lighthouse (right) to the Needles Fairway Buoy (left)

---

[21] No matter whether you agree with this or not, it seems to be quite memorable.

other, noting that the actual position of the lighthouse is the little white circle at the centre of the star, and the buoy is located at the centre of the circle on the symbol's baseline.

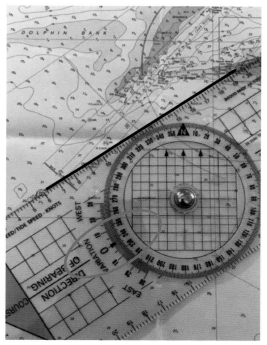

Plotter running along the line allowing you to read the True Bearing

- Set up the Portland Plotter with the edge of the plotter running along your pencil line
- Rotate the central dial so the grid in the middle is parallel to the north/south or east/west lines on the chart
- Read off the True Bearing: 236° True
- Apply variation: 1° W

Magnetic Bearing: 237° Magnetic

TAKING A BEARING

When you take a bearing of an object with a hand-held magnetic compass, you need to be standing somewhere safe, but where you feel comfortable and stable against the movement of the boat.

For preference, I tend to use a hand-held electronic compass, but I always carry an old-fashioned oil-filled compass too. No matter which one you use, this is at its best an imprecise science, so I normally take 3 to 5 bearings in close succession, a second or two apart, and then average the result.

Try to minimise the effect of the sea state by taking your bearings when the boat's movement reaches a lull. Even so, it would be a mistake to expect super-precise results.

DISTANCE

MEASUREMENT OF DISTANCE ON A CHART

There is only one way to measure distance on a Mercator or Transverse Mercator chart: by using the latitude scale alongside the distance to be measured.

**One minute of latitude equals
1 nautical mile
and
One degree of latitude equals
60 nautical miles**

Suppose you're planning to swim from Fort Albert on the Isle of Wight across the western entrance of the Solent to Hurst Castle (in view of the tidal streams, this is not something that I would recommend!). How far is it?

- First of all, measure the distance between the 2 points with a pair of dividers
- Then go to the right-hand margin of the chart at the same latitude – I've set the bottom point of the dividers against a line of latitude: 50° 42'N, and the upper point lands at 50° 42'.66N
- One minute of latitude is a mile, so this

distance is 0.66 nautical miles (nm)[22] – better known as a very long swim in cold water!

If the distance is too great to be covered in a single span of the dividers, set them at an easy distance (say 5 or 10nm), and pace the distance out, counting the paces and measuring the remainder.

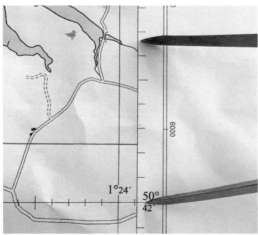

Measuring distance on a chart: measure the distance with your dividers and then read off the distance on the right-hand margin

MEASUREMENT OF DISTANCE AT SEA

There are a couple of quite interesting ways of measuring or estimating distance on the water without reference to a chart.

RADAR
The first, of course, is radar, which accurately measures the distance of a hard-surface, bluff object, like a cliff, a ship or a buoy, but which is rather less accurate on slanting surfaces like a sandy beach, or small objects that are obscured by the sea state, or when objects get so close that they are lost in the ground clutter. Providing that you accurately identify the object on your radar screen (and displaying the radar overlay on the chart plotter map is immensely useful for this), radar will usually give you an accurate range for an object (see Chapter 6).

DISTANCE TO THE SEA HORIZON
Another way to estimate distance is to calculate the range of the sea horizon. There are tables in the *Almanac* that do this for you. This is a more useful technique than you might imagine. It allows you to estimate the range at which you will see a big ship on a clear day, and how long you have before you need to alter course to avoid it. Also, at night this technique will give you a fairly accurate range at which a lighthouse light dips below the horizon – or appears above it.

The radius of the earth is fixed, so the distance to the sea horizon depends solely on your height of eye[23]. It's tabulated in the *Admiralty List of Lights*, and helpfully also appears in the 'Navigation' section of

---

[22] Since a nautical mile is about 6,000ft, or 2,000 yards, this is about 1,320 yards, – a very long way to swim.

[23] This assumes normal atmospheric refraction; the range at which objects can be seen can be distorted by abnormal refraction. You can sometimes tell this is happening if you see mirages hovering over the horizon.

Height (m)	Distance to the Sea Horizon (nm)
1	2.1
2	2.9
3	3.6
4	4.1
5	4.7
6	5.1
7	5.5
8	5.9
9	6.2
10	6.6
11	6.9
12	7.2
13	7.5
14	7.8
15	8.1
16	8.3
17	8.6
18	8.8
19	9.1
20	9.3
21	9.5
22	9.8
23	10.0
24	10.2
25	10.4
26	10.6
27	10.8
28	11.0
29	11.2
30	11.4

the *Reed's Almanac*. With permission, I've copied the table from the *Admiralty List of Lights* opposite.

So, if your height of eye when you're standing in your cockpit is 3m, which is about typical for the average yachtsman, the sea horizon is 3.6 nautical miles away.

Equally, if the bridge watch keeper on a merchant ship has a height of eye of 15m, the distance to their sea horizon is 8.1nm.

This gives you quite a useful way, on a clear day, of estimating when the superstructure of a big ship will appear over the horizon – when its range is:

3.6 + 8.1 miles distant = 11.7nm

It's not absolutely precise, but it gives you a reasonable ball-park figure to work with.

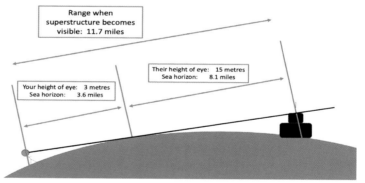

How to measure the distance when a ship's superstructure becomes visible

SPEED

Speed at sea is measured in knots:
- One knot is one nautical mile per hour
- A nautical mile is 1,852 metres, and a statute mile (which we use ashore) is 1,609 metres
- So, a knot is about 15% faster than a land mile per hour

Measuring speed on the water is confused by the fact that the water itself is almost always in motion, so you generally have to take account of two very different ideas of speed:
- **Boat Speed**: Displayed on your ship's log – your speed through the water

- **Speed Over the Ground** (SOG): The speed that your GPS tells you – your speed over the surface of the earth

The difference between the two is principally the effect of the tidal stream, or current, with perhaps a bit of leeway thrown in for good measure.

SOG is more relevant in respect to the land, or objects that are in some way attached to the land, like a buoy or an anchored ship.

Boat Speed is more relevant in relation to other freely moving objects on the water, like vessels that are under way.

CALCULATING SPEED OVER THE GROUND (SOG)

It's really helpful to have a way of connecting your boat's course and speed through the water, the direction and speed of the tidal stream, and your course and speed over the ground[24].

Suppose that you are heading 090° at 10 knots with a tidal stream setting you due south at 3 knots
What would your resulting course and speed be over the ground?

The easiest way to work this out is to draw a diagram:

- Start by drawing a line along your heading: 090° and mark the line with a single arrow. The length of this line is the distance that you would travel in 1 hour at 10kts: 10nm.
- From the end of this line, draw a second line to show the influence of the tidal stream – it will be 3 miles long in a direction of 180°. Mark this line with a triple arrow.
- You can then draw the diagonal which shows how far, and in what direction, you will have travelled over the ground in 1 hour (which is marked with a double arrow). In this case 10.4nm in a direction of 108°.

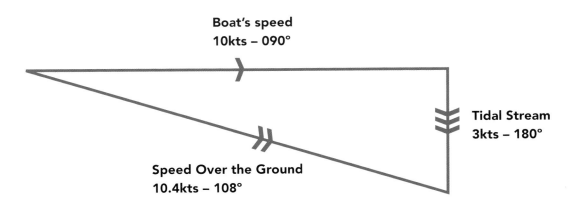

Boat's speed
10kts – 090°

Tidal Stream
3kts – 180°

Speed Over the Ground
10.4kts – 108°

Diagram to work out your SOG

So SOG is 10.4kts
And COG (Course over Ground) is 108°

---

[24] Course and Speed Over the Ground (COG and SOG) are sometimes referred to as Course Made Good (CMG) and Speed Made Good (SMG).

You can use the same triangle to work out what course you need to steer to stay on track in a tidal stream.

Suppose the tidal stream is setting 222° at 3.5kts
You are making 7kts through the water
And you want to make good a course of 180° over the ground
What course should you steer, and what will be your speed over the ground?

This is exactly the same triangle that we have just drawn, and the trick is to fill in the things that you do know, piece by piece, until it is complete.

- Start by drawing the one thing that you know all about: the speed and direction of the tidal stream (3.5kts at 222° – three arrows).
- Then draw the course that you want to make good, 180° (two arrows), which intersects with the 'going to' end of the tidal stream arrow. You only know the direction of this line at the moment, not the length.
- And finally, using a drawing compass, measure off 7kts from the 'going from' point of the tidal stream line, and mark where that intersects with the Speed Over the Ground Line. Draw the line between this point and the 'going from' point of the tidal stream line (1 arrow).

This gives you the answer
You need to steer a course of 162°
And you will make good 9.4kts over the ground

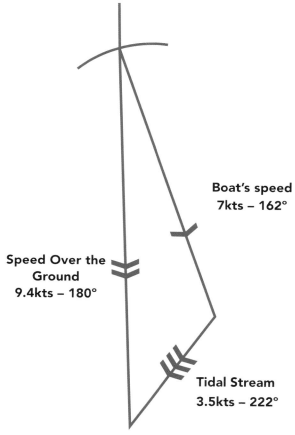

Boat's speed
7kts – 162°

Speed Over the Ground
9.4kts – 180°

Tidal Stream
3.5kts – 222°

The resulting diagram

These are incredibly useful calculations, particularly around Northern European waters where you can often find yourself working with strong tidal streams. For instance, if you're coming from the north and aiming at Braye Harbour on the north coast of Alderney, you may find yourself in strong tidal streams, pushing you east or west. You need to steer a course that will compensate for the tidal streams in order to keep the harbour entrance on a steady bearing. If so, it's useful to spend a couple of minutes on the chart beforehand, drawing out the speed triangle, to give you an idea of the best course to steer.

4
MOVEMENT OF WATER: THE HEIGHT OF TIDE

One of the things that makes marine navigation so interesting is the movement of water. If you're navigating through coastal waters, you face a double challenge: tidal streams that are always trying to sweep you off course, and the constantly changing depth of water as the tides ebb and flow. To be a proficient and safe navigator, you must be absolutely confident in your ability to calculate and use these tidal variations.

I have been aground – or almost been aground – in big ships and small yachts on a number of occasions, and from my experience I would say that just about every grounding is avoidable… and thoroughly annoying.

I remember watching the distress of a yacht crew one Sunday afternoon when their skipper drove them aground on the mud close by the entrance to Lymington Yacht Haven towards the end of a falling tide. They clearly hit the mud at a fair old speed because they couldn't get themselves straight back off again. No-one was hurt, and the boat floated off safely a few hours later on the flood tide, but it must have seriously messed up their plans for getting home that evening. And, like many navigation slip-ups, it was a very public display of one skipper's lapse in concentration.

© RNLI/Holyhead/Simon Price

TIDES, & THE MOVEMENT OF WATER

71% of the earth's surface is covered by a relatively thin layer of water. Most of this is fluid, and quite mobile when a force is applied to it – and there's no shortage of forces constantly trying to pull the water from one point on the earth's surface to another. These include:

- The gravitational pull of the moon and, to a lesser extent, the sun
- The centrifugal effect of the earth's rotation
- The wind, particularly the steady, constant winds like the Trade Winds
- Any unusually high or low areas of barometric pressure

By far the biggest and the most pervasive of all these influences is, however, the moon: a great big solid chunk of rock that orbits the earth at a distance of about 240,000 miles, from where – like the villain in a Bond movie, stroking a white cat – it exerts a massive influence on the oceans while the earth spins away below[25].

The earth rotates once every 24 hours, and the moon rotates around the earth once every 30 days or so. So the 'lunar day' (the time between each moonrise) is a little bit longer than the solar day – about 24 hours and 50 minutes. The oceans are locked into this timescale, and the water has to flow fast to keep up.

The moon's gravitational field applies a strong force on the waters of the oceans – a force that is strongest when the moon is directly overhead, and gradually reduces

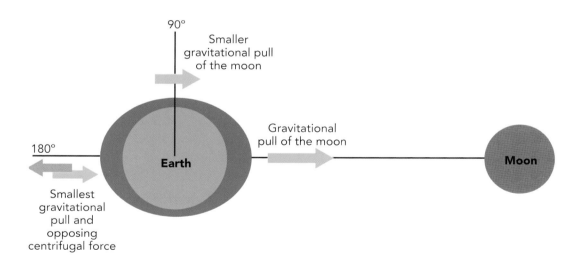

Gravitational pull of the moon

---

[25] The tides use up an extraordinary amount of power – something in the region of 3.75 terawatts (3.75 million, million watts) on average. This power comes from the rotational energy of both the moon and the earth, and it's actually slowing down the moon's orbit, increasing the distance between the earth and the moon by about 3.8cm every year. It's also slowing the earth's rotation – extending the length of a day by about 2 hours over the last 600 million years.

as you move around the earth:

■ Water that is directly underneath the moon experiences the strongest attraction

■ Water which is at 90° to the direction of the moon is also attracted to the moon, but less strongly

■ And the water facing directly away from the moon experiences the smallest pull of all

As a result, you get a concentration of water under the moon (resulting in a high tide), and a 'thinning out' of the water at 90° to the moon, which causes 2 low tides, one on each side.

From 90° to 180°, a second force comes into play. Although we consider the moon to be spinning round the earth, the moon and the earth actually form a sort of binary star, each spinning around the other. This creates a centrifugal force on the side of the earth facing away from the moon, where its gravitational pull is least, pushing the water away from the moon, and causing

a secondary high tide.

Meanwhile, the earth is rotating at a much faster rate than the moon's orbit, so these 2 standing waves are experienced on the earth as 2 high tides and 2 low tides each day (or, to be precise, each lunar day).

If the moon was the only heavenly body close to the earth, that would be it. However, the sun also exerts a force on the oceans which is a little less than half (44%) of the strength of the force exerted by the moon, but still quite substantial. So, when the sun and the moon are lined up, at the time of the full moon or the new moon[26], the force on the oceans is roughly 50% greater, and so the strength of the tides is greater. **This is called SPRING TIDES**.

When the sun and the moon are at 90° apart in the heavens, at a time when we see only a half moon from the earth, the gravitational force from the sun and the moon are pulling in different directions, and the tidal effect is reduced. **This is called NEAP TIDES**.

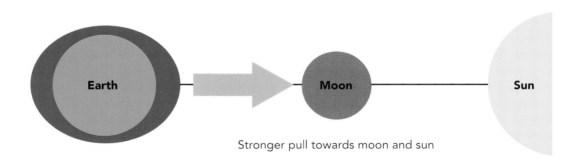

Stronger pull towards moon and sun

Spring Tides

---

[26] In fact, there's always a bit of a lag in the system, Spring Tides actually occur 2-3 days after the full moon and new moon, and Neap Tides happen about 3 days after half moon.

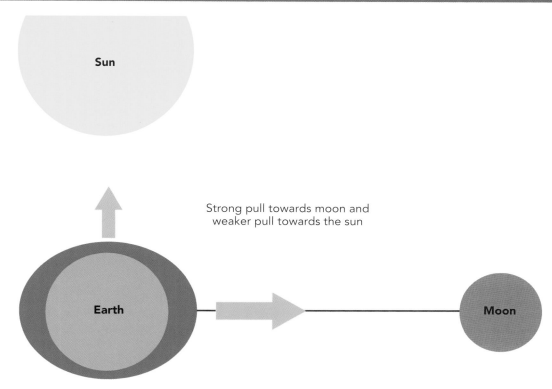

Sun

Strong pull towards moon and
weaker pull towards the sun

Earth

Moon

Neap Tides

The lunar cycle, from new moon to half moon to full moon and back to half moon and then new moon again, lasts a month. In that time, we experience 2 Spring Tides and 2 Neap Tides. So, the time interval between a Spring Tide and a Neap Tide is roughly one week.

The tidal effects are greatly reduced in inland seas, like the Mediterranean and the Baltic, where the entrance is too small to allow the regular passage of vast quantities of water. In other places, like the Bay of Fundy in Nova Scotia and the River Severn in the southwest of England, the funnel-shaped waterway actually amplifies the tidal effects and results in abnormally high tidal ranges.

The rotation of the earth normally results in 2 high waters and 2 low waters each day. This is called a **semi-diurnal tide**, and this is by far the most common form of

tide. However:

- Sometimes, land gets in the way of the water's flow, so that it can only manage one high and one low water each day. This occurs on the coast of Alaska, for instance, or in the Gulf of Mexico, and it's called a **diurnal tide**. This is much less common than semi-diurnal tides.

- Islands often cause unusual tidal flow patterns, such as the Isle of Wight, which allows the flood tide to enter from both ends of the Solent. This can cause a double high tide, or a **stand**. In fact, just about any offlying island will have a material effect on the water flow. For instance, the two largest ports in Patagonia, Punta Arenas on the Magellan Strait and Ushuaia on the Beagle Channel, are each fed by both Atlantic and Pacific tides, which results in unusual tidal shapes.

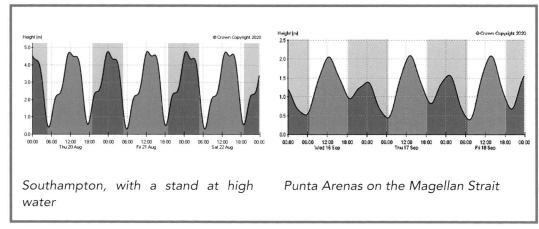

Southampton, with a stand at high water

Punta Arenas on the Magellan Strait

3-day tidal prediction graphs, for ports whch lie on waterways that are open at both ends taken from UKHO's EasyTide app

GETTING THE TERMS RIGHT

The tides play a massive part in any coastal passage, so it's quite important to get the terminology right.

- **Tidal Stream**: The tidal stream is the **periodic horizontal flow** of water caused by the gravitational forces from the moon and the sun
- **Current**: A current is a **permanent or semi-permanent horizontal flow of water**, normally in the ocean, and normally caused by a constant wind on the surface of the water
- **Height of Tide**: The Height of Tide is the **vertical movement** in sea level as a result of the gravitational influence of the sun and the moon
- **Tidal Range**: The tidal range is the difference between the height of high and low tide

Barring extreme events like a tidal surge, both the Height of Tide and the tidal streams are predictable to a high level of accuracy using the *Admiralty Tide Tables* and the *Tidal Stream Atlases*, or –

more accessible to a yachtsman – a good almanac, like *Reed's Nautical Almanac*.

TIDAL SURGES

Tidal predictions are almost uncannily accurate, but just occasionally, even around the UK coastline, things can get a little extreme.

Tidal surges tend to happen in relatively shallow and constrained water with the combination of a Spring Tide and a strong wind blowing onto, or away from, the shore. This can cause the water level to rise or fall by more than predicted, particularly when amplified by an area of unusually low or high atmospheric pressure.

A deep depression, or a strong northerly wind over the southern North Sea, for instance, can result in abnormally high tides and coastal flooding along the low-lying coastline of East Anglia and the Thames Estuary. It was to protect London from catastrophic flooding, that the Thames Barrier was constructed in the late 1970s. Since then there have been 186 flood defence closures[27].

Negative surges, with abnormally low

---

[27] Up to October 2019.

water levels, can occur when a strong wind blows water away from an area of shallow water.

Surges are normally well predicted and, when they do occur, they need to be taken seriously by any mariner.

On 29 August 2005, Hurricane Katrina swept ashore in Southern Louisiana in the United States of America, with all the makings of an extreme tidal surge: low pressure within the hurricane vortex, very strong onshore winds and a constrained coastline at the mouth of the Mississippi River, where the water flowing from the sea back into the river blocked its natural flow and caused a rapid increase in water level. The result was a 7-metre storm surge, about 3 metres higher than the height of the levees (the river's retaining walls). This caused flooding across almost 80% of the city and, tragically, the death of well over 1,000 people.

VERTICAL MOVEMENT OF WATER

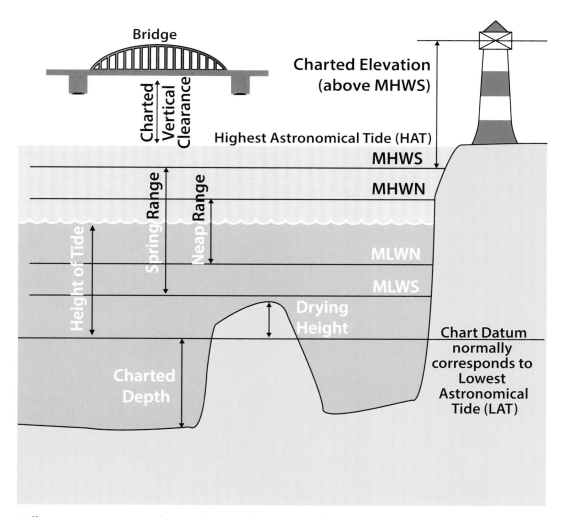

Different measurements of vertical heights (© Fernhurst Books)

CHART DATUM

All depths of water on the chart are referenced to a single datum level, carefully chosen by the hydrographer. This level is called the Chart Datum, and it is the key to working out the total depth of water:

- The **Charted Depth** is the distance between the seabed and Chart Datum
- The **Height of Tide** is the distance between Chart Datum and the water surface

So:

**The Total Depth of Water =
Charted Depth + Height of Tide**

Typically, Chart Datum is set at or around the level of the Lowest Astronomical Tide[28], which means that you can glance at a chart without working out the Height of Tide, and be reasonably confident that the depth of water will be greater than the depth shown on the chart.

There are 2 other datums that you should be aware of:

MEAN HIGH WATER SPRINGS (MHWS)

This is, as it says on the tin, the average level of High Water at Spring Tides. It's the level at which dry land is assumed to start on the chart, so MHWS defines the outline of dry land – dividing the yellow part of a chart (which is always dry) and the green, blue and white of the underwater topography. This boundary is portrayed on a chart by a thick black line.

MHWS is also used as the reference level for Charted Elevation of navigation marks, like lighthouses. So when the chart tells you that the elevation of La Veille Lighthouse on the tip of the Pointe du Raz in Brittany is 33m, it means that there's 33m

of vertical separation between the plane of the lighthouse and MHWS.

By happy coincidence, you will find that on many rocky parts of the coast there's a clear black line of marine growth which sits almost exactly at MHWS, corresponding nicely with the thick black line on the chart that divides dry land from the water. This can be very helpful when taking a bearing of the right- or left-hand edge of land.

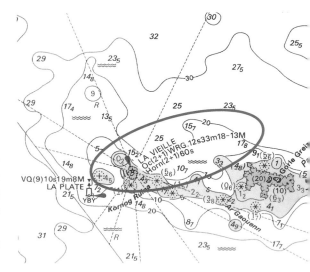

La Vielle Lighthouse with a Charted Elevation of 33m above MHWS

---

[28] The Lowest Astronomical Tide is the lowest level to which the tide routinely falls.

HIGHEST ASTRONOMICAL TIDE (HAT)

Highest Astronomical Tide is the highest level to which the tide routinely rises, and you will find the height difference between Chart Datum and HAT in Table V of the *Admiralty Tide Tables*, or in *Reed's Nautical Almanac*, at the bottom of the Standard Port tide tables. HAT is important because the 'Charted Vertical Clearance' – that is to say the air gap under an overhanging obstruction, like a bridge or power cables, is usually[29] shown on the chart as the distance from the level of HAT up to the obstruction[30]. This is done for reasons of safety, to ensure that the actual gap is almost always greater than that shown on the chart.

By the way, do you know the height of your masthead above the waterline?

DRYING HEIGHTS

The areas of the seabed that lie between Chart Datum and MHWS are neither properly 'sea' nor 'dry land'. They tend to cover and uncover as the tides rise and fall. These areas of the seabed are coloured in green on the chart and, their height above Chart Datum is displayed as a number with a line underneath it. This is called the **Drying Height**.

The progression from sea to dry land is nicely illustrated in this small chartlet of the Ile de Sein on the tip of Brittany. There is a clear transition:

- From white (more than 5m of Charted Depth)
- Through blue (5m to Chart Datum)
- Across Chart Datum
- To green (Chart Datum to MHWS)
- And finally, yellow for the land (above

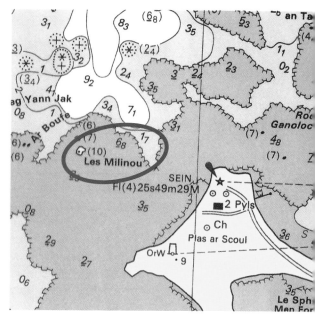

Different heights compared to Chart Datum are shown clearly by colours on the chart

MHWS)

Below Chart Datum (the blue and white areas), the depths are indicated as straightforward soundings: 1_7 indicates 1.7m below Chart Datum. In the green area, the soundings become Drying Heights, so 6_8 indicates that the seabed is 6.8m above Chart Datum (but still below MHWS). Eventually you get to the small islet of Les Milinou which stands 10m above MHWS, as indicated by its yellow colour and the notation (10).

By the way, always be wary of rocks with names. Fisherman are never going to go to the trouble of naming a rock unless it is either a source of wonderful lobsters or, more likely, a conspicuous danger to shipping.

---

[29] 'Usually', but not 'always'. Overhead clearances can sometimes be referenced to MHWS – so it's worth checking the chart Title Block if you're concerned about whether or not you will fit under a bridge.

[30] To work out the actual air gap, you would take the Charted Clearance, add the distance between HAT and Chart Datum, and then subtract the height of the tide above Chart Datum.

CALCULATING HEIGHT OF TIDE

STANDARD & SECONDARY PORTS

The tables used for calculating the Height of Tide are set out in the *Admiralty Tide Tables*, or more commonly for yachtsmen, in a reliable nautical almanac, like *Reed's Nautical Almanac*. Detailed tidal information is given for a series of 'Standard Ports', which tend to be the busiest and most important ports around the coast, and the Height of Tide calculations at these ports is normally pretty straightforward. The templates for the rise and fall of the tide at the Standard Ports is used for tidal calculations at a nearby location with similar tidal profiles. These are called Secondary Ports.

As yachtsmen and women, most of us reach for *Reed's Nautical Almanac* when we need information about the maritime environment, including tidal information. Much of this information is sourced from Admiralty publications, like the *Admiralty Tide Tables*, the *List of Lights* or the *Sailing Directions*, all of which are considerably more expensive than *Reed's*, and principally designed for the professional mariner. For copyright reasons, I have used Admiralty data in this book; you may spot a few minor differences in presentation (for instance, Admiralty publications are printed exclusively in black and white, while *Reed's* uses a lot of colour), but it's the same data, and I'll signpost any significant differences as we go along.

STANDARD PORTS

If you open up the *Almanac* or the *Tide Tables* on the pages of a Standard Port, you will see a dense table of dates and tide heights, and nearby a graph which shows the profile of tidal height with time.

Taking a closer look at the tide table (below), you will see that the tide times are displayed in UT – Universal Time, or GMT

ENGLAND — SOUTHAMPTON

LAT 50°53'N   LONG 1°24'W

TIME ZONE **UT(GMT)**   TIMES AND HEIGHTS OF HIGH AND LOW WATERS   YEAR **2020**

	MAY				JUNE				JULY				AUGUST		
	Time	m		Time	m		Time	m		Time	m		Time	m	
1 0342 3.7 1011 1.8 F 1631 3.7 2308 2.0			**16** 0555 3.6 1142 1.9 SA 1756 3.7			**1** 0557 3.8 1229 1.4 M 1843 4.1			**16** 0031 1.9 0631 3.5 TU 1250 1.8 1953 4.0			**1** 0031 1.5 0640 4.0 W 1300 1.4 1918 4.2			**16** 0024 1.9 0625 3.5 TH 1250 1.9 1905 3.8			**1** 0221 1.4 0834 4.0 SA 1445 1.5 2051 4.2			**16** 0151 1.7 0822 3.9 SU 1420 1.8 2041 4.0		
2 0456 3.6 1151 1.7 SA 1752 3.8			**17** 0024 2.0 0657 3.6 SU 1245 1.8 1857 3.7			**2** 0106 1.4 0709 4.0 TU 1332 1.2 1947 4.3			**17** 0127 1.8 0816 3.8 W 1343 1.7 1959 4.0			**2** 0136 1.4 0745 4.1 TH 1401 1.3 2016 4.3			**17** 0123 1.8 0744 3.7 F 1348 1.8 2009 3.9			**2** 0313 1.2 1013 4.2 SU 1535 1.3 2218 4.3			**17** 0250 1.4 0918 4.1 M 1515 1.4 2129 4.3		
3 0037 1.8 0625 3.7 SU 1309 1.4 1921 4.1			**18** 0123 1.8 0801 3.7 M 1341 1.6 1949 3.9			**3** 0203 1.1 0809 4.2 W 1425 0.9 2041 4.5			**18** 0214 1.6 0823 3.8 TH 1430 1.5 2049 4.1			**3** 0232 1.1 0843 4.2 F 1455 1.1 2104 4.4			**18** 0218 1.6 0845 3.9 SA 1441 1.6 2103 4.1			**3** 0400 0.9 1057 4.3 M 1621 1.1 O 2257 4.3			**18** 0340 1.0 1002 4.4 TU 1602 1.1 2211 4.5		
4 0143 1.4 0742 4.0 M 1406 1.1 2022 4.4			**19** 0213 1.5 0853 3.8 TU 1429 1.4 2041 4.1			**4** 0253 0.9 0901 4.4 TH 1514 0.8 2126 4.6			**19** 0256 1.4 0914 4.0 F 1512 1.3 2130 4.2			**4** 0323 0.9 1011 4.3 SA 1544 1.0 2228 4.5			**19** 0308 1.3 0935 4.1 SU 1530 1.4 2149 4.3			**4** 0444 0.8 1140 4.4 TU 1705 0.9 2337 4.3			**19** 0426 0.7 1042 4.6 W 1647 0.8 ● 2256 4.6		
5 0234 1.0 0836 4.3 TU 1455 0.7 2108 4.6			**20** 0256 1.3 0934 4.0 W 1511 1.2 2123 4.2			**5** 0340 0.6 1015 4.5 F 1600 0.6 O 2238 4.7			**20** 0335 1.2 0955 4.1 SA 1553 1.2 2212 4.3			**5** 0411 0.8 1100 4.4 SU 1632 0.9 O 2311 4.4			**20** 0354 1.0 1017 4.3 M 1616 1.1 ● 2231 4.4			**5** 0526 0.7 1223 4.4 W 1747 0.9 2349 4.2			**20** 0509 0.4 1143 4.7 TH 1730 0.6 2335 4.7		
6 0319 0.6 0924 4.5 W 1540 0.4 2150 4.7			**21** 0335 1.1 0944 4.1 TH 1550 1.1 2200 4.3			**6** 0425 0.5 1101 4.5 SA 1646 0.6 2321 4.6			**21** 0414 1.0 1031 4.2 SU 1633 1.1 ● 2249 4.4			**6** 0456 0.7 1150 4.4 M 1718 0.9 2354 4.4			**21** 0440 0.8 1058 4.4 TU 1701 1.0 2311 4.5			**6** 0606 0.7 1216 4.3 TH 1827 1.0			**21** 0550 0.3 1223 4.8 F 1811 0.5		

Tide table for Southampton

– so that you need to add one hour if you are using the tables during the summer months. This will convert the tables from GMT to British Summer Time. Helpfully, the editors of *Reed's Nautical Almanac* have shaded the days of GMT; if you use the *Admiralty Tide Tables*, you will have to work out the dates of BST for yourself.

In *Reed's Almanac*[31], the tide tables are marked up with the dates of Spring Tides in red and of Neap Tides in blue – so 5 August 2020 is a Spring Tide date, 2 days after the full moon on 3 August.

On 1 August, High Water is at 0834 UT (0934 BST) and 2051 UT (2151 BST), and the height of those tides is 4.0m and 4.2m above Chart Datum respectively.

	Time	m
1	0221	1.4
	0834	4.0
SA	1445	1.5
	2051	4.2

The Height of Tide graph shows the Height of Tide with respect to the time of Low Water at Southampton. In most Standard Ports, the graph is referenced to High Water, but uniquely in the Solent, where the tide floods from the east and the west at the same time, you tend to get a double high tide, or a 'stand', and so it's easier and more accurate to portray the Height of Tide in relation to the more sharply-defined time of Low Water.

Somewhere on the Height of Tide graph you will find a small text box (Circle 1) containing the Mean Ranges for Spring and Neap Tides: 4.0m at Spring Tides, and 1.9m at Neap Tides.

So, on the afternoon of 1 August:

- The Height of Tide at High Water is 4.0m
- The Height of Tide at Low Water is 1.5m
- So, the range of this tide is 2.5m (4.0 – 1.5 = 2.5)

Using a bit of eyeball interpolation, this is about $1/3$ of the way between the Mean Neaps Range (1.9m) and the Mean Springs Range (4.0m) (Circle 1), so you can call it 'one third Springs'.

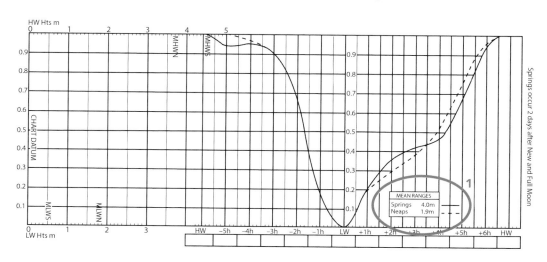

Height of Tide graph for Southampton

---

[31] But not in the *Admiralty Tide Tables*.

Don't worry if you're not so keen on 'eyeball interpolation'. The left-hand side of the tidal graph (see below), is actually an incredibly useful interpolation grid which you can use for a variety of calculations. In this case, I have marked the Mean Neap Range (1.9m) on the bottom line, and the Mean Spring Range (4.0m) on the top line and drawn a line (in red) between them.

We have already calculated the range on 1 August to be 2.5m, so I have drawn a vertical blue line from the bottom of the grid at 2.5m until it hits the red line, and then over to the left-hand margin. As if by magic, it hits the left-hand margin near a point marked 0.3. That is to say:

0.3 x (the difference between the Mean Spring Range and the Mean Neap Range)

… Or roughly 'one third Springs'.
You should also note that on the rising

tide (after Low Water), the profiles of Spring and Neap Tides are different on the graph, with Springs being shown in a solid line, and the Neap profile in a dashed line.

WORKING OUT THE HEIGHT OF TIDE AT A STANDARD PORT

Once you have the heights and the times of High and Low Water, it's not too difficult to work out your own 'Height of Tide table' for a Standard Port.

You are planning to be afloat from 1000-1800 BST in Southampton Water on 1 August 2020

You want to calculate the Height of Tide over that period

From the *Tide Tables* (remembering to correct for BST), find the relevant Tidal Points:

HW	0934 BST	4.0m
LW	1545 BST	1.5m
HW	2151 BST	4.2m

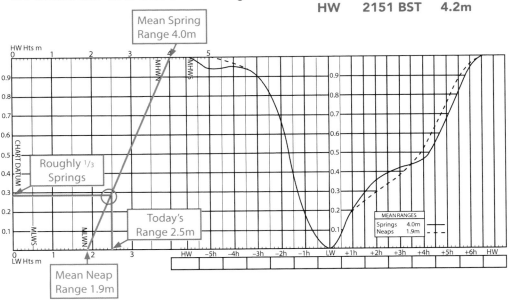

If you want to be sure, rather than 'eyeball interpolation' you can use the interpolation grid on the left-hand side of the tidal graph to work out the range between Neaps and Springs

Draw a line (red in this diagram) on the interpolation grid between High Water at the top (4.0m) and Low Water at the bottom (1.5m). Then note the time of Low Water (or High Water in other Standard Port graphs) in the bottom margin of the graph (1545 BST). I find it quite useful to write the time in pencil along this bottom margin at 2-hour intervals (shown in green).

If you want to find out the Height of Tide 2 hours before Low Water (LW) at 1345 BST, you draw a vertical line (blue in this case), starting at 1345 on the bottom margin, up until it hits the black tidal curve, along to the red line that you have already drawn, and finally up to the top margin... where, as if by magic, you can read off the Height of Tide: 3.1m.

It's slightly more interesting at LW + 2hrs (1745 BST), because you have to choose which tidal line – Springs or Neaps – to stop at. In fact, you have just worked out that this tide is about 'one third Springs', so you should stop one third of the way from the Neap curve to the Spring curve.

Height of Tide Southampton 1 August 2020		
Time (BST)		**Height of Tide (m)**
0934	HW	4.0
1045	LW –5	3.9
1145	LW –4	3.8
1245	LW –3	3.7
1345	LW –2	3.1
1445	LW –1	2.0
1545	LW	1.5
1645	LW +1	2.0
1745	LW +2	2.3

Following the same procedure as we went through above, the answer comes out at 2.3m.

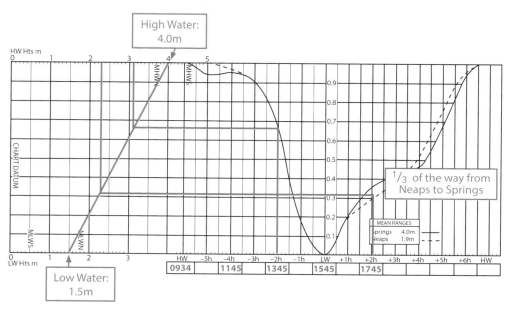

How you would use the Southampton tide graph to work out Heights of Tide for a Standard Port

You repeat this process for every hour over the period that you are interested in. This allows you to draw up a table (on previous page) in your navigation notebook with the heights of tide over the period 1000-1800 BST when you will be afloat.

In practice, you may find that you don't really need to actually draw the lines on the graph to read off the Heights of Tide; once you're used to the process, you can pretty much trace the lines by eye. This table is, by the way, quite remarkable, because you can see that the High Water stand lasts for about 3 hours, from 0945-1245 BST.

And that, in a nutshell, is how you do Standard Ports.

WORKING OUT THE HEIGHT OF TIDE AT A SECONDARY PORT

For reasons that I've never really understood, the two words: 'Secondary' and 'Ports' when bandied around in close proximity to each other, are enough to send a shock of chilled terror through the hearts of many yachtsmen. Which is a shame, because a Secondary Port calculation is really no different from the Standard Port calculations that we have just done for Southampton.

The **shape** of the tide at a Secondary Port is the same as its Standard Port: you just need to make adjustments to the **time and the height of High and Low Water**, and then you can treat it exactly in exactly the same way as a Standard Port.

Suppose that you want to calculate the Height of Tide in Salcombe, on the South Devon coast, to the east of Plymouth. Looking up Salcombe in the *Tide Tables* or *Reed's Almanac*, you find that Plymouth is the Standard Port to use when calculating the Height of Tide, and you will find a small table of corrections, as shown here in an extract from the *Tide Tables* shown below.

This table is replicated in *Reed's Almanac*, only with the addition of a helpful black arrow at the top, showing you which way to turn the pages to get to the Standard Port.

The columns that matter show the TIME DIFFERENCES and the HEIGHT DIFFERENCES. These are the corrections that you have to apply to the Standard Port data to work out the Salcombe tides. Annoyingly, these corrections vary with the time of the High and Low Water at the Standard Port, and the state of the tide from Springs to Neaps.

Starting from the left:
- If High Water Plymouth is at 0100 GMT or 1300 GMT[32], you make no correction to the times of High Water

No.	PLACE	TIME DIFFERENCES				HEIGHT DIFFERENCES (IN METRES)				ML	
		High Water		Low Water		MHWS	MHWN	MLWN	MLWS	Z_0	
		Zone UT(GMT)								m	
14	**PLYMOUTH (DEVONPORT)**	0100 and 1300	0600 and 1800	0100 and 1300	0600 and 1800	5.5	4.4	2.2	0.8		
20	*Salcombe River* Salcombe	+0000	+0010	+0005	−0005	−0.2	−0.3	−0.1	−0.1	3.14	c
21	Start Point	+0015	+0015	+0005	+0010	−0.1	−0.2	+0.1	+0.2	3.20	★c
23	*River Dart* DARTMOUTH	STANDARD PORT					See Table V			2.93	★
23a	Greenway Quay	+0030	+0045	+0025	+0005	−0.6	−0.6	−0.2	−0.2	2.84	c

Corrections for Secondary Port Salcombe from the Tide Tables

---

[32] If using the *Almanac*, it's worth checking which time zones these times refer to. It's usually the same time zones as used for the Standard Port tide table.

- If High Water is at 0600 GMT or 1800 GMT, you add 10 minutes to the Standard Port time
- For Low Water at 0100 or 1300 GMT, you add 5 minutes
- For Low Water at 0600 or 1800 GMT, you subtract 5 minutes

The right hand side of the table tells you that the correction to the height of MHWS is –0.2m (when the Height of Tide at Plymouth is 5.5m), and the correction to Mean High Water Neaps is –0.3m (when the Height of Tide is 4.4m)… and so on.

Using these headline corrections, you just need to interpolate sensibly to find the corrections for High and Low Water. You can interpolate by eye, or by drawing a graph, or with your calculator – whichever you feel happiest with.

We want to calculate the tides in Salcombe on the morning of 4 July 2020 Between 0800 BST and midday

Making allowance for the fact that on this date the UK will be working in BST, you can note down the relevant Plymouth tides in your notebook:

HW   **0444 GMT   0544 BST   5.1m**
LW   **1107 GMT   1207 BST   1.0m**

4		Time	m
		0444	5.1
		1107	1.0
	SA	1708	5.3
		2331	1.0

The range of this tide is 4.1m
From the text box on the Height of Tide diagram (see below), the range for Springs is 4.7m and 2.2m for Neaps, so you can use the interpolation grid to work out that this range is just over ¾ **Springs**.

Now you just need to do a bit more interpolation to find the adjustments for time and Height of Tide at Salcombe.

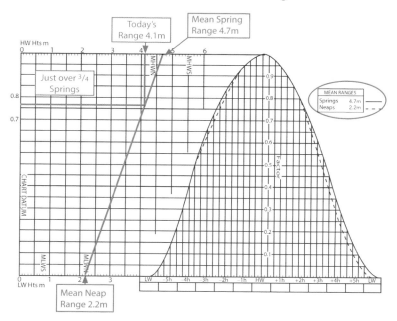

Using the interpolation grid you can work out that this range is just over ¾ Springs

Correcting the Time

The important thing is to avoid any confusion over the time zone. The tide tables are almost certainly shown in UT (GMT), as are the Secondary Port corrections, and you'll be using BST in your boat. It's often easier to use both GMT and local time in parallel when calculating these tides.

The headline corrections for adjusting the time of High and Low Water at Salcombe (see p60) are:

High Water
- 0100 GMT 0200 BST
  0 min correction
- 0600 GMT 0700 BST
  +10 min correction

Low Water
- 0600 GMT 0700 BST
  −5 min correction
- 1300 GMT 1400 BST
  +5 min correction

You have already worked out that, at Plymouth, the Standard Port on this day (4 July 2020):
- HW is at: 0444 GMT   0544 BST
- LW is at: 1107 GMT   1207 BST

Plot the GMT times on the red and blue lines of the time interpolation graph, and you can read off the corrections for 0444 GMT and 1107 GMT, respectively:
- HW Correction: +8 minutes
  (approximate is fine here)
- LW Correction: +2 minutes

Now, apply these corrections to the times of High and Low Water at Plymouth...

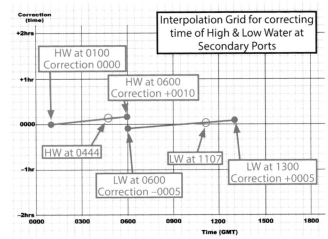

Plot the corrections on the interpolation grid and read off the correction for the particular times[33]

- So, High Water Salcombe is:
  0452 GMT   0552 BST
- And Low Water Salcombe is:
  1109 GMT   1209 BST

Correcting the Height of Tide

You go through exactly the same process to correct the Height of Tide, only using the height correction figures (p60).

You have already worked out that at Plymouth that morning:

HW   0444 GMT   0544 BST   5.1m
LW   1107 GMT   1207 BST   1.0m
The range of this tide is 4.1m

And your corrections (p60) are:
MHWS (5.5m)   correction: −0.2m
MHWN (4.4m)   correction: −0.3m

MLWN (2.2m)   correction: −0.1m
MLWS (0.8m)   correction: −0.1m

So on the height interpolation graph, you can draw these data points. Again, I have drawn the High Water line in red, and the

---

[33] Blank versions of these grids can be downloaded from www.fernhurstbooks.com – search 'Mastering Navigation at Sea' and click on 'Other Resources'.

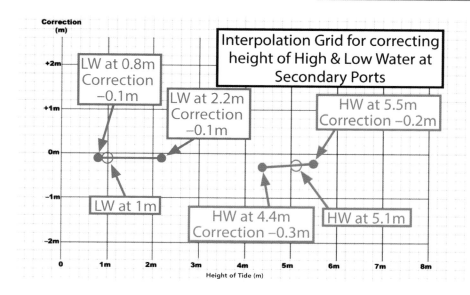

Again, you can use the interpolation grid to get the correction[33]

Low Water line in blue.

HW Plymouth: 5.1m   correction: –0.2m
LW Plymouth: 1.0m   correction: –0.1m

All that remains to be done is to apply these corrections to the Height of Tide graph at Plymouth that morning and write down the results in your notebook.

At this point, I'm just going to use BST, because that's the time zone you will almost certainly be using for navigation.

Tide Times & Heights at Salcombe 4 July 2020				
	High Water		Low Water	
	BST	m	BST	m
Plymouth	0544	5.1	1207	1.0
Correction	+0008	–0.2	+0002	–0.1
Salcombe	0552	4.9	1209	0.9

This gives you the time, and the height of both HW and LW at Salcombe that day.

This feels like a bit of a long-winded process, and you can of course do the interpolation by eye if you prefer. In any case, once you're used to it, it doesn't take so long, and it's actually quite satisfying.

All you need do now is to go straight back into the Plymouth Height of Tide graph for a simple Standard Port calculation using the corrected times and heights for Salcombe.

The time of HW Salcombe (0552 BST) goes in the bottom margin, and HW and LW Salcombe (4.9m and 0.9m respectively) allow you to draw the red line.

At HW + 3 (0852 BST), I have gone 3/4 of the way between the dashed line (Neap Tides) and the continuous (Spring Tides) line because, as we established earlier, this tide is 3/4 Springs. This gives a Height of Tide of 3.3m.

You now just repeat the process until you have filled in the table. By the way, you may find that if you work through this you will come up with differences of a few minutes; don't worry too much about small discrepancies – in my experience Secondary Port calculations are as much art as science, and a few minutes here or there really doesn't make a lot of difference in practice.

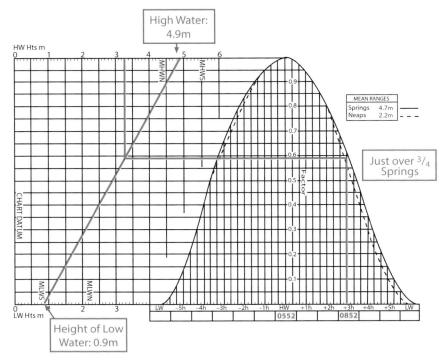

High Water: 4.9m

HW Hts m

MEAN RANGES
Springs 4.7m
Neaps   2.2m

Just over ³/₄ Springs

Factor

CHART DATUM

LW Hts m

0552   0852

Height of Low Water: 0.9m

Now use the Standard Port Plymouth's Height of Tide graph

Height of Tide Salcombe 4 July 2020		
Time (BST)		**Height of Tide (m)**
0752	HW +2	4.2
0852	HW +3	3.3
0952	HW +4	2.3
1052	HW +5	1.5
1209	LW	0.9

And that, really, is how to do Secondary Ports. A little time and patience, some interpolation, either using a grid or by eye, and a couple of tables.

USING THE HEIGHT OF TIDE TABLES
You're in the vicinity of Salcombe on the morning of 4 July

You want to pass over a bank with 0.7m Charted Depth of water at 1000 BST

If your boat has a draught of 1.5m, how much under-keel clearance would you have?

The total depth of water = Charted Depth + Height of Tide

Height of Tide at 0952 = 2.3m
Total depth of water: 0.7 + 2.3 = 3.0m

If your draught is 1.5m, you will have 1.5m of clearance under your keel

TIDAL ANOMALIES IN THE SOLENT
The water flow in and out of the Solent (between Christchurch and Selsey Bill) is complicated by the fact that the flood tide comes into the Solent from both the east and the west. This distorts the normal flow

of water, giving a double high tide, or a stand, at many of the ports and anchorages (as we have already seen for Southampton, p57). Working out the Height of Tide in these ports is not really any different from the normal calculations for Standard and Secondary Ports, except that for additional accuracy, the *Tide Tables* often contain specific curves for individual ports – rather than using the Standard Port curve. And because typically these ports have an extended period of High Water, the curves are indexed around Low Water, which tends to be rather better defined than High Water (as we saw for Southampton).

So, for these ports:

- You do all your corrections, as before, for the times and Heights of Tide
- You also work out where you are between Neap and Spring Tides
- Then, instead of using the Standard Port curve, you go to the curve for the individual port you are working in, interpolating as before between the sometimes very different curves for Spring and Neap Tides

- Finally, note down the results of your calculations in the notebook, and cast your eye over them one more time, just to check that they make sense

As an example, I have included one calculation using this method in Chapter 19.

WORKING OUT THE HEIGHT OF TIDE ONLINE

If this all seems a bit like hard work, you can always use an online app to calculate the times and the heights of tide.

The UKHO hosts an app called *Easy Tide*, which I love: **www.ukho.gov.uk/ easytide/EasyTide/index.aspx**. This provides a free service over a limited forecasting period. If you want predictions for an unlimited period into the future, you have to pay.

You could also find an app like *My Tide Times* in the iTunes App Store. I can't vouch for the accuracy of this app and would advise you to check the accuracy of any commercial app before you use it in anger.

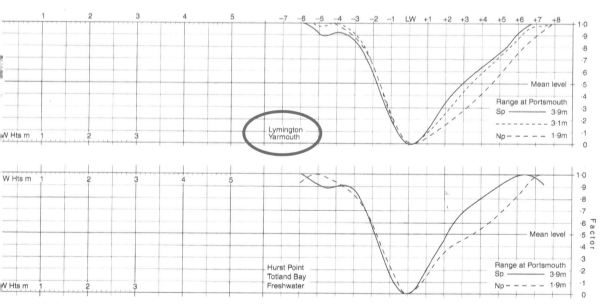

Tidal curves for ports near the Solent

5

MOVEMENT OF WATER: TIDAL STREAMS & CURRENTS

The waters of the ocean are in perpetual motion:

- Sometimes, driven by the motion of the earth, sun and moon, this motion is periodic and repeats itself in a daily, or half-daily cycle. These cyclical flows of water are the **tidal streams**.
- Sometimes the motion of the water is constant, or virtually so, driven by steady winds, like the trade winds, blowing over the earth's surface and setting up massive flows of water around the oceans – like the Gulf Stream in the North Atlantic. These constant flows of water are called **ocean currents**.

In general, you will encounter tidal streams in coastal waters, and on the continental shelf, where water depth is less than 200 metres. Ocean currents are more common in the deeper ocean waters, sometimes flowing in different directions at different depths.

OCEAN CURRENTS

Accurate predictions for the speed and direction of currents are contained in the *Admiralty Sailing Directions*, and currents are often drawn on small scale charts as well, depicted as a sort of wavy, corrugated line.

As a rule of thumb, the speed of a wind-generated surface current is roughly 1/40th of the mean, sustained windspeed.

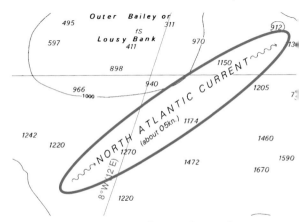

How ocean currents are depicted on a chart

So, a 25-30 knot trade wind, blowing from the east, will set up a westerly set in the water of about 0.75kts in the open ocean.

Sometimes, the border of a current is quite well-defined, and is marked by a change in sea colour or temperature.

This can often be associated with fog, as can often be found on the Grand Banks of Newfoundland in eastern Canada, where the cold Labrador Current runs into the much warmer Gulf Stream, giving this part of the Atlantic Ocean one of the highest incidences of fog in the world.

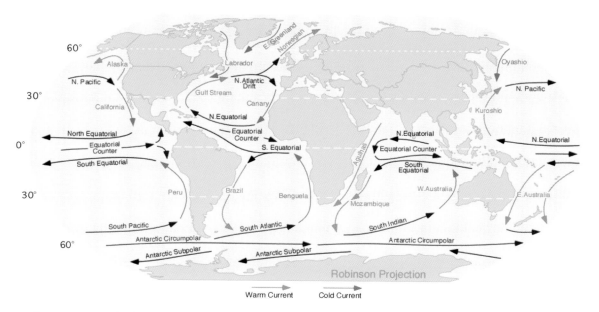

Ocean currents (NOAA)

TIDAL STREAMS

CALCULATING THE SPEED & DIRECTION OF TIDAL STREAMS

Around UK waters, there are two commonly used methods of predicting tidal streams. Both are derived from the same data and both, in theory at least, give the same results. These are the **Tidal Diamonds** which you find on coastal charts, and *Tidal Stream Atlases*.

TIDAL DIAMONDS

Suppose that you were contemplating a passage through the Swinge, the turbulent channel to the west of Alderney (this is dangerous and unstable water – and I really wouldn't recommend going there without careful preparation).

On *Chart 60*, there is a diamond right in the middle of The Swinge, labelled D. This letter refers to the Tidal Data block, which can normally be found in the margins of the chart.

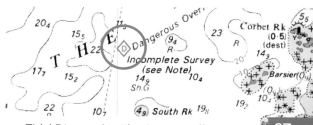

Tidal Diamond in The Swinge, off Alderney

Each diamond has its own table with 13 rows and 3 columns:

- The rows give tidal stream predictions at hourly intervals, from HW –6 hrs to HW +6 hrs
- The first column gives the direction of the tidal stream (°T)
- The second column is the speed of the tidal stream (kts) at Springs
- The third is the speed (kts) at Neaps

Tidal Streams referred to HW at SAINT HELIER

Hours		Geographical Position			Ⓐ 49°44'54 N 2 11·88W		Ⓑ 49°38'44 N 2 11·88W	
Before High Water	6 5 4 3 2 1	Directions of streams (degrees)	Rates at spring tides (knots)	Rates at neap tides (knots)	-6 267 -5 275 -4 269 -3 271 -2 067 -1 075	3·4 1·5 3·1 1·4 2·4 1·1 1·1 0·5 0·9 0·4 3·3 1·5	232 231 232 193 069 065	3·6 1·5 3·3 1·4 2·2 1·0 0·6 0·2 2·1 0·9 4·0 1·7
High Water					0 091	3·1 1·4	057	4·1 1·7
After High Water	1 2 3 4 5 6				+1 267 +2 287 +3 285 +4 273 +5 259 +6 264	0·3 0·2 1·9 0·8 2·3 1·0 3·3 1·5 3·1 1·4 3·2 1·4	047 040 340 255 242 234	3·3 1·4 1·9 0·8 0·6 0·2 1·5 0·7 2·9 1·2 3·6 1·5

	Ⓒ 49°41'24 N 2 14·58W		Ⓓ 49°43'24 N 2 14·98W		Ⓔ 49°44'14 N 2 18·78W	
-6	234 2·8 1·1		227 6·5 2·6		218 5·0 2·0	
-5	186 1·4 0·6		222 6·8 2·7		210 5·1 2·1	
-4	100 1·4 0·6		183 4·8 1·9		207 3·9 1·6	
-3	078 1·5 0·6		170 1·2 0·5		202 2·2 0·9	
-2	062 1·6 0·6		051 2·6 1·0		072 1·1 0·4	
-1	054 1·6 0·6		041 4·6 1·8		051 2·8 1·1	
0	047 1·7 0·7		047 5·5 2·2		024 5·5 2·3	
+1	020 1·2 0·5		038 5·1 2·0		018 4·8 2·0	
+2	354 0·5 0·2		037 5·5 1·6		018 3·4 1·4	
+3	278 0·5 0·2		041 1·9 0·8		014 1·9 0·8	
+4	252 1·7 0·7		161 0·5 0·2		186 0·6 0·2	
+5	250 3·1 1·2		231 5·1 2·1		201 2·8 1·1	
+6	239 2·9 1·2		229 6·2 2·5		214 4·3 1·7	

The tidal data block on the chart

Tidal information on this chart is referenced to High Water in St Helier.

So, at Spring Tides, 5 hours before HW St Helier, the rate of the tidal stream at diamond D is 6.8 knots in a direction of 222°T. By any standards, that represents an impressive flow of water. And in shallow water, over an uneven seabed, a tidal stream of this rate will certainly throw up serious and dangerous overfalls.

What is the tidal stream in the middle of The Swinge at 10am (BST) on 5 July 2020?

Go to the Tide Tables for St Helier (a Standard Port). On 5 July 2020:

	Time	m
5	0035	1.8
	0617	10.3
SU	1259	1.9
O	1837	10.6

High Water at St Helier is:
    0617 GMT   0717 BST   10.3m
Low Water is:
    1259 GMT   1359 BST   1.9m
And from the tidal graph (see opposite):
The Mean Spring Range is: 9.6m
And the Mean Neap Range is: 4.1m

So 10am BST is just short of 3 hours after HW St Helier. And the range of this tide is 8.4m (10.3 – 1.9 = 8.4).

According to the *Tide Tables*, 5 July is 6 days after Neaps and 2 days before Springs. So this is ³/₄ Springs.

Alternatively you can use an interpolation grid (see opposite), which gives a result of just over ¾ Springs.

Now, you go back to the Tidal Data block, diamond D, at HW +3, which says that the stream is 1.9kts at Springs and 0.8kts at Neaps in a direction of 041°T.

So finally, you can either use an interpolation grid (opposite) to work out what the rate will be with a range of 8.4m (¾ Springs), or you can estimate the answer by eye.

In either case, the predicted tidal stream is:

1.7kts in a direction 041°T

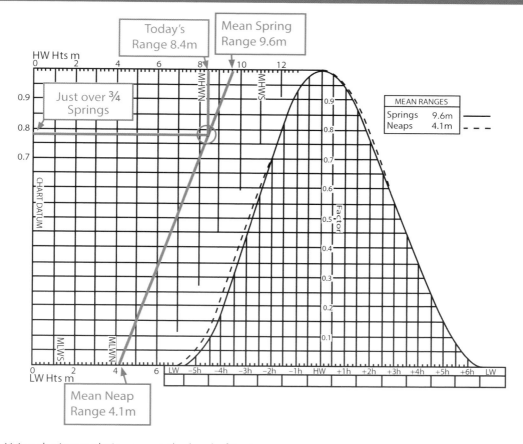

Using the interpolation to get the level of Springs

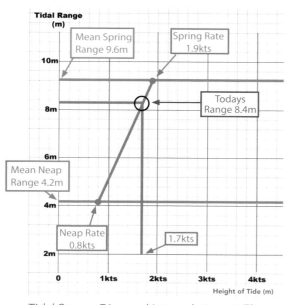

Tidal Stream Diamond interpolation grid[33]

TIDAL STREAM ATLAS

The UKHO has published an extensive series of *Tidal Stream Atlases*, spanning the waters of northwest Europe from Shetland to the mouth of the Loire, and from the west coast of Denmark to the east coast of Ireland. It's worth having a selection of these invaluable books on board, covering any sea areas that you are likely to visit; they don't go out of date and I use them constantly, both for planning and when I'm on passage.

Information from the *Tidal Stream Atlas* is reproduced in a number of places – in *Reed's Nautical Almanac*, for instance, and also on some local charts. Personally, I have a preference for the booklets: I annotate each page with the appropriate time (in 2B pencil so I can rub it out), and this becomes an invaluable point of reference on passage.

Information for The Swinge is contained in the *Tidal Stream Atlas* for the Channel Islands. This *Tidal Stream Atlas* is calibrated against both HW Dover and HW St Helier. The closest diagram in the Atlas to 10am on 5 July 2020 is titled:

2 hours before HW Dover.
2h 50m after HW St Helier

On 5 July, that is 1007 BST[34].

There's a lot of information in this diagram that's not apparent in the Tidal Diamonds, like the northeasterly set of the stream, curving round to the north as it passes Burhou. You can also see the southwesterly counter flow of the stream close to the Braye Harbour breakwater. It's easy to compare these flow lines with the hours before and after, just by turning the page.

At 1007 BST in the middle of The Swinge, there is a north-easterly arrow annotated with the numbers **08,21**.

These numbers are the Neap and Spring tidal stream rates in tenths of a knot. I have no idea why they are written this way – it's one of the many mysteries of seafaring. Clearly, the Neap rate is less than the Spring rate, so you don't need a degree in oceanography to remember which is which!

So, at Neap Tides, the tidal stream flows at 0.8kts in a direction of about 050°, and at Spring Tides, the speed of the tidal stream is 2.1kts in the same direction.

Once again, you can either interpolate with a grid[35] or by eye, giving a result that at 1000 BST on 5 July (¾ Springs), the predicted tidal stream is:

1.8kts in a direction 050°T

This is not too far off the prediction that we got from Tidal Diamond D.

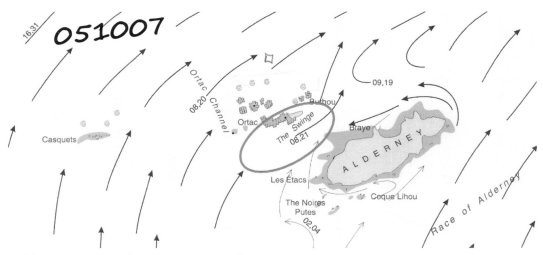

Tidal stream diagram for 1007 BST on 5 July

---

[34] I have marked this diagram '051007' to signify 1007 BST on 5 July. I put a 2-digit date before a 4-digit time, because it helps to reduce confusion if, like me, you don't always rub out your workings at the end of a passage.
[35] Helpfully, the *Tidal Stream Atlas* has an interpolation grid inside the front cover.

SHOULD I USE THE TIDAL STREAM DIAMONDS, OR THE *TIDAL STREAM ATLAS*?

You should use both. If you're doing pilotage in and out of the western Solent, for instance, or into Braye Harbour on the island of Alderney, you should work out the tidal stream at each diamond adjacent to your track, because it will give you a precise and very accurate prediction at that point and time.

But you will probably also want to know how the tidal stream is flowing around you, and for that the best reference is the *Tidal Stream Atlas*, annotated for the right time. On a cross-Channel passage, for instance, I mark up every page of the Channel *Tidal Stream Atlas* in advance so that I can quickly check the tidal stream predictions all the way across. It takes almost no time, and it's incredibly useful in helping you keep track on your progress and ETA.

But at the end of the day, these are just predictions, and you should never give up an opportunity to check them against the actual tidal stream. So, whenever you go past an object that is firmly moored to the seabed – rocks, navigation buoys, anchored ships, navigation beacons or fishing floats – check the rate and direction of the tidal stream and compare it to the predictions.

When I'm estimating the flow of water past a stationary object, I compare the speed of the water with my normal brisk walking pace, which is about 2.5kts: if I were able to walk on water[36], could I keep up? If I would have to break into a trot, or even run to keep up with the buoy, I would estimate the tidal stream as 3, 4 or 5 knots

– or possibly more.

I took this photo in the splendidly named Peril Strait in South Alaska, where the tidal stream can run at up to 9 knots... which is well beyond my running ability!

Check the rate and direction of the tide when you pass objects fixed to the seabed

TIDAL RACES

Beware of tidal races. There is absolutely no sense in going through a race if you can possibly avoid it, and if you do have to sail through one, make sure that your timing is perfectly accurate so you get through as fast as possible, with the minimum amount of turbulence. Tidal races tend to happen when big tidal streams are forced past an obstruction, or through a narrow passage. This speeds up the waterflow, and often causes turbulence – sometimes severe turbulence – particularly when the seabed is uneven, or when the wind is blowing against the tidal stream.

You will find tidal races all around the UK, and in many other areas as

---

[36] I make no pretensions towards holiness, but it reminds me of the Russian pilot who came onboard when I took my ship to Russia shortly after the fall of the Iron Curtain. He stood with me on the bridge as I brought her alongside the jetty at St Petersburg without tugs. After we were safely alongside, he shook me warmly by the hand, and said: "Very god." Sadly, I think this was more a reflection on his limited English than a comment on my ship-handling.

well: Portland Bill has a notorious race, as does the east coast of Alderney. The Gulf of Coryveckan between the islands of Bute and Jura in the Hebrides, and the Pentland Firth on the north coast of Scotland. There are more; they're all written up in the appropriate *Sailing Directions*, and you need to treat them with respect, whether in a big ship or in a small leisure yacht.

TIDAL STREAM INDICATORS ON THE CHART

In many parts of the world, for instance the eastern tip of Tierra del Fuego and the off-lying Isla de los Estados, just northeast of Cape Horn, there are no tidal stream atlases available. But the water flows are

clearly marked on the chart:
- The flood streams are marked with arrows with 6 small feathers on the back (Circle 1)
- Ebb streams are marked with simple arrows with just an arrowhead at the front (Circle 2)
- The double sets of ripples (Circle 3), show where you can expect overfalls
- And running along the bottom of the chart is the corrugated symbol of the Cape Horn Current (Circle 4)

Note, too, the broken contour lines (Circle 5) which indicate unreliable soundings, and which should always sound a big warning alarm in the mind of a navigator.

This is not particularly friendly water.

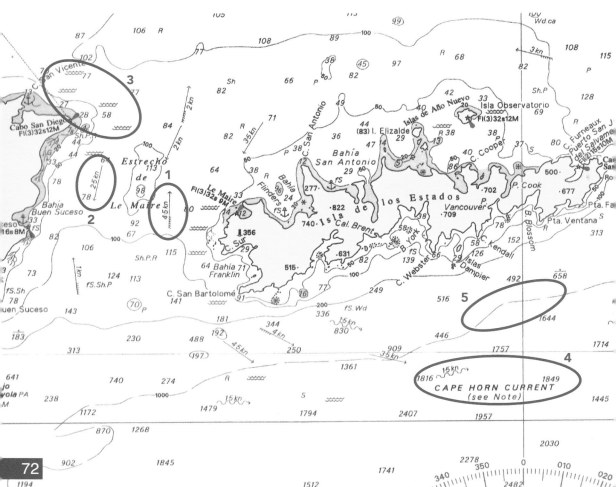

6
THE FIX

The moment that you let go of your mooring lines, your boat takes on a life of its own, moving not just where you steer it, but also influenced by the tidal streams, the current and the wind.

To a large extent, tidal influences are predictable. You can predict, with a fair degree of accuracy, what the tidal stream will be doing at any time and in any place, and so you can calculate its likely effect on your course and speed over the ground. But no matter how hard you try, your best estimate of position will progressively become less and less accurate as time passes – as a variety of small inaccuracies gradually creep in. Things like:

- Inaccuracies in your steering and your speed through the water
- Variations in the tidal stream
- Leeway
- The ocean current

None of these can be predicted with 100% accuracy. And over time these errors can amount to quite significant differences between where you think you are, and where you actually are.

One of my most embarrassing navigation moments occurred when I was navigating a conventional submarine, well before GPS became available. When operating around the European coastline we would use Decca as the principal radio navigation aid. Decca was fine. It was a bit temperamental and moody at times, but you could live with that. The difficulty was that it wasn't universally available. So when we were sent down to the Western Approaches to the Straits of Gibraltar for a 2-week intensive exercise with some surface ships, we had to rely largely on DR (Dead Reckoning) and EP (Estimated Position), together with an occasional snatched sun sight during periods when other ships didn't want to play with us.

Over the course of the fortnight we found that fewer and fewer ships were turning up for our planned exercises. And then, on the last couple of days of the exercise, none turned up at all. We assumed that they had all broken down, or that they were lost.

Eventually the time came for us to surface and head in towards Gibraltar.

I drew a line on the chart, and we set off for the Straits at breakfast time. By mid-afternoon we unexpectedly came across a steady stream of shipping, all crossing our track at an angle of about 30°. "*No problem*", I told the Captain, "*they're probably all heading to Casablanca. I'm quite confident of our position, and I'll confirm it with a star sight tonight.*"

The Captain gave me one of those looks and said, "*Even so, I think we might just tag along with them, and if we do end up in Casablanca I'll just have to apologise.*" Wise man. We followed the line of shipping … and sure enough the next morning we found ourselves passing through the Straits of Gibraltar.

It was an embarrassing 48 hours, and my colleagues never let me forget the incident. We had been at least 25nm out of position when we surfaced, despite all of my best efforts to keep track of where we were. I learnt how important it is to allow for this growing 'pool of errors' which is an inevitable result of a long period without fixing. I also learnt the great seafaring skill of trusting your instinct, as the Captain had done. And from a navigation perspective, I realised that the shipping lanes, which are so predictable, can, under certain circumstances, give you a badly needed and very helpful position line.

FIXING INTERVAL

To avoid this sort of embarrassment, you should have a structured routine for plotting a fix on the chart at regular intervals whenever you're underway:

- In coastal waters your fixing interval may be every 10 minutes or half hour – and sometimes even more frequently, depending on the proximity of danger
- Crossing the Channel, and away from immediate navigation dangers, I tend to

plot a fix on the chart every hour
- And on long offshore passages, I plot a fix once in every watch

Whatever period you choose, make sure that it becomes a standard part of your watch-keeping routine. There are a number of good reasons for this:

- Firstly, it stops you having to follow a line of shipping into port – which would be just as embarrassing in a yacht as it was in a submarine.
- Secondly, in the event that you unexpectedly lose the ability to fix, the most recently recorded fix will serve as your last known position, from which you can continue your passage.
- Thirdly, it gives you an opportunity each hour to assess your progress, confirm that you are steering the right course, and work out your ETA. It also gives you 5 minutes of quiet time to study the chart, and your progress across it.
- And finally, it's an hourly prompt to fill in the logbook; more on this later in the chapter.

It's so easy when plotting a fix to always fall back on GPS, writing down the co-ordinates and plotting them on the chart. I have to say that I often do just that. However, when a conspicuous bit of the coast is in sight, or at least a landmark or two, I quite often try to confirm the GPS position with a bearing (corrected for variation, of course) just to make sure that the little grey electronic box hasn't suddenly developed a wild and malicious sense of humour.

On coastal passages, with a number of landmarks in sight, I occasionally plot a fix by other means – visual bearings, radar ranges or transits – or any combination of these. These are quite often less accurate than GPS, but they provide an independent check on your position, and they also give you a chance to practise a skill that is often quite challenging in a small boat.

In pilotage waters, I nearly always navigate with head marks and transits, and generally don't plot fixes on the chart, unless I need some greater clarification of my position (see Chapter 13).

Finally, it's easy enough to talk about 'a fix', but of course a fix is no more than a historical record of your position, showing where you were some time ago. It doesn't tell you where you are right now, or where you will be in the future. So, try to get yourself into the habit of supplementing every fix with a **Dead Reckoning** position or two, and an **Estimated Position** or two as well. The **DR** and **EP**, as they are known, will give you the most accurate estimates of your position between one fix and the next (see p82).

GPS

GPS is probably one of the most universally valuable bits of technology to be introduced during my lifetime. Almost anything can now be tracked with great accuracy: your boat, the airplane that takes you on holiday, your car, your bike, your phone – even your dog – can all fix their position to within metres anywhere in the world, thanks to GPS.

This marvel of engineering is achieved with about 30 satellites, owned and operated by the US Military, that are in constant polar orbit around the earth. The orbits of these satellites are arranged in such a way that 4 will always be 'visible' to a GPS receiver, anywhere on the earth's surface. Every satellite contains a very accurate atomic clock, and they can track their position in orbit to a high level of accuracy.

Each satellite transmits a radio signal containing its exact position, and the precise time, both of which are updated from ground stations on every orbit. Your GPS receiver picks up signals from at least 3 satellites[37], measures the distance from each, and calculates your position. Not only does this give you a constant, accurate position reference, but it also provides the best possible time reference, so if you ever want to know the actual time, ask your GPS – it will know. It's all a little bit magical.

The US Government estimates the accuracy of the civilian version of GPS to be about 4.9m (16ft) under open sky. Which is quite accurate enough for most of us in our boats or our cars – and a far greater level of accuracy than you or I would ever need in the open ocean. With this level of accuracy, why wouldn't we use GPS for all of our navigation?

Well, of course, we do, and it's absolutely fine to use GPS as the primary navigation reference in open waters. When you're working close to navigation dangers, however, or conducting pilotage, you may find that visual navigation techniques, backed up with sound preparation, will give you a faster and more accurate indicator of whether you're safe or not. It also gives you more time to watch the water around you, which is so important for your overall safety. When I'm operating in pilotage waters, I normally switch to visual navigation techniques, although I keep the chart plotter close at hand, so that if things don't look right I can always get a second opinion from the GPS.

It should also not be forgotten that

---

[37] You need just 3 satellites to provide an accurate fix at sea level. The 4th satellite helps your GPS set to compute the time more accurately – and so gives a more accurate position, including a 3D fix if operating above (or below) sea level.

somewhere there is a big switch with **'GPS. ON – OFF'** inscribed into the wall beside it.

It would only take someone a few moments to throw that switch from **ON** to **OFF**, and suddenly you and I (and just about everyone else on the planet) would be left without any immediate navigational reference. Which would be scary.

More likely, a power failure in your boat, or a full short of your batteries, could cause both your GPS set and your chart plotter to suddenly fail with no warning at all. So try not to become too dependent on the magic grey box for all your navigation needs. And do carry a battery-powered GPS handset onboard (with a big pile of spare batteries) as a spare, just in case your boat has a major power failure in mid-Channel.

FIXING YOUR POSITION

There are many ways to determine your position at sea, and they all come down to the humble **position line**. The position line is a single line on which you can be certain (or at least fairly certain) that the ship lies. It can be a bearing from a fixed object, or a transit (that is to say when two charted objects are in line). It could be a radar range, which takes the form of an arc of a circle. I have sometimes also used sounding lines, or lines derived from a radio fixing aid or a bearing from a radio beacon. A position line can also be obtained by taking a sight of an astronomical object… Or even crossing a busy shipping lane. And finally, of course, your GPS set provides you with 2 position lines: latitude and longitude.

So there are lots of ways of generating a position line, with varying degrees of accuracy. To fix your position, you need to generate 2 or more position lines which cross each other. To make it a reliable fix, these lines should intersect at an angle greater than 30°, and less than 150°.

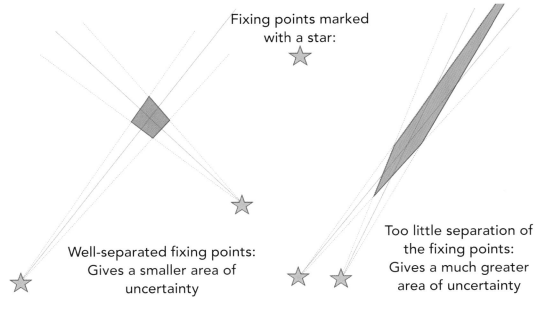

Fixing points marked with a star:

Well-separated fixing points: Gives a smaller area of uncertainty

Too little separation of the fixing points: Gives a much greater area of uncertainty

The effect of having well-separated and poorly-separated fixing points

WHY DOES THE ANGLE THAT POSITION LINES CROSS EACH OTHER MATTER?

It's important to get a decent angle of separation between two position lines because the greater the angle, the more accurate the fix is likely to be. Suppose that the accuracy of your hand-held magnetic compass ±4°.

If your 2 fixing points are widely separated, as in the left-hand illustration, you get a well-contained area of probability, as shown by the blue shading. However, if the fixing points are too close together, as in the right-hand diagram, the position lines cross at a narrow angle and the area of uncertainty is extended, reducing the accuracy and the reliability of the fix

THE 3-POSITION LINE FIX

Every position line that you take in a small boat, except possibly a good, well-charted transit, will carry some level of inaccuracy. A 2 position line fix may look superficially appealing, but you can't be certain how accurate these lines are: the cut of a third position line will give you much greater confidence in your position. I have, on a number of occasions, mis-identified a fixing mark, particularly in poor visibility, or on an unfamiliar stretch of coast, and a third position line will instantly bowl out an error like this. So always try to fix with 3 position lines, which will give you much greater confidence in the accuracy of your position. It doesn't matter whether the position lines are visual bearings, radar ranges, a transit – or a mix of the whole lot: 3 position lines are nearly always better than 2. If you can only get 2 lines, and you're over a sloping or uneven seabed, try taking an echo sounding and use that to corroborate the position that you get from the first 2 lines.

THE 'COCKED HAT'

More often than not, a 3 position line fix will result in a 'cocked hat', or a triangle, instead of the pin-point fix that we all aim for, where the position lines all pass through a single point. This isn't a problem as long as the cocked hat is not too large (in which case, you will need to re-take the fix), and it's generally quite acceptable to put the fix position at the sort of 'centre of gravity' of the triangle.

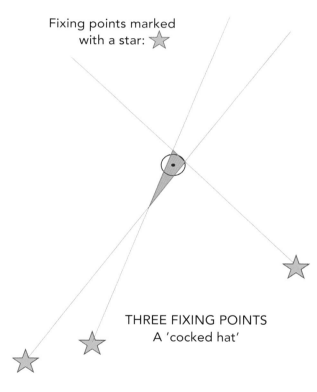

Fixing points marked with a star:

THREE FIXING POINTS
A 'cocked hat'

However, if you draw out the area that lies within the compass accuracy – in this case ±4° – of all 3 position lines, you create an area (that I have shaded blue), over half of which lies outside the cocked hat. Your actual position is equally likely to be anywhere within this blue area, and there's quite a large part of the cocked hat where you're unlikely to be.

Fixing points marked with a star: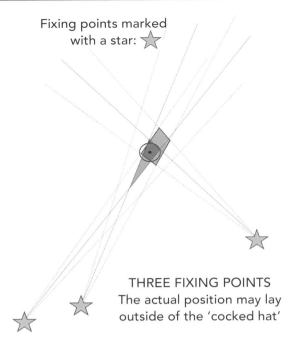

THREE FIXING POINTS
The actual position may lay outside of the 'cocked hat'

Use the cocked hat by all means – we all do – but never forget that fixing is an imprecise art, and you should always take the results with a pinch of salt, even when the fix itself looks quite convincing. If you are passing close to a danger it may be prudent to position your fix at the corner of the cocked hat that is closest to the danger.

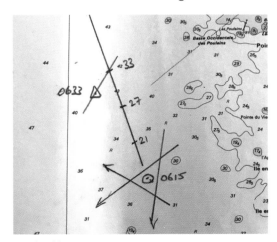

Cocked hat

This is a 3-point visual fix taken on a passage northwest along the coast of Belle Ile, on the south coast of Brittany. It's resulted in a cocked hat about half a mile across, which is about as big as I would accept this close to a rocky shore.

- I've marked the fix with a spot and circle and a four-figure time
- From the fix I've drawn a Dead Reckoning (DR) position for the next 18 minutes (that's to say, 3 intervals of 6 minutes)
- And I've put an Estimated Position (EP) on the third DR, making allowance for the southwesterly tidal stream

VISUAL BEARING LINES

The easiest position line to take is normally a visual bearing of some fixed, charted landmark, using a hand-held magnetic compass.

HAND-HELD MAGNETIC COMPASS

In a yacht it is unlikely that you would be able to use the steering compass for taking visual bearings, so most of us go to sea with a couple of hand-held magnetic compasses[38]. These can be oil-damped magnetic cards, normally with some form of sighting device on top of the glass or perspex cover, or they can be electronic flux-gate compasses. Both are damped as much as possible to reduce the inaccuracy caused by the boat's movement, but you will find that they still swing around a fair amount in any sort of seaway.

Whichever sort of hand-held magnetic compass you use, you should recognise that these are not precision instruments, and there is a fair amount of inaccuracy built into any bearing that you take. To reduce the errors, I often take a rapid series

---

[38] Take one for everyday use, and a second as a spare.

of about 5 bearings of each object and use the average. Even so, I wouldn't count on getting an accuracy greater than ±2°, and in any sort of seaway I would consider ±4° to be a more accurate figure.

FLUX-GATE COMPASS

Flux-gate compasses are quite neat, and you almost certainly have one as part of the system that drives your chart plotter. You can also buy small, light hand-held flux-gate compasses which appear to be just as accurate as the conventional oil-damped compasses.

Flux-gate compasses work by sensing the earth's magnetic field using coils of wire wrapped round a core of magnetic material. This gives a read-out of Magnetic Bearings which can easily be digitised and used in other applications – like chart plotters. Although quite small and rather sexier than a standard magnetic compass, flux-gate compasses suffer from all the same inaccuracies as a standard compass, and you will, of course, need to apply variation to the reading to convert from Magnetic to True Bearings.

RADAR POSITION LINES

Radar works by sending out a series of fine, directional radio beams, bouncing them off other objects (like a ship, a cliff or a lighthouse), and timing how long they take to get back. All radio signals travel at the speed of light so it is quite easy to time the returning echoes and get an accurate range from your radar set.

For reasons of accuracy, I would only ever advocate using a radar range for fixing; radar ranges tend to be quite accurate – and far more accurate and reliable than radar bearings, which suffer from all the inaccuracies of a magnetic compass, amplified by additional issues in the way the radar beam is formed. So I would avoid using radar bearings unless absolutely necessary. When taking a radar range, you must always make sure that you're ranging on the right object – a task that is very much simpler when the radar display is superimposed on the chart plotter. It's best to range only on the closest point of an object, which is less likely to be thrown out by other returning echoes and will give you the most accurate range.

A radar position line is plotted as a circular arc, using a pair of drawing compasses, and it is generally drawn with an arrowhead at each end.

TRANSITS

If I had to name my favourite position line, it would be the transit – for the reason that it's very low maintenance and very accurate. As a navigator, you should always keep an eye out for useable transits – whether it's a charted transit between 2 leading marks, or simply an unofficial one that you have spotted between a church spire in the distance and a pink house on the waterfront. It's a brilliant way of effortlessly staying on track and out of harm's way.

When you are lucky enough to be able to use a transit for a fix, you absolutely know that you are on that line. Given this level of accuracy, it's OK to make a fix with just one other bearing line, so if there's a transit available, you will often get a more accurate fix by delaying the fix until you cross the transit line.

Admiralty charts publish a number of tried-and-trusted transits around the coast, although I would always advise reading the *Sailing Directions* or a good local pilot book before embarking on an unfamiliar transit. They're fun to use. I have used many charted transits to squeeze through narrow passages, particularly on the North

Brittany coastline and, with care, it's a safe and quite exciting form of navigation.

If you look out for them, you can generally find useful transits at the entrance to many ports. This one is at the entrance to Portsmouth Harbour, marked by the War Memorial on the waterfront in line with a conspicuous block of flats and, behind that, the spire of St Jude's Church. When these three marks are in line, you can be confident that you're on a trusted route across the Spit Sand into the main entrance channel to Portsmouth Harbour. The photo is taken from a position well to the north of the transit.

In harbours used by commercial or naval shipping, the main entry channels are well marked, often by lit transits that are visible by day or night. In this case, also in the entrance to Portsmouth Harbour, the

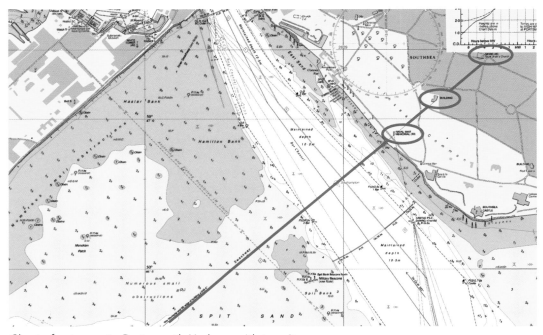

Chart of entrance to Portsmouth Harbour with transit

The 3 transit marks (not in line)

track up towards Fort Blockhouse is marked by a single directional light[39] situated on the eastern side of the harbour entrance. The light is designed so that, when you are on track you will see a white light occulting every 4 seconds (that is to say, briefly switching itself off every 4 seconds). When you are to the west of the main channel, the light will change and alternate white and red. And when you are to the east, you will see it alternate white and green. Further out still, it occults red (to the west) and green (to the east) every 4 seconds.

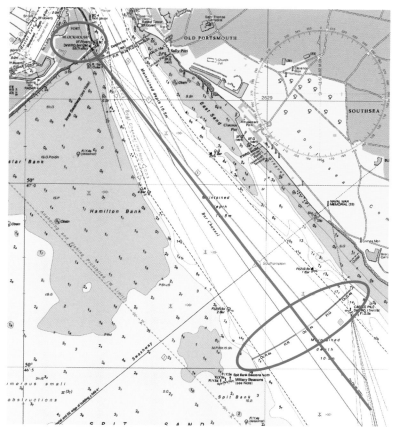

Chart showing how the lights at the entrance to Portsmouth Harbour could be used as a transit

You could find a natural transit between that light and the block of flats behind it, which, for small ships at least, would be just as accurate.

There are a couple of rules to observe when using a transit:

■ Before using a transit, make sure that you have identified both marks of the transit correctly. It is incredibly embarrassing to find that the leading mark is not a beacon after all but a small boat being used for a spot of Sunday morning fishing.

■ Make sure that there is sufficient distance between the front and back marker of a transit. The greater the separation, the more sensitive the transit becomes.

■ Be aware that one or other of the marks may disappear behind an obstruction half-way along the planned transit. The transit into the pretty anchorage of Harvre Gosselin on the west coast of Sark is marked on the chart (see overleaf) and so it must be – you might think – an entirely reliable headmark. However, as you approach, Sark Mill rather depressingly drops below the line of the cliff, leaving you running in on the monument alone. Even transits can let you down from time to time.

---

[39] A single directional light is not of course a transit, but it can be just as accurate, particularly when the sectors are narrow, like this. It's included here as a sort of 'Honorary Transit'.

The transit on Sark which disappears from view as you approach

DEAD RECKONING (DR) & ESTIMATED POSITION (EP)

As I've shown in the image opposite, there is a little bit of homework to do once you've plotted your fix on the chart.

- First of all, mark your most likely position with a spot, a circle and a 4-figure time – that's your fix
- You then need to convert the fix, which is by now a historical record of where you were, into a more useful prediction of where you will be in the future
- So, once the fix is plotted, take the time to plot forward your future position – I normally try to estimate my future position over the timespan of the next 2 or 3 fixes

You do this with **Dead Reckoning** and **Estimated Positions**.

From the starting point of the most recent fix, draw a line along the bearing that you're steering, and mark it off with the distance that you will travel through the water over each of the next 2 or 3 fix intervals. Those positions, which are derived solely on steered course and log speed, are called the **Dead Reckoning Positions (DRs)**. They take no account of the tidal stream or leeway.

A more accurate estimate of future position would take account of the tidal stream, so with each DR position, you can apply a further correction that makes allowance for the flow of the predicted tidal stream. These positions, which are typically marked with a dot and a triangle, are called **Estimated Positions (EPs)**.

- **Dead Reckoning Positions** are marked by a tick across the future track of the ship
- **Estimated Positions** are marked with a dot inside a triangle; you would normally mark them with a 2-figure time showing the minutes after the hour for which they apply

LEEWAY

When drawing your EP, you may also want to take account of the boat's leeway if it is proving to be a significant component of your course and speed made good.

I have to say that I have never felt the need to do this, but it is certainly something to be aware of, particularly if you are moving at slow speed, or if you decide to heave-to in a strong wind. Depending on the design of your boat, the relative speed and direction of the wind, and your own speed through the water, the leeway could vary from zero to something quite significant.

If necessary, you could make allowance for leeway in your EP. Sometimes, when calculating a course to steer to make a particular waypoint, you may want to ask the helmsman to steer a few degrees closer to the wind to make good your desired course.

AN EXAMPLE

Suppose that you are approaching Braye Harbour from the northwest, heading 152°M with a log speed of 6 knots. You estimate the tidal stream to be 240°M at 2 knots. With a strong tidal stream, and this close to an unfriendly shoreline, you're fixing every 6 minutes.

At 1332 BST you take a 3-point visual fix which gives the following bearings:
Chateau a L'Etoc 156°M
Right-hand edge of Alderney 200°M
Right-hand edge of Burhou Island 228°M

You plot these 3 bearings (with arrow heads to show that they are visual position lines), and it makes a respectably small cocked hat. You mark the fix at the centre of this cocked had with a spot, surrounded by a circle and a 4-digit time.

With the fix plotted:

■ You draw a line along your heading of 152°M[40]

■ You can then tick off the DR marks: 6 minutes at 6 knots = 0.6nm, so each tick is 0.6nm down the track

■ Each DR position is marked with a 2-digit

time

■ Finally, you apply the tidal stream vector in a direction of 240°M – which at 2 knots will push you 0.2nm in 6 minutes and 0.4nm in 12 minutes: this allows you to position your EP triangles

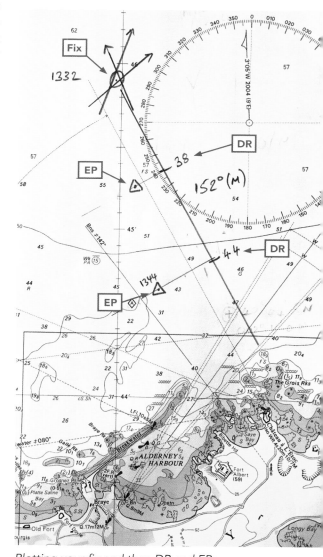

Plotting your fix and then DR and EPs

---

[40] There's no hard-and-fast rule about doing your chartwork in Magnetic or True – the choice is yours, as long as you are consistent. Personally, in a sailing boat, I do all my navigation in degrees (Magnetic), even though the chart is drawn up against true north. I find it quite simple to work this way and it means that you can give the helmsman and your crew a simple magnetic course to steer with the ship's (magnetic) steering compass.

Don't be dismayed by all of this – it is much quicker to do than to read, and importantly it gives you a pretty clear indication of where you are, and where you will be, over the next 2 fixing intervals.

In this case, although you are heading for the harbour entrance, the 1344 EP highlights the need to alter course to port if you want to avoid the shoal area at the end of the breakwater.

One final note: as you approach the shore, always be cautious of changes to the wind speed and direction, caused by the proximity of land, and be particularly aware of any changes to the tidal stream as you get closer. Close inshore you can expect the tidal stream to slow down, speed up or even reverse course, depending on the shape of the seabed and the coastline. The same often applies to the wind. You can normally spot such changes by differing patterns on the water, and by unexpected changes in the way that you are moving against the landscape. This is a time when you need to be properly alert.

RUNNING FIX

Running fixes are handy when you are starting to run out of fixing options. It's not a technique that's used very often because, frankly, it takes quite a lot of effort. What's more, there is a lot of opportunity to build errors into the fix, so it may not be particularly accurate. To be honest, I doubt if I would use it when simpler fixing methods are available. But it's one more option to have up your sleeve and it's saved my bacon on more than one occasion.

With a running fix, you only use one fixing mark, but you use it more than once, to give you a multiple position line fix.

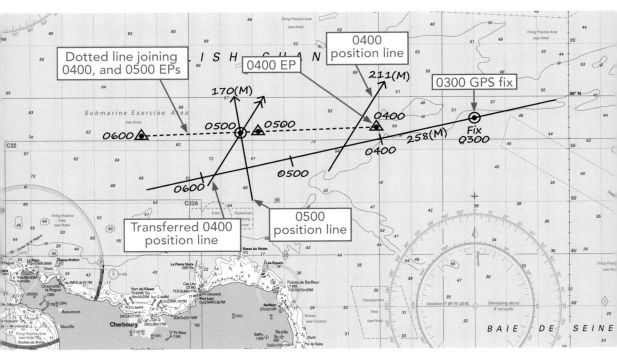

Plotting a running fix (Imray chart 12)

Suppose you're heading southwest down the Channel[41]. It's the middle of the night and you are just coming up to the Cotentin Peninsula with Cherbourg on your port bow. You have no radar and the GPS stopped working when your daughter's teenage boyfriend tried out a new pair of pliers that he had been given for his birthday, and inadvertently cut through the GPS aerial cable in the cockpit. The visibility is poor, limiting your visibility to just a few miles.

You are steering a course of 258°M at a log speed of 10 knots
The tidal stream is flowing at 310°M, 2kts[42]
Variation on the chart is 0° 42'W (in 2020)

Your last fix, before your daughter's boyfriend got cracking with his pliers, was an accurate GPS position at 0300 BST. You have plotted a DR on the chart for 10kts for 0400, 0500 and 0600, and you have also laid off EPs from these DR positions at a distance of 2, 4 and 6nm to the northwest of the respective DR positions.

Suddenly, at 0400, the visibility clears for long enough to take a bearing of Pointe de Barfleur Lighthouse on the northeastern corner of the peninsula. The bearing is 211°M.

You plot this position line on the chart[43], which gives you some reassurance because it passes close to the northwest of your 0400 EP. You could, if you wish, 'update' your 0400 EP to the closest point on that bearing line. But you haven't yet got enough for a reliable fix: you need a second, crossing bearing line.

As luck would have it, at 0500 you get a second bearing of Pointe de Barfleur Light, now on a bearing of 170°M. You plot that bearing on the chart and again it passes a mile or so to the west of your 0500 EP. But again, this alone isn't a fix.

However, if you were to move your 0400 position line in the same direction and the same distance as the boat has moved (that is to say EP to EP) from 0400 and 0500, you could justifiably use this transferred position line to give you a cut and a reasonably accurate 2-position line fix.

Now for the clever bit...
To transfer the 0400 position line:
- First of all, draw a dashed line on your chart joining the two EPs at 0400 and 0500
- Set up your dividers with one point on the 0400 EP and the other on the 0500 EP
- Now, without disturbing the separation of your divider points, shift the '0400 point' along the dashed line until it hits the 0400 bearing (211°M)
- Mark the spot on the dashed line where the '0500 point' of the dividers has now shifted to
- Draw a line parallel to the 0400 bearing (211°M) through that spot; this is your transferred position line, and the convention is that you mark it with a double arrow
- Where the 0500 position line (bearing 170°M) cuts the transferred 0400 position line (211°M), you can now justifiably put your spot and circle, and call it the 0500 fix

---

[41] In this example I have used *Imray chart C12*.

[42] Stretching reality, I have assumed that the tidal stream is constant over the 3 hours of this example.

[43] In order to plot the bearing of 211°M on the chart (where the compass rose is set up for True North) you will of course need to take account of variation. As it happens, the closest compass rose in the illustration shows that variation here is almost zero in 2020, so in this case the True Bearing to plot would be 211°T.

At the end of the day, this is just a 2 position line fix, and even then it is only as good as your DR and your assessment of the tidal stream, but when you are scrambling around for a fix, you would be surprised how welcome even this can be. And you can of course subsequently add a third bearing line to increase the accuracy of the fix.

This sounds long-winded, because I have deliberately taken the procedure step-by-step, but with practice it can be done quickly and easily at sea. You will seldom use a running fix, even if you spend a lot of time at sea, but it's worth tucking the technique away because, when you run out of fixing options on a stormy night, it's pure gold dust.

ECHO SOUNDINGS

As a young submariner, one of the most common questions that I was asked by various captains (normally when they were feeling scratchy) was "*What is the distance to the closest point of land?*" I would dutifully rush off to the chart table and come back with something like "*The coast of Norway, sir, which is 72nm to the southeast.*" There would follow a theatrical silence, followed by: "*Rubbish! The closest point of land right now is 200 feet right under the keel, and if you don't do a better job of keeping the submarine on depth, you'll find out the hard way in just a few seconds.*" There was a sort of predictability about this exchange which had all the other watch keepers in the Control Room almost singing along with the punchline – but it taught me a big and important lesson… **never forget the third dimension.**

This lesson has stayed with me ever since. Whether navigating a big ship, a submarine or a small yacht, you must never ignore the depth of water. If you do (I speak as someone who has been there on a number of occasions), you will suddenly be disturbed from your lunch by an uncomfortable graunching sound from deep down in the ship's structure, followed by a lurch as you bounce off the seabed. Inevitably this event is followed by a great deal of explaining and paperwork, not to mention repairs to the hull. All of which, frankly, you can do without.

One of the most useful tools to help us avoid running aground is the humble echo sounder.

Get into the habit of noting down the sounding every time you take a fix: it's a very useful double check on the accuracy of your position. A sounding that just doesn't look right is the best and quickest indicator that something is wrong with your navigation.

The echo sounder sits quietly on the edge of you instrument panel, giving you a constant (and very accurate) read-out of the depth of water. And yet more often than not, we just ignore it. Try to get into the habit of looking at the sounding from time to time, particularly in inshore waters, to make sure that you have a comfortable amount of water under your keel. If it's starting to look a bit shallow, slow down or stop, and give yourself a few moments to work out what to do.

NAVIGATIONAL ACCURACY

You should always be aware of the accuracy of your navigation equipment.

RELYING ON GPS

Nothing in navigation – not even your trusty GPS set – is ever 100% accurate, and there are scars on the bows of my yacht to prove it. We decided to leave the Treguier River in North Normandy one morning before dawn, making an early start to catch the tidal stream up to the Casquets before returning across the Channel. It had been a short night; I was tired, and I was stupidly treating my chart plotter as an oracle of unshakeable truth. Only, it wasn't an oracle of unshakeable truth at all. It led us squarely into an unlit navigation buoy when we thought that we were right in the middle of the navigable channel, albeit on a narrow section of the river, and we finished our holiday with a very embarrassing green scrape down the boat's port side. My pride was damaged, but happily the boat was otherwise unscathed. Had we been just 5 metres further left, we would have gone careering into the rocks, so I suppose that we got off comparatively lightly. But it wasn't my greatest feat of navigation.

The thing is that I had been lulled into a false sense of security, thinking that my chart plotter was totally reliable. It wasn't; at that precise moment it was probably about 20m in error, but there was no indicator to tell me that. In general, you should expect your GPS fixes under clear skies, and free from obstructions, to be in the order of ±5m[44], but I would probably allow ±20m to be on the safe side.

VISUAL BEARING LINES

When using a hand-held magnetic compass in a small boat, I usually take about 5 bearings in quick succession, and use the average. In general, I would expect individual bearings to be within 4 or 5° degrees of the mean. The accuracy of the mean bearing in calm weather is unlikely to be better than ±2°, and I would estimate ±4° or worse in lumpy conditions. To put that in perspective, an error of ±2° gives a lateral error of ±200 metres at a range of 3nm.

RADAR RANGES

The accuracy of a radar range depends wholly on the nature of the object being used for fixing. A vertical cliff will give you a clear, precise and sharp echo that carries very little in the way of potential errors. But a long, low sloping beach like Lytham St Annes in Lancashire (which can be up to a mile wide at Low Water), and where lines of breakers often extend the radar return to seaward, may well give you a much less accurate range. On the whole, provided that you use a sharp cliff edge and a reliable radar set, you should get ranges accurate to ±0.1nm.

TRANSIT

When you are on a transit, and you're certain of your transit marks, you have one absolutely rock-solid position line: ±0°.

SOUNDINGS

Soundings can give you a very accurate position line, particularly when going over an abrupt change of depth in the seabed, like the Hurd Deep north of Alderney where the depth of water doubles within the space of a few miles, or when crossing a small, sharply-defined bottom feature. But over a flat seabed with few distinguishing features it is less likely to give you an accurate position line. Even so, it's good practice always to record the sounding when you take a fix, and to check the actual against the expected depth of water.

THE 'POOL OF ERRORS'

The thing about navigation errors is that they're cumulative, and if you're going for any length of time between fixes, it can be instructive (and a bit scary) to plot the accumulated 'Pool of Errors' on your chart.

---

[44] www.gps.gov – the 'Official US government information about the Global Positioning System'.

It starts with the accuracy of your last fix. I would assume that my GPS gives a position that is accurate to ±0.1nm, and that a reasonably good visual fix is accurate to ±0.25nm.

And then on top of this, the other errors come piling in….

Without resorting to an autopilot, I doubt if I could steer a small boat in a seaway for any length of time with greater than about ±5° of accuracy. Even using an autopilot, the accuracy is unlikely to be better than ±3° (±3° gives a lateral error of ±1nm for every 20nm travelled).

On top of that, my boat's log has never been properly calibrated, and I wouldn't trust it to be more accurate than ±5%, which gives an additional potential distance error of ±1nm for every 20 nm travelled.

The log and steering errors mean that the accumulated errors on your DR position alone is roughly a circle expanding by 1nm for every 20nm travelled.

In addition, you should add the errors in your estimation of the tidal stream. A lot of work goes into making tidal stream predictions as accurate as possible, but the actual tidal rates are affected by the wind, by atmospheric pressure, and can change quite markedly from place to place. So, it would be safe to give the tidal stream predictions an additional ±5-10% margin of error as well. In tidal streams of about 2kts, which is fairly typical around the south coast of the UK, this adds a further margin of ±0.1-0.2nm per hour to your 'Pool of Errors'.

So bringing the numbers crudely together, I would say that, for every 20 miles travelled (about 3 hours of passage time for my boat), the radius of my 'Pool of Errors' expands by approximately 1nm from DR errors, and by about 0.5nm from errors in the prediction of tidal stream. And that's if I'm really concentrating on the accuracy of my steering.

In other words, there's an expanding circle around my EP, with a radius growing by 1.5nm every 3 hours, and that's on top of my original fixing error of a circle with a radius of 0.25nm from a visual fix.

So, to put all that into context, on the 60nm passage from the Needles to Bray Harbour in Alderney, a 7kts passage would take about 9 hours. In the absence of any fixing during the passage, your 'Pool of Errors' would have a radius of:

$$0.25nm + 3 \times 1.5nm =$$
$$\text{a radius of } 4.75nm$$

Since Alderney is only about 3nm in length, you could quite easily miss the island by a fairly substantial margin.

There are 2 important take-aways from this:

- It's important to get into a routine of regular GPS fixing, particularly on long-ish passages – because each time you put a fix on the chart you knock that pool of errors back down again, and greater certainty in your position means that you and your crew are safer.
- If you are ever without fixing for a while, you need to work out your 'Pool of Errors' and keep the whole envelope clear of potential dangers. This may often mean taking a more conservative track.

CROSS-TRACK ERROR

Cross-Track Errors (or XTE in its abbreviated form) is the parameter that your GPS uses to let you know how far you are off your planned track, and you will almost certainly find a setting on your GPS set that gives you a real-time read-out of XTE.

When you set your autopilot to follow a track between waypoints, it will try to minimise XTE by steering to keep you on track, no matter what the tidal stream and other influences are doing to you. If, however, you ask your autopilot to steer a given course, you may well find yourself diverging from your planned track, and potentially racking up a sizeable XTE as a result of the tidal stream.

In all honesty, XTE is not a parameter that I use a great deal, and it probably has more relevance in powerboats where the speeds are higher and the effect of the tidal stream is less significant. I prefer the simpler method of fixing with a DR and EP, or watching the Course Over The Ground (COG) indicator on my chart plotter.

KEEPING A SHIP'S LOG

You should keep a ship's log whenever you undertake anything but the most trivial passage in your boat. In fact, you would be crazy not to do this.

Navigating a small yacht is not as rigorous as the Royal Navy or the Merchant Navy, where you are obliged to keep a log, and the contents of that log are well-defined. No-one will prosecute you if you don't. But the log is your official record of the passage; it can be used to prove your whereabouts if you are ever called to account by the authorities (which has happened to me on a couple of occasions). It also provides your point of reference for navigation, weather and other events if things go catastrophically wrong.

The routine of regularly filling in the logbook brings you to the chart table every hour. So while you're there, you might as well put a fix on the chart to check progress and to run your eye over the chart. These few moments contemplating the chart will make you more aware of where you are, and the environment in which you're working. And finally, the logbook gives you a wonderful record of your sailing adventures in future years, particularly if you take time to record sightings of unusual objects and ships, marine mammals and strange weather conditions.

I have never bought a pre-printed ship's logbook in my life (although there are some excellent ones available from Fernhurst Books). I tend to keep the ship's log in a big exercise book with small 5mm squares, which is enough to keep the columns of information more or less in order.

Be selective about the information you want to record. I put in quite a lot, with columns for:
- Time
- Log reading
- Latitude
- Longitude
- Course steered
- Log speed
- Wind speed and direction
- Distance to next waypoint
- Barometric pressure

My logbook – not pretty, but effective

7
VISUAL AIDS TO NAVIGATION

There are many features, some of them natural and some of them man-made, that you can use for navigation. Many of these time-honoured marks, like the daymark above the harbour entrance at Dartmouth, have been used for generations, and still today provide an invaluable fixing aid for mariners.

DAYMARKS & LANDMARKS

Ever since I first saw a navigation chart, on which a cliff-top building was marked with the legend: '**White House (conspic)**', I have wanted (and consistently failed) to live in a house that passing ships can use as a fixing point. But in all honesty, any visible landmark, when plotted on the chart can be used as a fixing point; and in this we are greatly helped by the skill and the experience of the cartographers, who remove masses of irrelevant detail from the charts, leaving only those features that they believe to be of use to the mariner. As a result, land features are pretty sparse on most charts. Towns are shown only in ghostly outline. Roads are drawn almost casually, because they are seldom visible from seaward.

But the features that you can see, and which you may wish to use for navigation, are pinpointed with forensic accuracy.

Here, for instance, on the western tip of the Isle of Wight, the land contours are much less well-defined than they would be on an Ordnance Survey land map, but at the same time real emphasis is given to the features that you could use for navigation – like Tennyson's Cross (Circle 1), a radio mast (Circle 2), a conspicuous hotel in Alum Bay (Circle 3), the highest point of Headon Hill (Circle 4), and the tower of St Saviour's Church at the back end of Totland (Circle 5). These are all perfectly respectable fixing points; don't overlook them just because they aren't 'classical' navigation marks, like a leading light, or a lighthouse with red stripes around it. To add to this, you can often find more details about the appearance of the coastline and its individual features in the *Sailing Directions*, or the *Shell Channel Pilot*.

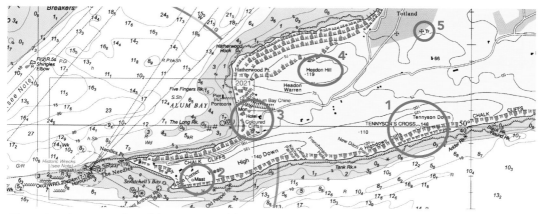

Chart showing several useful navigational features on land

In areas that we frequently visit, I sometimes take photos of navigation marks, or even pick up postcards with aerial images of the coast and local landmarks, taping them onto the relevant page of the pilot book. Five years later, when you return, these often rather quirky snaps will remind you what to look out for; and sometimes an aerial photo will show you where the navigable channel, or the visitors' pontoon, lie. Of course, this is not an entirely reliable way of navigating; the postcard photo may have been taken 20 years ago – but it can be useful for orientation.

Postcards can also be useful, here showing the entrance to Loctudy on the south coast of Brittany

LIGHTHOUSES

Lighthouses are excellent fixing points by day or by night, and they are well marked on the chart with a black, hollow-centred star and a diagonal magenta lozenge sprouting out of it, which indicates the presence of a light that can be used for navigation.

The Needles Lighthouse on the western tip of the Isle of Wight is more complex than most because it is sectored. That is to say that the characteristics of the light vary, depending on the direction from which you observe it. A light is normally sectored to indicate shoals, or areas which may be dangerous for navigation: in this case the

Photos can be useful navigational reminders, like this one, taken on the entrance to the Odet River in South Brittany

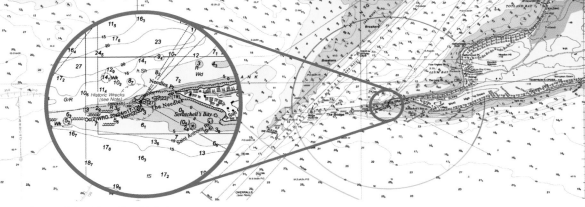

Chart of the Needles Lighthouse

red sectors warn of the Shingles Bank to the northwest, and some ugly rocks to the southeast. This light also has a narrow white and green sector to the northeast which is carefully angled to help mariners negotiate the Needles Channel.

Written below the lighthouse symbol is the legend:

Oc(2)WRG.20s24m17-13M
Horn(2)30s

You can find the formal decode in *Chart 5011 Symbols and Abbreviations Used on Admiralty Paper Charts.*

This notation details the characteristics of the navigation light and fog signal. Specifically:

- The light occults twice every 20 seconds, and is coloured white, red or green depending on the sectors from which you are looking
- The lens of the light is 24m above Mean High Water Springs
- The light has a Nominal Range (see p94) which varies from 17nm to 13nm, depending on the sector that you're looking at
- There is also a fog signal: a horn which makes 2 blasts every 30 seconds

At the start of each geographical area in *Reed's Almanac* there is a useful and lightly-trodden section, titled 'Lights, Buoys and Waypoints'. Here you will find a great deal of information about specific navigation lights, copied from the *Admiralty List of Lights,* specifically:

- The latitude and longitude of the light
- The characteristics of the lights
- Nominal Ranges of the various sectors
- The arcs over which they shine
- And the paint scheme of the structure

Looking at the entry for the Needles Lighthouse, you can see that the Nominal Range of the white sector is 17nm[45], the 2 red sectors 14 and 13nm respectively, and the green sector 14nm. It also specifies the paint scheme: a red band and lantern.

CHARACTERISTICS OF NAVIGATION LIGHTS

This may be a useful moment to consider the different types of lights that are used on navigation marks:

---

[45] Charts and reference books usually abbreviate nautical miles to 'M' and metres to 'm'. To reduce any possibility of confusion within my very limited brain, I always abbreviate nautical miles to 'nm', and I do so in this book.

Flashing Rhythm	Used on Chart	Description
Fixed	F	The light, which may be of any colour, stays on continuously.
Occulting	Oc	The total period of light is longer than the total period of darkness. I remember this as a light that is predominantly on, but which is 'flashing' periods of darkness at regular intervals. May be: ■ Single occulting: One period of dark in any cycle ■ Group occulting: More than one period of dark in any cycle, but gathered together as a group ■ Composite group occulting: More than one period of dark in a cycle, but gathered together in more than one group
Isophase	Iso	The duration of light is equal to the duration of darkness. These lights have a very regular rhythm, with the light on for a period, and then off for the same period. It stands out very easily from flashing and occulting lights.
Flashing	Fl	Total duration of the light is less than the total duration of darkness. In other words, it is precisely what it says on the tin. May be: ■ Single flash: One period of light in any cycle ■ Group flashing: More than one period of light in a cycle, but gathered together as a group ■ Composite group flashing: More than one period of light in a cycle, but gathered together into more than one group ■ Long flash: Where the length of the flash is 2 seconds or more
Quick	Q	A repetition rate of between 50 and 79 flashes per minute (although for simplicity it is generally either 50 or 60 flashes per minute). May be: ■ Continuous quick flash: No breaks in the sequence of flashes ■ Group quick flashing: More than one flash, grouped together, in each cycle ■ Interrupted quick flash: A continuous quick flash, but with a break between cycles
Very Quick	VQ	As for Quick Flash, with the same groupings, but with flashes repeating at a rate of 80 to 159 flashes per minute. Usually either 100 or 120 flashes per minute.
Ultra Quick	UQ	A light with flashes repeating at a rate of not less than 160 flashes per minute.
Alternating	Al	The light alternates between two colours, each exposed for the same length of time, and with no periods of dark between them.
Morse Code	Mo	A light which shows groups of long and short flashes which are designed to represent characters of the Morse Code. For instance, a light which is marked **Mo(K)W** would be a white light flashing the Morse Code for 'K', or '– · –'

HOW FAR AWAY CAN YOU SEE A NAVIGATION LIGHT?

When you're at sea, it's quite useful to be able to work out how far away you will pick up a light. There are 3 critical measurements for working out the range at which you will see a light:

- **Nominal Range**: This is the range at which you would expect to see the light under normal night-time atmospheric conditions, and with a Meteorological Visibility[46] of 10nm. The Nominal Range is printed on the chart, underneath the lighthouse symbol and in front of the capital 'M'. It's a measure of the light's intensity.
- **Luminous Range**: This is the range which you can expect to see the light, *'determined only by the intensity of the light and the visibility at the time. It takes no account of the elevation, the observer's height of eye or the curvature of the earth'*.[47] In other words, we know how intense the light is (Nominal Range); given the current weather conditions, this is the distance that we should expect to see it through the murk.
- **Geographical Range**: This is the range at which, in perfect visibility, the light would appear above the horizon, making allowance for normal conditions of atmospheric refraction.

These ranges may all be quite different (and in any case on a really clear night you can often see the loom of a distant light

some time before the light itself becomes visible above the horizon). But for most of the time, the range at which you will see a light:

- **At night** will be limited either by the weather conditions, or by the curvature of the earth; that is to say it is either the Luminous Range or the Geographical Range (whichever is less)
- **By day**, the distance at which you will see a feature is either the Geographical Range or the Meteorological Visibility (whichever is less)

Suppose that you're approaching the Needles Lighthouse from the south How far away would you see the light in perfect visibility?

From the chart (see p92), from the *Almanac*, or from the *Admiralty List of Lights* (section 7.2), you can see that:

- The White Sector has a Nominal Range of 17nm
- And the elevation of the lantern is 24m above MHWS

Assume that your height of eye, standing in the cockpit of your boat, is 3m.

To work out the Geographical Range, you simply go into the Geographical Range table from the *Admiralty List of Lights*, reproduced here, but also available in the Navigation Tables of *Reed's Almanac*.

You go into it with your height of eye (3m) across the top, and the elevation of the lantern (24m) down the side, you can quickly read off the Geographical Range:

---

[46] The authoritative reference for Meteorological Visibility in this context is the IALA website: https://www.iala-aism.org. It specifies that Meteorological Visibility is *'The greatest distance at which a black object of suitable dimensions can be seen and recognised by day against the horizon sky, or, in the case of night observations, could be seen and recognised if the general illumination were raised to the normal daylight level. The term may express the visibility in a single direction or the prevailing visibility in all directions.'* In short, when the visibility is 10nm, you should be able to see and recognise significant objects when they are 10nm away!

[47] Reference: *The Mariner's Handbook*, NP100, Section 2.76

Geographical Range is 13.5nm

That is the range at which the lantern of the lighthouse would appear above the horizon in perfect visibility.

However, in less-than-perfect visibility, the range may be less than this. The Shipping Forecast is quite Delphic in its description of visibility:

- **Very poor or Fog**: Visibility less than 1,000 metres
- **Poor**: Visibility between 1,000 metres and 2 nautical miles
- **Moderate**: Visibility between 2 and 5 nautical miles
- **Good**: Visibility more than 5 nautical miles

Elevation ft	Elevation m	3 / 1	7 / 2	10 / 3	13 / 4	16 / 5	20 / 6	23 / 7	26 / 8	30 / 9	33 / 10	39 / 12	46 / 14	52 / 16	59 / 18	66 / 20	72 / 22	79 / 24	85 / 26	92 / 28	98 / 30
0	0	2.0	2.9	3.5	4.1	4.5	5.0	5.4	5.7	6.1	6.4	7.0	7.6	8.1	8.6	9.1	9.5	10.0	10.4	10.7	11.1
3	1	4.1	4.9	5.5	6.1	6.6	7.0	7.4	7.8	8.1	8.5	9.1	9.6	10.2	10.6	11.1	11.6	12.0	12.4	12.8	13.2
7	2	4.9	5.7	6.4	6.9	7.4	7.8	8.2	8.6	9.0	9.3	9.9	10.5	11.0	11.5	12.0	12.4	12.8	13.2	13.6	14.0
10	3	5.5	6.4	7.0	7.6	8.1	8.5	8.9	9.3	9.6	9.9	10.6	11.1	11.6	12.1	12.6	13.0	13.5	13.9	14.3	14.6
13	4	6.1	6.9	7.6	8.1	8.6	9.0	9.4	9.8	10.2	10.5	11.1	11.7	12.2	12.7	13.1	13.6	14.0	14.4	14.8	15.2
16	5	6.6	7.4	8.1	8.6	9.1	9.5	9.9	10.3	10.6	11.0	11.6	12.1	12.7	13.2	13.6	14.1	14.5	14.9	15.3	15.7
20	6	7.0	7.8	8.5	9.0	9.5	9.9	10.3	10.7	11.1	11.4	12.0	12.6	13.1	13.6	14.1	14.5	14.9	15.3	15.7	16.1
23	7	7.4	8.2	8.9	9.4	9.9	10.3	10.7	11.1	11.5	11.8	12.4	13.0	13.5	14.0	14.5	14.9	15.3	15.7	16.1	16.5
26	8	7.8	8.6	9.3	9.8	10.3	10.7	11.1	11.5	11.8	12.2	12.8	13.3	13.9	14.4	14.8	15.3	15.7	16.1	16.5	16.9
30	9	8.1	9.0	9.6	10.2	10.6	11.1	11.5	11.8	12.2	12.5	13.1	13.7	14.2	14.7	15.2	15.6	16.0	16.4	16.8	17.2
33	10	8.5	9.3	9.9	10.5	11.0	11.4	11.8	12.2	12.5	12.8	13.5	14.0	14.5	15.0	15.5	15.9	16.4	16.8	17.2	17.5
36	11	8.8	9.6	10.3	10.8	11.3	11.7	12.1	12.5	12.8	13.2	13.8	14.3	14.9	15.4	15.8	16.3	16.7	17.1	17.5	17.9
39	12	9.1	9.9	10.6	11.1	11.6	12.0	12.4	12.8	13.1	13.5	14.1	14.6	15.2	15.7	16.1	16.6	17.0	17.4	17.8	18.2
43	13	9.4	10.2	10.8	11.4	11.9	12.3	12.7	13.1	13.4	13.7	14.4	14.9	15.4	15.9	16.4	16.8	17.3	17.7	18.1	18.4
46	14	9.6	10.5	11.1	11.7	12.1	12.6	13.0	13.3	13.7	14.0	14.6	15.2	15.7	16.2	16.7	17.1	17.6	18.0	18.3	18.7
49	15	9.9	10.7	11.4	11.9	12.4	12.8	13.2	13.6	14.0	14.3	14.9	15.5	16.0	16.5	17.0	17.4	17.8	18.2	18.6	19.0
52	16	10.2	11.0	11.6	12.2	12.7	13.1	13.5	13.9	14.2	14.5	15.2	15.7	16.2	16.7	17.2	17.7	18.1	18.5	18.9	19.2
56	17	10.4	11.2	11.9	12.4	12.9	13.3	13.7	14.1	14.5	14.8	15.4	16.0	16.5	17.0	17.4	17.9	18.3	18.7	19.1	19.5
59	18	10.6	11.5	12.1	12.7	13.2	13.6	14.0	14.4	14.7	15.0	15.7	16.2	16.7	17.2	17.7	18.1	18.6	19.0	19.4	19.7
62	19	10.9	11.7	12.4	12.9	13.4	13.8	14.2	14.6	14.9	15.3	15.9	16.5	17.0	17.5	17.9	18.4	18.8	19.2	19.6	20.0
66	20	11.1	12.0	12.6	13.1	13.6	14.1	14.5	14.8	15.2	15.5	16.1	16.7	17.2	17.7	18.2	18.6	19.0	19.4	19.8	20.2
72	22	11.6	12.4	13.0	13.6	14.1	14.5	14.9	15.3	15.6	15.9	16.6	17.1	17.7	18.1	18.6	19.1	19.5	19.9	20.3	20.7
79	24	12.0	12.8	13.5	14.0	14.5	14.9	15.3	15.7	16.0	16.4	17.0	17.6	18.1	18.6	19.0	19.5	19.9	20.3	20.7	21.1
85	26	12.4	13.2	13.9	14.4	14.9	15.3	15.7	16.1	16.4	16.8	17.4	18.0	18.5	19.0	19.4	19.9	20.3	20.7	21.1	21.5
92	28	12.8	13.6	14.3	14.8	15.3	15.7	16.1	16.5	16.8	17.2	17.8	18.3	18.9	19.4	19.8	20.3	20.7	21.1	21.5	21.9

Geographical range table from the Admiralty List of Lights

If the Meteorological Visibility is 'Moderate' – say 5nm – and you have a copy of the *Admiralty List of Lights* onboard, you need to find the Luminous Range Diagram – or, of course, you can use the diagram below.

Start on the top margin with the Nominal Range of the light (17nm); down until you hit the curve of Meteorological Visibility (5nm) and over to the left-hand margin to read off the Luminous Range.

By day, you will see the Lighthouse Lantern at the least of the Geographical Range (13.5nm) and the Meteorological Visibility (5nm), so you should start looking for it at 5nm (although white objects – like lighthouses – are notoriously difficult to see at a distance in any sort of reduced visibility).

The Luminous Range is 10.2nm

This is 3.3nm less than the Geographical Range – so the likelihood is that you will first see the light when it's 10.2nm away.

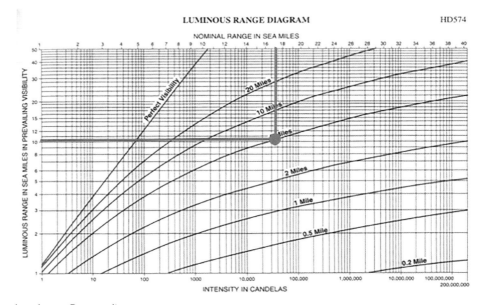

LUMINOUS RANGE DIAGRAM   HD574

NOMINAL RANGE IN SEA MILES

LUMINOUS RANGE IN SEA MILES IN PREVAILING VISIBILITY

Perfect Visibility

20 Miles

10 Miles

Miles

2 Miles

1 Mile

0.5 Mile

0.2 Mile

INTENSITY IN CANDELAS

Luminous Range diagram

NAVIGATION BUOYS

Wherever you go in the world you will find navigation buoys, which are absolutely invaluable for mariners entering and leaving harbour.

In the Navy, we were rightly discouraged from using navigation buoys for visual fixing: they can sometimes shift their moorings, and so they can't always be relied upon. Even so, my first ever port entry as a submarine navigator was into Vlissingen in Holland, which required me to follow the narrow, sinuous channel through 40nm of mudbanks that guard the mouth of the Westerschelde, most of it well out of sight of land. While I had a team putting regular Decca[48] fixes on the chart in the Control Room, I found that on the bridge I was almost exclusively using the network of buoys to guide me safely through the channels.

In a small boat, you have much greater freedom of movement than a deep-draught submarine, so an errant buoy is less of a concern. As a result, I have often navigated my yacht using the buoys – both to guide me in and out of port, and for fixing. Where possible, I use land-based fixing marks, but if not, I use a buoy, and it seems to work well enough.

Since 1980, the majority of maritime states have adopted the IALA[49] Combined System of Buoyage. This system has now been implemented through much of the world, with only a few areas diverging. North America, for instance, and the inland waterways of Europe, use the IALA System, but with specific modifications which you would have to check in the *Sailing Directions* before entering those waters.

To all intents and purposes, however, the IALA Buoyage System defines the 5 types of navigation buoy that you and I are most likely to come across on the water. These can be seen below.

Lateral	Green and red, according to the side of the marked channel	Used to indicate the limit of a navigable channel.
Cardinal	Yellow and black in horizontal bands, depending on the direction of the obstruction	Indicates the direction of safe water, in reference to the cardinal points of the compass. For instance, a northerly cardinal mark lies to the north of an obstruction, and vessels should pass to the north of the mark.
Isolated Danger	Red and black in horizontal bands	Marks isolated dangers of limited size with navigable water all round.
Safe Water	Red and white in vertical stripes	Shows that there is safe and navigable water all round. Used for landfall and mid-channel marks.
Special	Yellow	No navigational purpose: used to mark a feature like a racing mark, or the end of an outfall pipe, etc.

[48] Decca was the electronic navigation aid for coastal navigation that was widely used around the coast of Western Europe, and elsewhere, before the advent of GPS.

[49] IALA is the International Association of Lighthouse Authorities, a multi-national body that brings states together to produce ever-safer aids to navigation.

These types of buoy can all happily co-exist in any given stretch of water. For instance, on the way out of the Needles Channel you will find a varied collection of buoys, starting with the Sconce northerly cardinal buoy (Circle 1). Round the corner you will come across the NE Shingles easterly cardinal buoy (Circle 2). You pass to the north and east of these, respectively.

This is followed, further down the Needles Channel, by the green lateral buoy called Warden (Circle 3). You pass between this buoy and the red lateral Mid Shingles buoy (Circle 4), before heading down to the westerly cardinal Bridge buoy (Circle 5) and the red pillar lateral SW Shingles buoy (Circle 6). And finally, a mile further southwest, you reach the Needles Fairway Buoy (Circle 7), a Safe Water Mark, painted in red and white vertical stripes, which is the starting point for ships entering the Needles Channel.

Each of these buoys has an individual design and a specific, unambiguous meaning.

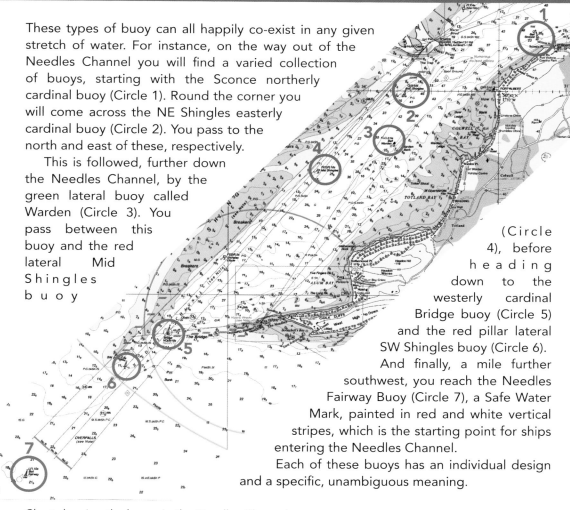

Chart showing the buoys in the Needles Channel

LATERAL BUOYS

Lateral Buoyage is used to indicate the limit of a navigable channel and is designed to be simple – so that there really is no room for confusion.

Having said that, there are two systems of Lateral Buoyage in service around the world, which are imaginatively titled '**IALA System A**' and '**IALA System B**'. These systems are geographically defined, so the great majority of recreational yachtsman will only ever come across one system.

- **System B** is employed in North and South America, Japan and the Philippines
- **System A** is in use everywhere else in the world, including the UK and Europe

For European sailors, unless you are planning to charter a boat in the USA or Canada, you really only need to be aware of IALA System A.

IALA SYSTEM A

IALA System A could not be simpler. The buoys are coloured red or green: the red buoys are described as 'can-shaped'; and the green buoys are 'cone-shaped'.

If you are travelling with the **flood tide**, you keep the **red buoys to port**, and the **green buoys to starboard**.

And just in case you are confused about the direction of the flood stream (this isn't so daft – in the Solent it floods from both ends at once), you will often find a big, chunky hollow arrow on the chart, nudging its way between 2 circles. This symbol identifies the direction of the flood tide.

The lateral buoys are easy to distinguish, because the authorities go to great trouble to make them different – in colour, shape, numbering and in the topmark. I have never had any difficulty in telling one from the other.

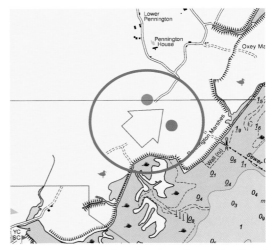

Chart symbol showing the direction of the flood stream

Port-hand buoy (when moving with the flood stream)	**Starboard-hand buoy** (when moving with the flood stream)
■ Painted red ■ 'Can' shape ■ Red light at night ■ Would normally have a cylindrical or square topmark ■ Even numbered ■ Leave to port when moving with the flood stream	■ Painted green ■ 'Conical' shape ■ Green light at night ■ Would normally have a triangular topmark ■ Odd numbered ■ Leave to starboard when moving with the flood stream

Red port-hand buoy	*Green starboard-hand buoy*

IALA SYSTEM B

IALA System B is similar to System A, except that when entering the harbour (going with the main flood tide), you leave the red buoys to starboard, and the green buoys to port. The US Navy has quite a nice mnemonic for this:

'RED – RIGHT – RETURNING'

Port-hand buoy
(when moving with the flood tide)

- Painted green
- Square shape
- Green light at night
- Odd numbered
- Leave to port when moving with the flood stream

Starboard-hand buoy
(when moving with the flood tide)

- Painted red
- Square shape but can be slant-sided
- Red light at night
- Even numbered
- Leave to starboard when moving with the flood stream

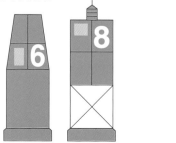

THE CARDINAL SYSTEM OF BUOYAGE

The Cardinal System is universal, and it's used on buoys, beacons, poles and other fixed navigation marks as well. It is used to indicate where safe water lies.

The marks are organised around the cardinal points of the compass. They tell you unambiguously which side of a danger you need to stay in order to remain safe, and the buoys in each quadrant are designed to be readily distinguished by colour, topmark, and light characteristics.

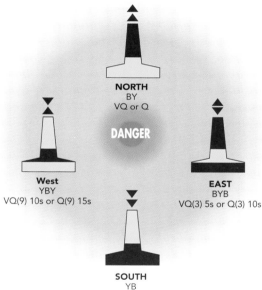

Cardinal buoys (© Fernhurst Books)

It takes a little bit of learning, but there are some valuable mnemonics that can help you through this.

The best way to remember the Cardinal System is to start with the topmark:

- The cones on the Northerly marks point north
- Those on the Southerly marks point south

99

- The Westerly Cardinal Buoy's cones form the shape of a crude 'W' on its side
- And the Easterly Cardinal Buoy's cones looks like a sort of primitive 'E'

Westerly buoy
topmark

Easterly buoy
topmark

Having sorted out the shape of the topmarks, you can move onto the colour of the marks themselves. One way to remember this is that the cones point towards the black bits of the marks themselves:

- **Northerly Mark**: The cones point upwards, and the black painting is at the top
- **Southerly Mark**: The cones point downwards, so the black painting is on the base
- **Westerly Mark**: The cones point towards the centre, so the black is sandwiched between two bands of yellow
- **Easterly Mark**: The cones are pointing outwards, so the black banding is at the top and the bottom

	North	East	South	West
Topmark Cones	Point up / north	Form a primitive 'E' on its side	Point down / south	Form a crude 'W' on its side
Colours – Cones point towards the black bits	Cones point up, black at top (black over yellow)	Cones point out, black at top & bottom (black, yellow, black)	Cones point down, black on base (yellow over black)	Cones point inwards, black in centre (yellow, black, yellow)
Lights – configured like the time on a clock face	Quick or Very Quick flashes	Flashing (3)	Flashing (6), followed by one long flash	Flashing (9)
Safe water	To the north	To the east	To the south	To the west

You will, of course, find cardinal marks of all shapes and sizes around the coast. Here's a stone beacon that I found on the south coast of Brittany:

Stone beacon cardinal mark in South Brittany

Just looking at this, you will see from the colour scheme that this is a southerly beacon with safe water to the South. At night you would expect it to show a light quick flashing 6 with one long flash.

The joy of the cardinal systems is that you don't even need a chart in order to stay safe. You can just look at the colouring of the mark, or its light characteristics, and know which side of it to pass.

OTHER MARKS

SAFE WATER MARK
Safe water marks can be found right around the coastline. They are often laid as the stepping-off point for pilotage into a harbour, like the Needles Fairway Buoy which lies at the start of the channel into the Western Solent.

Safe Water Mark © Bob Jeffrey, RNLI Eastbourne

These are painted with red and white vertical stripes. Please note that the golden anchor top mark in this photo is misleading. Operationally, these buoys generally have a circular topmark, painted red. The crew of the Eastbourne RNLI Lifeboat, however, is the real thing.

ISOLATED DANGER MARK
You really do need to be able to recognise this mark which gives you warning of an isolated danger in an area which otherwise is safe for navigation. I took this photo at half-tide in the entrance to Granville Harbour in Normandy. On an otherwise even, sandy bottom there is a rock, covered at High Water, which is marked with this beacon. The colours of this mark are, if my memory serves me right, in exactly the same as Dennis the Menace's shirt[50].

Isolated Danger Mark

---

[50] For those of us lucky enough to have read *The Beano* in our youth.

NEW DANGER MARK

These buoys are used to mark newly-discovered hazards to navigation, most commonly (but not exclusively) new wrecks in busy shipping lanes. They will stay in place until a permanent mark is laid, or the obstruction has been removed. Where more than one mark is required, they will be identical, with synchronised lights.

You don't see these buoys very often, but if you do the message is unambiguous – stay well clear!

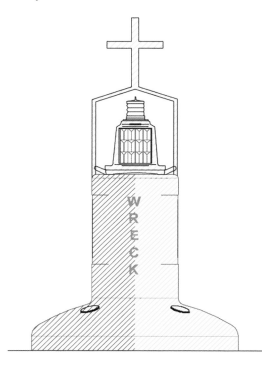

New Danger Mark (© Trinity House)

Multiple pileups can, and do, happen in the busy shipping lanes, and it was one of these that led to the introduction of this mark. On 14 December 2002, the car carrier *Tricolor* and the container vessel *Kariba* collided in the entrance to the north-south shipping route through the English Channel. The *Kariba* struck the *Tricolor* on the port side, and the car carrier quickly took on water,

capsized and sank.

Two days later, the German cargo vessel *Nicola* struck the wreck of the *Tricolor*. Tugs pulled the cargo ship from the wreck on the same day. Then, two weeks after that, on New Year's Day 2003, the *Tricolor* was struck for a third time. On this occasion, the Turkish tanker *Vicky*, carrying 77,000 tons of gas oil, hit the wreck. These wrecks in the Dover Strait led to the creation of a rapid intervention service to prevent any further such multiple accidents. One of these interventions was the introduction of the New Danger Mark.

SPECIAL MARKS

These are not strictly speaking navigation marks, but you will see them from time to time, and you should be able to recognise them.

This is a racing mark in the Solent, but they can be used for a variety of non-specific purposes and they are generally marked on the chart.

Special Mark

	Safe Water Mark	Isolated Danger Mark	New Danger Mark	Special Mark
Topmark	Circular Red	Circular x 2 Black	Upright cross Yellow (if fitted)	Diagonal cross Yellow (if fitted)
Colour	Red & white vertical stripes	Red & black horizontal stripes	Blue & yellow vertical stripes	Yellow (usually name painted in black)
Light	White Isophase or occulting, one long flash every 10 seconds May also show Morse character 'A' (· −)	White Flashing (2)	Alternating blue & yellow flashing light May have racon Morse Code 'D' (− ··) or AIS transponder	Yellow (if fitted)
Meaning	Safe water all around	Hazard with safe water all around	Marking a new & uncharted danger	No navigational meaning – often racing marks

ROCKS & WRECKS

To navigate safely, you have to be able to interpret the symbols for rocks and wrecks on the chart, which are quite detailed and can often be a little confusing. This has the additional benefit of helping you decide whether you can use charted rocks and wrecks for navigation: they can often provide a valuable headmark or fixing point as long as you are careful, and (to state the obvious) as long as they're standing proud of the water at the time that you want to use them.

ROCKS

From a navigational perspective, there are so many types of rocks that it is sometimes easy to become a little confused. Overleaf is just one small sample of the menagerie of rocks and hazards that you can find within a mile of Bray Harbour entrance in Alderney:
Circle 1: Overfalls. These are not strictly speaking rocks, but very much the effect of: rocks + an uneven seabed + strong tidal streams: you will find overfalls right around

the coast of Alderney.

Circle 2: The 'green cauliflower'. This is the symbol for a cluster of rocks that cover and uncover with the tide. The rocks stand 5.5m above Chart Datum, as you can see from the notation $\underline{5}5$. This in a port where, at Mean High Water Springs, the sea level is 11.0m above Chart Datum, and at Mean Low Water Springs it is 1.4m. It's coloured green because it lies between Chart Datum and MHWS. The symbol is shaped like a cauliflower to show that it's an expanse of rock, rather than a single rock.

Circle 3: The vertical cross with one spot in each quadrant. This is a rock which is awash at Chart Datum, so it could be a danger to shipping, even though it's likely to be covered most of the time.

Circle 4: The spotted necklace is a Danger Line. It is used to indicate an area with multiple dangers, through which it is unsafe to navigate. You can see 2 star-shaped symbols there, standing 0.3m and 1.2m above Chart Datum, respectively. These rocks may or may not be visible, depending upon the Height of Tide.

Circle 5: This circle contains a wonderful assortment of rocks and demonstrates just

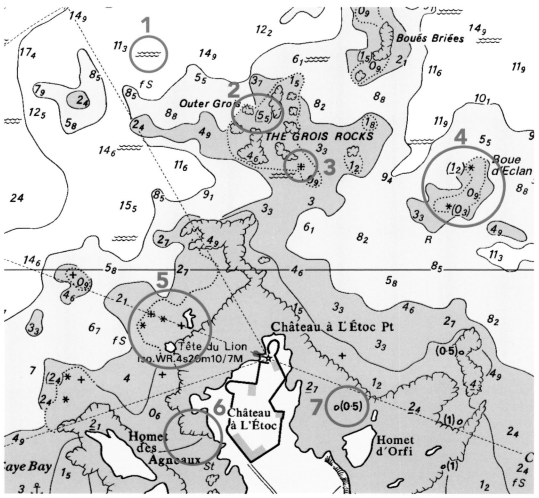

Two charts showing rocks near Alderney

how carefully these charts are drawn up. The single vertical cross in the middle of the circle indicates an individual rock, the depth over which is unknown, but which nevertheless may be a danger to navigation. It sits between two small, yellow-coloured islets, one of which is called 'Tete du Lion'. The yellow colouring indicates that these 2 islets stand above MHWS, and so are always visible. Rocks like this sometimes have a Charted Elevation ascribed to them in brackets: e.g. (14), which would indicate that it stands 14m above MHWS[51]. On the shore side of the circle, the 'green cauliflower' has reappeared: a cluster of rocks that cover and uncover with the tide. This time, no height above CD is shown. Then, to seaward, there is a 6-pointed cross – more of a star – which indicates a solitary rock that covers and uncovers, but whose precise height above Chart Datum is not known. And finally, the vertical cross with spots in each quadrant – a rock that's awash at Chart Datum. All of these rocks are sensibly fenced in by a spotted danger line, showing that this area is unsafe for navigation.

Circle 6: This is an interesting area of the chart, where the cauliflower-shaped outline of a rock shelf gives way to the smooth outline of a seabed that is either sand or mud.

Circle 7: A small column of rock, this stands 0.5m above MHWS.

WRECKS

Wrecks are inherently dangerous to shipping, and whether you are a yachtsman, a trawler skipper, the Captain of a VLCC, or the navigator of a nuclear submarine, you really don't want to hit one. So the position of the wreck, and the least depth over its structure, are of material importance to all seafarers, and there are a variety of wreck symbols, each of which tells a slightly different story. Most wrecks lie well under water but there are some which stand proud of the water at all times, and which can sometimes provide a useful fixing mark for passing mariners.

Close to the entrance to the Gareloch on the River Clyde, where the UK's submarine force is based, the wreck of the sugar ship *MV Captayannis*, has lain on her side for the last 40 years, providing a familiar 'welcome home' landmark for returning submarines. I have often used this wreck as a fixing mark for my submarine, when weaving my way in and out of the Gareloch.

The wreck of the MV Captyannis (© Keith Shipman and the Helensburgh RNLI crew)

The various wreck symbols used on the chart are all laid out in *Chart 5011 Symbols and Abbreviations Used on Admiralty Charts*. There is no need to learn them all; but it is important to recognise which may be a danger, and which are not.

---

[51] Note the subtle change in notation: when the chart indicates a 'Drying Height' above Chart Datum (but below MHWS), the sounding is underlined. When the object is permanently dry – that is to say, it stands above MHWS – the elevation is just noted in brackets or stands alone on the yellow background.

8

RADAR & RADIO AIDS TO NAVIGATION

I have never been entirely comfortable navigating with radar, and today GPS will give you a more accurate position, more quickly than you will ever achieve with a radar set, particularly in a small boat. In large ships I have, when necessary, felt my way into harbours in fog using radar for blind pilotage – a technique that doesn't easily read across to the less user-friendly displays in a small boat.

To me, the real value of radar in a small boat is for collision avoidance in poor visibility. When you can't see the other ships around you, radar is a godsend, particularly if it's tied to your AIS receiver and your chart plotter, and for that reason alone I carry radar on my boat.

HOW RADAR WORKS

Radar works by sending a stream of radio pulses out from a rotating aerial. Each pulse is transmitted down a specific bearing, and if there is a solid object in the way of the pulse, it will create an echo, which returns to the aerial. The radar set measures how long it takes the echo to get back and, from

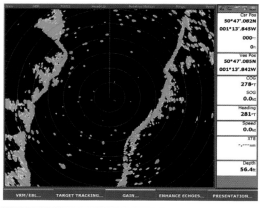

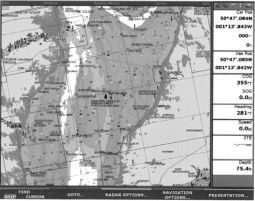

Example of a radar picture overlaid onto a chart plotter display. Top: radar picture. Bottom: combined display. (© Raymarine)

the direction of the aerial and the time interval, it's able to position the object on a radar screen or chart plotter. In a single rotation of the aerial, your radar scans the entire horizon around the ship.

The radio pulses travel in a straight line, so in normal atmospheric conditions the range of the set is limited to the visual horizon, as seen by your aerial. So, the higher the aerial, the further it will be able to see.

In most small boats, the radar is displayed as an additional layer on the chart plotter, so it's relatively easy to correlate the echoes with known objects like land or buoys, or to identify vessels that are in your vicinity. Over a period of time you can estimate the other ship's course and speed, and from that work out its Closest Point of Approach (CPA). This process is greatly helped by ARPA and AIS[52]. While neither of these is flawless, they will often help you weed out dangerous tracks from those that are less of a problem, and hopefully take well-informed collision avoidance decisions.

THE ACCURACY OF YOUR RADAR

Before you use any radar information you need to make sure that your radar is set up as well as possible. You normally have a choice of displaying radar data **'North Up'** or **'Ship's Head Up'**. Either of these can work for you, as long as you give yourself time to get used to the display. I always tend to use the radar on 'North Up', because the display remains stable when you alter course. It's also a lot easier to correlate with the chart – which means that it's easier to pick out shipping from

navigation marks and buoys.

You should make sure that the bearing display is accurately aligned with the boat's compass. This matters because most of us now superimpose our radar display onto the chart plotter, so the two need to be aligned. Depending on the quality of your set, you may also be able to adjust the gain to reduce sea clutter around the boat. This can be a bit of a 2-edged sword: reducing the clutter can make it easier to see close contacts; but, if you are a bit heavy-handed on the gain control, it can suppress small, close contacts altogether. So you need to operate this control with care.

HOW RELIABLE IS YOUR RADAR?

RANGE

The one thing that radar does really well is to measure range. The trick is always to measure the closest point of an object – a ship or a land feature – and if you do, you can be pretty confident that you will get an accurate range. When using radar to fix on the coastline, try to find bits of the coast that are sheer and rocky; this too will give you an accurate range.

BEARING

There are times when it's so, so tempting to use radar to give you a bearing to fix with. All I can say is that even in a super-sophisticated warship with radar equipment that was vastly more expensive than anything I had in my yacht, I would try to dissuade the watch keepers from using a radar bearing line.

The radar set works by using the long, flat aerial to shape a narrow and precisely targeted radio beam, and the laws of

---

[52] ARPA – Automatic Radar Plotting Aid; AIS – Automatic Identification System. Both systems provide information on course, speed and CPA for other contacts in your vicinity. ARPA information is derived from your radar, and AIS from the GPS information in other ships, broadcast on VHF (see p109).

physics dictate that the longer the radio aerial, the better job it will make of this complicated task. So the relatively short radar aerial that you and I carry in our yachts gives us quite a chubby radar beam, which is unlikely to provide better than 1-2° of accuracy. If you add the inaccuracies caused by a small flux-gate compass and the random movements of your boat, and you should probably allow an accuracy of ±4 or 5° on radar bearings taken in a small boat – so you will nearly always get a better and more accurate fix using radar ranges.

Don't expect miracles of your radar; it can only see the things that you could see if the visibility was good enough: it can't see over the horizon; it can't see round corners; and it can't see behind things. Also, give yourself time to interpret the radar picture. It's not always easy to identify all of the many echoes around you and, even when you have identified them, you still need to work out which echoes to worry about, and which are relatively harmless.

RADAR FIXING

In principle, radar fixing is no different from fixing with visual bearings. You need to identify three distinct and identifiable points that are painting clearly on radar, ideally separated by more than 30°. As accurately as you can, put the radar cursor on the closest point of those features, note down the ranges, and plot them with a compass and a soft pencil on your chart.

In this example, I have plotted a fix using three ranges:

- Burhou (1): 14.7nm
- Closest Point of Alderney (2): 13.0nm
- Cap de la Hague (3): 2.5nm

… and it has produced a fairly respectable fix.

There is no exclusivity in radar fixing; it is entirely possible to get a good fix with 2 ranges and a visual bearing, or 2 visual bearings and a single radar range.

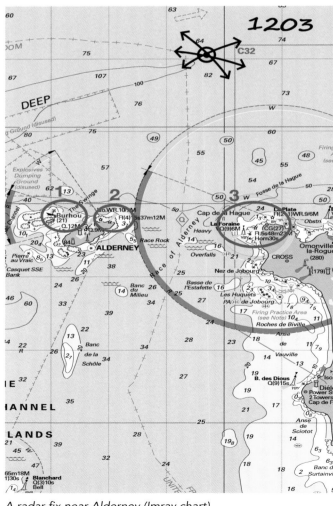

A radar fix near Alderney (Imray chart)

RADAR COLLISION AVOIDANCE, ARPA & AIS

Radar is a useful tool for fixing, and it can be used for blind pilotage, but its real value lies in giving you a much better awareness of your surroundings in poor visibility. Having spent much of my professional life on or close to the sea, I can honestly say that poor visibility in a ship of any size frightens me far more than heavy weather. That's because, even with a really good radar set, you never quite know what's out there – and even when you do know that there is something there, it takes a little bit of magic to work out its course, speed and CPA. Having a radar is far, far better than not having a radar, but even today it's risky being out on the waters in fog, particularly in a small vessel, so I would strongly advise yachtsmen to avoid sailing in poor visibility if at all possible. Even so, you will occasionally be caught out in fog. When this happens, you have to be able to navigate safely, and perform competent collision avoidance in these much more demanding circumstances.

And that's where ARPA and AIS come in.

ARPA

ARPA is built into most modern radar sets. It analyses a series of radar echoes from each contact, removing own ship motion, and provides you with a course, speed and CPA for the contact. In a small boat it's battling with a lot of variables: your own course and speed, which are constantly varying in any sort of a seaway; plus the accuracy and any lag in the flux-gate compass from which the radar set gets its heading information; plus any variations in course and speed in the other vessel. And finally, particularly at longer ranges, you may only be receiving intermittent paints from the contact on your radar.

So, while I have always valued ARPA, I tend to treat the information that it gives me as helpful collateral rather than absolute truth.

AIS

I find AIS to be more reliable than ARPA, because it picks up VHF transmissions from other ships, in which they broadcast their identity, their position and their course and speed. So, it's easier for your AIS set to plot this information on your display and give you an accurate CPA. This helps greatly with situational awareness and collision avoidance.

AIS is great, but it's not infallible. To be accurate and fool proof, it requires every other vessel to switch on their AIS transponder. And that's probably not going to happen: many small boats still don't have an AIS transponder and small boats are, of course, the most difficult to detect on radar. So be careful; the best advice I can give you, on a sunny day or in fog, is to keep your eyes up – out of the electronic screens – and to always keep a good visual lookout.

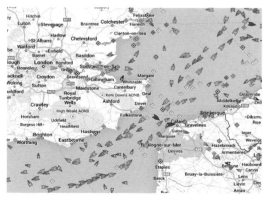

Typical AIS display for the Straits of Dover – things can be quite busy around here (Also Maritime AS)

RADAR BEACONS

RACONS

Around the coast, and particularly in busy shipping lanes, you may find marks – buoys, lightships, light houses or beacons – that carry a radar transponder so that they are able to identify themselves on a ship's radar. This is particularly valuable in places like the Dover Strait where shipping density is high, and where mariners need to be able to quickly tell the difference between a ship's radar return and that of a navigation buoy.

Here, in the Dover Strait, the Varne Light Buoy carries the legend: Racon (T) which signifies that it will periodically identify itself on your radar screen with the Morse character 'T' (–), painting directly behind the return from the buoy itself.

Other Racons are identified by different Morse characters. Racons that are identified with the Morse symbol 'D' (– · ·), are used to mark new and uncharted hazards to navigation, like a recently sunk vessel. A Racon transmitting the Morse Symbol 'D' is likely to be temporary, and so uncharted,

and it may be mounted on a New Danger Mark (see p102).

RAMARKS

You will occasionally encounter Ramarks, which transmit continuously, and are not triggered by a ship's radar. In all honesty I find these slightly annoying; they paint on your radar screen as a single radial line in the direction of the Ramark but give no range information. Happily, they are not that common: I have only come across them a couple of times, and with luck you won't either.

OTHER RADIO NAVIGATION AIDS

As recently as 10 years ago, there would have been a long section here about radio navigation aids, like Decca and even possibly Loran-C, not to mention radio direction-finding. These systems have all been superseded by GPS. They are no longer a part of the RYA navigation syllabus.

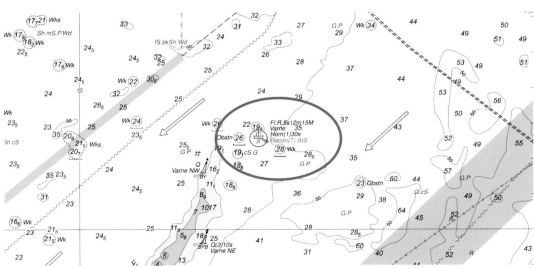

The Varne Light Buoy in Dover Strait carries a radar transponder

9

NAVIGATION EQUIPMENT

"I must go down to the sea again, to
the lonely sea and the sky.
And all I ask is a tall ship, and a star to
steer her by."

Much as I love this poem, *Sea Fever* by
John Masefield, I have to say that I would
question the resilience of his navigational
arrangements. To navigate safely and
reliably, you do need the right kit. And to
be honest, it costs quite a lot to buy the
right equipment: kit that is reliable and can
function in the demanding environment of
a small boat, with severe turbulence and
salt-laden air. You may well be tempted
to try to get away with cheaper, inferior
equipment, but all of my experience tells
me that it's worth paying for reliability –
good stuff to look after you on the water.
You can't just pop down to the nearest
chandlery when you're half-way across the
Bay of Biscay, and even in some foreign
ports it's a struggle to get the precise bits
that you need.

I'm still scarred from my very first visit to
an Italian chandlery in a port called Porto
Ercole, trying to buy a specific nut for

the outboard motor when the only Italian
words I could speak were 'spaghetti' and
'piano'. If possible, the storekeeper spoke
even worse English than I spoke Italian.
We got there in the end, with a couple of
Oscar-winning mime performances, but
not before he had randomly offered me a
pair of sailing wellies, a bilge pump and a
packet of frozen peas – on the off-chance
that they might be what I was looking for.

This chapter is not meant as an
equipment inventory for small boats; I have
just listed some of the things that I consider
absolutely essential to safe navigation.

EQUIPMENT

ANCHOR & ANCHOR CABLE

Your anchor sits patiently on the bow, and
most of us are guilty of paying it only scant
attention until the moment comes to drop
it unceremoniously over the bow once
more, onto a dark and muddy seabed. But
you should give it a bit of attention from
time to time:

■ Is it the right size and shape for your

boat (the best anchor may not be the one that came as part of the package when you bought the boat)?

- Have you got sufficient anchor cable, at the right weight?
- Is your cable marked off so that you know at a glance how much you have veered over the bow?
- And is your anchor shackle secure and properly moused?

You will often have to anchor – to ride out a storm; to wait for a favourable tide, or just to spend the night somewhere safe, so a good anchor, attached to a good length of weighty cable, will give you real peace of mind, and it means that you really can sleep well at anchor.

STEERING COMPASS

There really is not much to say about your steering compass; it will be part of the inventory when you buy your boat; it should be big enough for the helmsman to read clearly, and well enough lit to allow you to use at night.

It should also be accurate. In a Navy warship we used to spend half a day every year sitting at a buoy with a tug pulling at our stern, while the Compass Swinging Officer, whose knowledge of the arcane science of compasses swinging gave him the aura of a latter-day druid. He would come onboard, armed with a big suitcase of magnets, and spend the day on the bridge, taking bearings, making notes and quietly muttering under his breath before suddenly appearing in the Wardroom at teatime where, with a conjuror's flourish, he would drop a completed Deviation Card on the table.

In a yacht, we're more fortunate because in most cases, a non-ferrous hull causes minimal deviation of the steering compass. However, if you have a boat with a steel hull, or if you're concerned that the deviation may indeed be substantial, it is worth getting a Swinging Officer to conduct a compass swing for your boat, and to draw up a Deviation Card for you.

Steering compass (© Kamila Koziol / shutterstock.com)

CHECKING DEVIATION OF THE STEERING COMPASS ON A SMALL YACHT

Despite the rather magical nature of the Swinging Officer's art, you can check the accuracy of your steering compass yourself. This should be done with the boat stationary in calm water and away from other magnetic influences (like a pontoon).

Point the boat directly at a remote but unambiguous landmark and check the ship's head on the compass. At the same time, take the most accurate fix you can – GPS would be good for this – and plot your position on the chart. Finally, compare the heading on the steering compass with the charted Magnetic Bearing of the distant object, not forgetting to apply variation. The difference between the two is deviation.

You can do this even better, and more accurately, by pointing your boat directly down the line of a known transit and checking the charted Magnetic[53] Bearing of the transit against your heading on the ship's steering compass.

To create a Deviation Card, you should repeat this process on a variety of headings, every 45° or less, (ideally every 22.5°) right round the compass. This is likely to test the patience of even the most patient crew, and in any case I doubt if you would be able to find enough distant objects to point at right round the horizon. So you might instead consider completing the process over a period of time, slowly compiling the data until you have enough.

BINOCULARS

You should not go to sea – in anything – without a couple of pairs of high quality, waterproof binoculars, ideally with a rubber sheathing to prevent them being damaged. You don't need anything fancy; just good, reliable binos that you are happy with, and which don't mind getting wet. I have never seen the need for stabilised binoculars, or binoculars with a compass read-out superimposed on the picture. You don't need additional complications, and you don't need the higher magnification that comes with image stabilisation. Unstabilised binoculars with 8x magnification are quite good enough.

I use a pair of high-quality rubber-sheathed Nikon Monarch binoculars which have good optics and, at 8x42[54], pretty good low-light performance. They haven't let me down.

Always have a secure lanyard on your binoculars, and always put it round your neck when you're using them!

My binoculars

HAND-BEARING COMPASS

The hand-bearing compass is the Eeyore of my yachting inventory. Just as the Winnie the Pooh books would not really work without Eeyore, so you couldn't very well go to sea without a hand-bearing compass… but even so I find it a thoroughly annoying piece of equipment that's neither fun nor easy to use. The trouble is that in any sort of a swell the reading bounces around all over the place, so it can be a bit of a challenge to take an accurate bearing of Portland Bill Lighthouse, and you also have to work quite hard to get a sufficiently accurate bearing of an approaching ship to check its bearing movement.

In the end, I decided to switch from a classical oil-damped card compass to a hand-held flux-gate compass (after one particularly fraught mid-Channel battery crisis, I now make sure that I take plenty of spare batteries with me), and I find that I get the best results when I take about 5 bearings in succession, and use the average.

---

[53] That is to say, the True Bearing, with variation applied to it.

[54] All binoculars carry a similar designation. 8 is the level of magnification provided by the binoculars, and 42 is the diameter of the lens that you point towards the thing you're looking at. The bigger this 'objective lens' is, the better low-light performance you get from the binoculars.

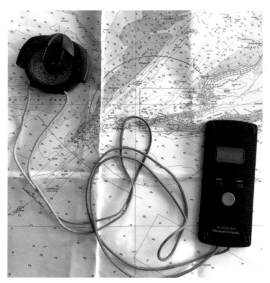

Hand-bearing compasses: the traditional oil-filled (left) and electronic (right)

OTHER EQUIPMENT

POLAROID SUNGLASSES

A pair of polarising sunglasses is incredibly useful. Mine are a pair of worn-out pear-shaped Aviator glasses; a left-over from the 1980s, when we all wanted to look like Tom Cruise in *Top Gun*. As a middle-aged man who looks nothing at all like Tom Cruise, I recognise that I may appear faintly ridiculous wearing them, but on a sunny day with a lot of reflection from the water, the polaroids are just brilliant for cutting out the glare from the water when you're looking up-sun, and they also allow you much better vision into the water as well.

TORCHES – BIG & SMALL

You need a big, powerful torch that you can shine onto the water to search for a buoy at night or – God forbid – someone who has fallen overboard. In addition, each crew member should carry a small pocket torch at night, so they can move around the boat and operate safely, at sea or in harbour. Choose a brand that you're happy with, and which is moderately waterproof. Personally, I use Maglite torches, which come in a variety of sizes. They're robust, sufficiently waterproof, and they have stood the test of time.

YOUR EYES

I know that it's a bit cheesy putting this into the 'equipment' section. But I have done so because it matters more than you can possibly imagine that you keep looking outside the boat. We've all had a variety of instruments and screens installed around the cockpit to help us navigate, and they do help. But your eyes, and the thoroughness of your lookout, are probably the most important component of safe navigation – and they don't cost you a penny to install!

Use them well; if you wear glasses, make sure that they're the right strength, and that you have a spare pair onboard. And encourage all the crew to just keep looking all round the horizon (including the bit of sea right behind you). Even on a warship, with no end of sophisticated equipment onboard, the bridge lookouts were nearly always the first to spot an object in the water, or a submarine at periscope depth.

INSTRUMENTS

ECHO SOUNDER

It's so easy to overlook this quiet and unassuming little instrument; yet it's a vital tool for safe navigation, and it deserves your attention. Make sure that you can read the sounding from both the cockpit steering position and the chart table.

SETTING THE ZERO ON YOUR ECHO SOUNDER

You can adjust the reading on your echo sounder to display:
- The total depth of water (i.e. from the

waterline to the seabed)
- The depth of water under the transducer
- The depth of water under the keel

The choice is up to you – there is no right or wrong answer. But whichever way you go, both you and your crew must know precisely what the numbers on the display mean.

For what it's worth, I have always felt most comfortable with my echo sounder displaying the total depth of water – that's to say distance from the waterline to the seabed.

You can find the instructions for setting the zero in the manufacturer's handbook, and they should also be available online.

CALIBRATING YOUR ECHO SOUNDER

Echo sounders are pretty accurate, but you should periodically check that it is displaying the right depth.

This is an enjoyable job for an idle day when you're alongside in a marina. Just drop a weighted line over the side and compare the depth of water with the echo sounder reading. On the basis that the seabed might have a bit of a slope on it, it's worth putting the weight over both sides and taking an average.

ELECTRONIC LOG

Most yachts have an electronic log (or speed sensor) which is operated from a small impeller sticking out from the bottom of the boat in a place where there is a more-or-less unimpeded flow of water. The speed of the impeller's rotation is picked up by an onboard sensor and translated, quite accurately on the whole, into a read-out of the boat's speed through the water. This in turn is converted into distance travelled (again through the water).

The disadvantage of these impellers

is that they periodically get fouled by seaweed or other rubbish in the water, which usually takes an awkward 20 minutes in the bilge, clearing the obstruction and swearing fluently. A useful alternative is the ultrasonic speed sensor, which has no tiny paddle-wheels to catch seaweed.

Either way, this instrument gives you speed and distance travelled through the water, and, in my experience, they tend to be quite accurate.

These, with the magnetic compass, are the raw components of essential navigation, and I would find it very difficult to navigate accurately without them.

WIND INSTRUMENT

A wind instrument showing wind strength in knots, and wind direction (switchable to show either true or relative wind) should be part of your boat's standard outfit. This is another piece of vital equipment.

The weather forecast around UK waters, particularly for the next 24-48 hours is generally pretty accurate, but at the end of the day, it's just a forecast and the only thing that matters on the water is what the wind is doing around you.

THE BEAUFORT SCALE

Wind strength is measured in the Beaufort Scale with 0 being flat calm and 8 and over being a gale. It is quite easy to estimate the Beaufort Force of the wind by dividing the true wind strength (in knots) by 4. So, a 20-knot wind is Force 5, and a Force 8 gale is about 32-36 knots.

You will tend to get white horses on the water at wind strengths greater than 20 knots (Force 5 and above), and I always fancy that I can feel a sort of venom in any wind over Force 8, which can be quite frightening, even for experienced mariners.

10
REFERENCE BOOKS

You do need a reasonably extensive and well-stocked bookshelf, filled with the current editions of reference books, all of which should ideally be situated within easy reach of the chart table. When you visit other peoples' yachts, take a sneaky look at their chart table book selection; it's quite revealing. Some people half-fill it with accounts of single-handed round-the-world voyages. Some with reference books that are greatly loved, but patently out-of-date. And on some there is a well thought-out selection of useful books. Here are some of my greatest hits.

ALMANAC

If you're sailing around the UK and the waters of Western Europe, there is really only one almanac to buy. This is **Reed's Nautical Almanac**. You can't miss it; visit almost any chandlery over the winter months, and you will find yourself tripping up over copies of this heavy tome piled up on the floor. For any mariner, and actually for anyone with an interest in the sea, this book provides hours of fascinating reading.

And it's quite useful too.

There is masses of information in this book that is reviewed and updated annually, and just about all of it is relevant to you and me when we're on the water.

The *Almanac* runs to over 1,000 pages and contains just about everything that you need to know for safe cruising around the coasts of the UK and Western Europe, from Shetland to Denmark in the north, round Ireland and down to Gibraltar, including the Canary Islands, the Azores and Madeira.

It contains tide tables for Standard and Secondary Ports, copies of the *Tidal Stream Atlases*, pilotage information for ports and waterways, small chartlets of harbours, communications frequencies and port facilities; not to mention passage information and distance tables.

You can, of course, get all of this information from other sources, but I haven't found anywhere else that presents it as well as *Reed's*, or in such a compact format. It is carefully and diligently curated, and you can download monthly updates from January to June by registering at: **www.reedsnauticalalmanac.co.uk**

This should be an essential part of your boat's library, and you really should get a new copy each year, not least for the tidal information that it contains.

PILOT BOOKS

The complimentary publication to the *Almanac* is the pilot book. In their most formal and all-encompassing form, the *Admiralty Sailing Directions*, published by the UK Hydrographic Office are expensive and may be rather too detailed for the average recreational sailor. But at the same time, they are beautifully written and comprehensive descriptions of the coast and the sea conditions that you can expect to find around the world.

I would not perhaps go as far as W Somerset Maughan, writing in 1951, who wrote lyrically about the *Admiralty Sailing Directions* in his book *The Vessel of Wrath*:

"These business-like books take you upon an enchanted journey of the spirit…, the stern sense of the practical that informs every line cannot dim the poetry that, like the spice-laden breeze that assails your senses when you approach those magic islands of the eastern seas, blows with such sweet fragrance through the printed page."

They are enjoyable reading, nonetheless.

As you can see from the chart, the 76 volumes of the *Admiralty Sailing Directions* cover all of the world's oceans, and they do so in great, and painstaking detail. I have to admit to having spent a lot of quiet night watches browsing through some of the more arcane volumes that used to be stowed away in my submarine's chart table – just in case we should be deployed to the islands in the southern Indian Ocean…. I am not sure that I would necessarily go to the expense of buying a copy for my yacht.

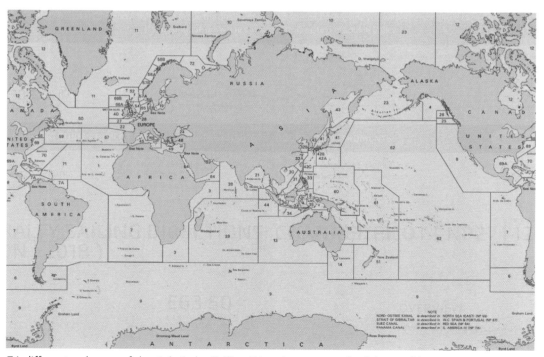

76 different volumes of the Admiralty Sailing Directions cover all of the world's oceans

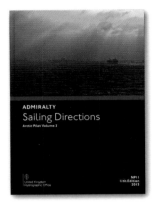

Admiralty Sailing Directions: beautifully written but possibly too detailed for the recreational sailor

of this book onboard. It is outstanding.

Other parts of the British Isles have equally impressive and well-compiled pilot books, like the Clyde Cruising Club's *Sailing Directions and Anchorages* – or Fernhurst Books' *Cruising Companions*, covering East Coast Rivers, North Brittany & Channel Islands, Solent and West Country. These books are easy to find and can normally be bought online – why wouldn't you use the experience and knowledge of local sailors when planning a trip through their waters?

It may, however, be the case that you want to take your boat to more distant waters, like the Baltic, Norway, the Mediterranean or indeed the Caribbean. If so, the minimum that you will need is a copy of the *Tide Tables* (I would check the Admiralty Publications list as a first port of call for these). You will also want a pilot book or two to guide you round. There is no shortage of these in the reference bookshelves of good chandleries, and most can also be bought online.

We discovered a particularly lovely collection of pilot books while cruising from Nanaimo on Vancouver Island[55]. These have been compiled by the husband-and-wife team Anne and Laurence Yeadon-Jones, cruising the coast of British Columbia

But if I were cruising a long way from home, I would certainly consider carrying one or more of these marvellous books onboard.

They are available in paper, or in a less expensive online download, and they carry detailed information on navigational hazards, buoyage, pilotage, regulations, general notes on countries, port facilities, seasonal currents, ice and climatic conditions. In addition, they contain diagrams and photographs of the coast and harbour entries to give you a better understanding of the coastline.

For those of us who routinely sail around the English Channel, the go-to pilot book is the *Shell Channel Pilot*, written and edited by Tom Cunliffe. And to be honest, I would not cruise the Channel ports without a copy

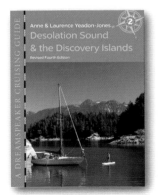
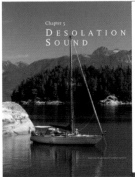

The beautifully presented Dreamspeaker Cruising Guides for British Columbia

55 Nanaimo Yacht Charters and Sailing School; www.nanaimoyachtcharters.com

in their yacht, *Dreamspeaker*. These *Dreamspeaker Cruising Guides* have the dual advantage of being both accurate and beautifully presented, with the anchorages and passages portrayed in hand-painted watercolours.

TIDAL STREAM ATLAS

You don't have to carry a *Tidal Stream Atlas* onboard; around UK and NW European waters, you can generally rely on tidal stream information in the charts, the *Almanac* and the *Sailing Directions*, not to mention your chart plotter tidal stream overlay.

Admiralty Tidal Stream Atlas

But personally, I would always carry these little booklets with me as part of my chart table collection. They don't go out of date, so you only ever have to buy them once, and they give you the full picture of local water movement, how the tidal stream is running around you, and how the strength and direction of the stream will change with time.

These books make it much easier to time your passage round big grizzly tidal hotspots, like the Raz de Seine (which can be awkward if you get it wrong) or the Alderney Race.

The portfolio of *Tidal Stream Atlases* covers the waters around the United Kingdom from the top of Shetland, and

Skagen in north Denmark, right down the French coast to South Brittany and the mouth of the Loire.

The coverage of the Admiralty's Tidal Stream Atlases

THE *MARINER'S HANDBOOK*

The *Mariner's Handbook* would be my *Desert Island Discs* indulgence. The UKHO describes it as:

"The Mariner's Handbook (NP100) contains clear guidance to help Mariners improve their understanding of maritime navigation, sea and ice conditions, meteorology and regulations."

That's all true, of course, but this book is more than that: it has been with me throughout my career, as a literary refuge during long sea voyages. It's a sort of elephant's graveyard for all the information that a mariner might need, but which the hydrographer hasn't managed to squeeze into any of his other publications. I love it; it has of course changed over the years, and it has sadly now lost the engaging section in the 1972 edition which deals with Arctic Survival....

"The survivor of a shipwreck is invariably faced with little choice but that of fighting for continued existence.... [but] despite the inhospitability of the Arctic... his case may not be as hopeless as first seems apparent. Sources of food, drink and shelter can be found...."

Homeric stuff.... And where else would you find a learned and earnest text about 'Navigation Amongst Kelp', or 'Underwater Volcanoes and Earthquakes', not to mention an explanation of the difference between Purse Seine fishing and

My Desert Island Disc's luxury: The Mariner's Handbook

Gillnetting?

It also contains a wealth of useful information about currents, the weather and cloud formations, sea conditions, the limitations of GPS, and much more that is relevant to you and me as recreational sailors. Pricey, but priceless.

ADMIRALTY CHART CATALOGUE

Until recently, I always used to carry an extract of the *Admiralty Chart Catalogue* to help me choose the right charts for the passage that I was planning.

As a leisure sailor, you no longer need to do this. Excellent websites like OneOcean's www.bookharbour.com (shown below with the Imray filter) allow you to check the chart coverage of Admiralty and Imray charts, and order them directly online. It also has an extensive collection of navigation publications too, including a variety of *Sailing Directions*.

As part of your pre-season preparations, I would strongly recommend that you check that you're carrying all the charts that you will need, and that you spend a day or so bringing them up to date.

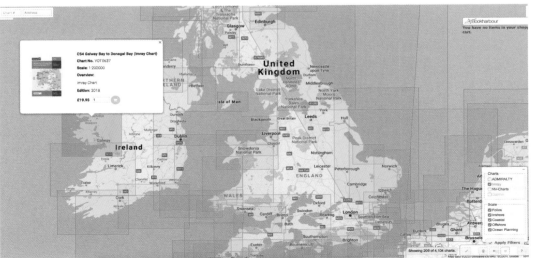

Bookharbour's webpage of chart coverage, here with an Imray filter

CHART 5011 – SYMBOLS AND ABBREVIATIONS USED ON ADMIRALTY PAPER CHARTS

Charts are paper knowledge, and this booklet (it's not a chart – don't ask me why it has been given a chart designator) is the key to unlocking a large part of that knowledge. There's a great deal of interesting, curious and genuinely important information in this book and if you don't have a copy onboard, you really should. Alternatively, my book *Understanding a Nautical Chart* contains the complete *Chart 5011* as an appendix (see p33).

ADMIRALTY TIDE TABLES

These books are essential on bigger ships, but something of a luxury on a small boat where all the tidal information that you might require is available in the *Almanac*. You may find it interesting and useful to have a copy of this onboard for longer

The Admiralty Tide Tables are essential on bigger ships but a luxury on a small boat

offshore passages, but I would not consider it essential for coastal cruising. It is updated annually. The tables can be downloaded digitally, and they are updated, if necessary, through *Notices to Mariners*.

Don't forget too that the UKHO provides us with free 6-day Height of Tide predictions online with *EasyTide*: **www.ukho.gov.uk/easytide/EasyTide/index.aspx**

This is quite a good way of getting the Height of Tide data quickly and accurately. This example is a 6-day prediction for Burnham-on-Sea in the Bristol Channel.

Duration: 7 days

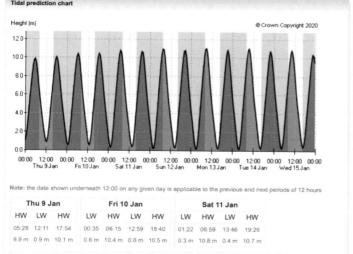

Tidal prediction chart

Height (m) — © Crown Copyright 2020

Adjust chart time axis

Daylight saving: 0 hours

Max graph size: 7 days

Apply

Daylight Saving Warning

EasyTide predictions are based on the standard time of the country concerned.

For the UK this is GMT. The "Daylight saving" drop-down box in the top right-hand corner of the screen can be used to convert the predicted times to "Daylight Saving Time".

For information on Daylight Saving Time in the UK, known as British Summer Time (BST), please visit https://www.gov.uk/when-do-the-clocks-change

Note: the date shown underneath 12:00 on any given day is applicable to the previous and next periods of 12 hours

Thu 9 Jan			Fri 10 Jan				Sat 11 Jan			
HW	LW	HW	LW	HW	LW	HW	LW	HW	LW	HW
05:28	12:11	17:54	00:35	06:15	12:59	18:40	01:22	06:59	13:46	19:26
9.9 m	0.9 m	10.1 m	0.6 m	10.4 m	0.6 m	10.5 m	0.3 m	10.8 m	0.4 m	10.7 m

A 6-day prediction for Burnham-on-Sea in the Bristol Channel on EasyTide

11
A FEW THOUGHTS ABOUT SAFE NAVIGATION

Safe navigation is not just about putting fixes and EPs on the chart or working out Secondary Port tides. It's a responsibility that lies with the skipper of any vessel to make sure that his or her crew, ship and cargo arrive at their destination in one piece. That demands a mindset that is firmly rooted in doing things the right way and doing them safely.

I have no wish to take the fun out of sailing – quite the opposite. There's a whole tradition of seafaring that has come down through the generations as 'good seamanship', which is all about keeping your crew safe and it's worth picking up on some of these pearls of wisdom when you come across them. Things like:

- Not leaning on the guardrails (they DO come unfastened from time to time)
- Having one hand for the boat and one for yourself
- Wearing a lifejacket at sea
- And making sure too that your crew wear 'proper' footwear when going out on deck at sea

These things matter, and they all sit on your shoulders as the skipper – so be thoughtful of your crew and keep them safe. I've put down a few thoughts in this chapter.

1. ALWAYS PLAN TO HAVE ENOUGH WATER UNDER YOUR KEEL

One of the traditional toasts of the Russian Navy (there are quite a lot of them) is for 'Six clear feet of water under the keel.' I couldn't argue with that. I too like to have a good 2 metres of water under my keel, and I'm even happier with 5 metres or more, especially when the chart relies on old surveys, with limited accuracy.

One of the places where I've always felt the need for an additional margin of safety is the passage inside the Ile de Batz on the north coast of Brittany. This is a relatively simple and well-marked navigational short-cut, used by a lot of yachts making their way down the coast to the Point of Brittany. But it isn't a channel to be undertaken lightly: the tidal streams run up to 3.5 knots, and the seabed was last surveyed by leadline in 1930, so it would be imprudent to rely on the soundings being entirely accurate. It's a

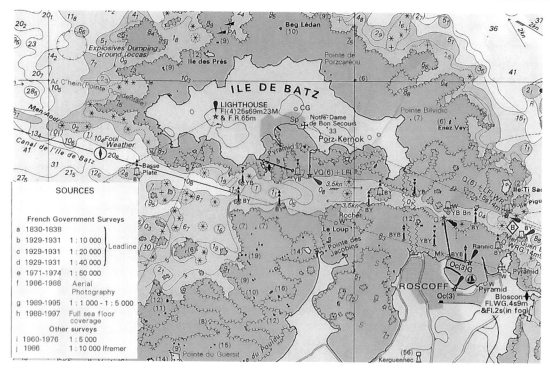

The passage inside the Ile de Batz was last surveyed by leadline in 1930 and is unlikely to be 100% accurate

passage to plan in advance, but with good planning, sufficient water under the keel, and a gentle tidal stream behind you, it is perfectly achievable, and a lot of fun.

2. KNOW YOUR LIMITS, AND THOSE OF YOUR CREW

The sea is quite an alien place if, like the great majority of us, you spend most of your time ashore. More so if you've never been to sea in a boat before; and more so still if you don't have complete faith in your skipper.

For those of us who are lucky enough to own a boat, there is a real imperative to think ahead, to prepare thoroughly and to ensure that the whole experience is enjoyable and rewarding for everyone onboard. So, at some point it is worth just reflecting on the conditions that you,

personally, are happy to take your boat out in, and how they might change with a more timid, or less experienced crew.

I have never believed anyone who stands on the bridge of a ship, or a cockpit of a yacht in a storm, stretches out their arms and tells you with a determined look on their face that they LOVE rough weather. No professional mariner that I have ever met loves rough weather. At best, it's cold, wet and uncomfortable and it interferes with your food and your sleep. More importantly, it interferes with your ability to keep a good lookout, and it also stops people from thinking clearly.

On our boat, we don't go out if we think we will have more than 20 knots of wind over the deck. That's downwind in about Force 5 and upwind in Force 3-4. We do this not because we're frightened of the weather; I have been at sea in some simply horrific weather. We do it because beyond that point we start enjoying it less. You may well have different limits but do try to work out what they are. And if you find yourself at sea, starting to feel uncomfortable with a rising wind, or a swell larger than you expected, don't be too proud to shorten sail and run for cover. It is, after all, meant to be fun!

Many of us are prone to that terrible affliction called 'press-on-itis'. This is an old submarine term for the person's frame of mind when they keep stubbornly bashing on with a plan that's clearly no longer feasible. To be frank, it doesn't fool anyone – it just makes you look like a bit of an idiot. I once sailed back across the Channel from Guernsey with a skipper who refused to be halted by forecasts of a westerly 8 gusting 10 coming up from the southwest. We needn't have set out – actually with an inexperienced crew onboard we shouldn't have set out. We could easily have taken the ferry home, or stopped at Alderney after the first couple of hours – but the skipper was determined to keep going regardless. The worst of it was that he spent the entire passage in his bunk with seasickness, while my wife and I kept watch in the cockpit… right across the Channel.

And always, always be conscious of how your crew are feeling: you have a genuine responsibility to look after them. If they spend long periods of time feeling cold and wet – or both – or if they're frightened, too far out of their comfort zone, or just feeling seasick, they will no longer be enjoying the experience, and you have probably lost any hope of taking them to sea with you again. Just as importantly, if half your crew are feeling rotten, you have fewer eyes to keep a lookout, to steer and to take a watch. And that puts more pressure on everyone else.

3. PLAN YOUR PASSAGE INTELLIGENTLY

I have lost count of the number of boat owners that I've met who express a desire to sail across the Atlantic, or round the world. Sometimes, these are people with little or no yachting experience under their belt. I know that this is a dull thing to say, but when you're deciding what to do with your boat, and where to go, choose a passage that is within your abilities. I'm told that a fair number of yachts that set out to cross the Atlantic never get further than Portugal, when the reality of the challenge starts to set in. And let's face it, you don't have to sail across the Atlantic to have a lot of fun, and a lot of challenges, in your boat.

Before any trip, even a weekend out on the Solent, think it through and prepare well. Make sure that you have the right equipment onboard; that you're topped up with fuel and water; that you've worked out the tides; that you have an up-to-date weather forecast; and that the boat is in good shape.

Don't plan to go too close to potential dangers. It is always so tempting to go close inshore, or close to something interesting in order to have a good look, but the closer you get to something hard and spiky, the more planning you have to do in advance.

Shortly after we started cruising, we took a yacht over to North Brittany, and on the chart I spotted the wreck of the *Amoco Cadiz*, a tanker that had run aground on the Portsall Rocks, right on the tip of Brittany, in the late '70s. None of the wreck was showing above the water and, while the chart gave a clear position for the wreck, there was no depth information. Nevertheless, with a sort of reckless curiosity, I took the boat closer and closer until we were almost on top of it… at half tide… but with no idea how much clear water I had. We didn't see anything, and soon turned away to get on with our holiday. But how crazy was that? With 6 other people onboard, I had absolutely no way of knowing whether we were safe or not. If I had really wanted to do this (and with the benefit of hindsight I can see no good reason for doing so), it would have been much better to stop, spend 15 minutes making a respectable, safe navigation plan, and then following it.

Without a navigation plan you might get too close – as Costa Concordia did (© Gerasy Movych Olcksandr / shutterstock.com)

Amoco Cadiz wreck – not worth risking safety to have a look

I'm not the only one to take it into my head to do a bit of unplanned sightseeing. The Captain of the Italian liner, *Costa Concordia* was also a fully signed-up member of the reckless navigation club. Sadly, he was not so fortunate: when he attempted a close pass by the island of Giglio, just off the west coast of Italy, he struck the rocks outside the harbour entrance, fatally holing his ship. 32 people died in this incident. If he had only taken a few minutes to make a formal navigation plan for his close pass, this distressing incident would have been avoided.

Don't cut corners. Metaphorically or literally. When you plan your route, give yourself adequate clearance from any dangers, and plan alterations of course to maintain those separations. You will no doubt start to get impatient as you plough on towards the planned 'wheel-overs'. It's always tempting to 'warm the bell' and

start nudging round sooner. But when you cut a corner, you reduce your clearance from the dangers, and that increases the risk. Think it through first. If it takes you closer to potential dangers, you may wish to increase the frequency of your fixes or use a radar clearing range to help you stay safe.

And finally, if I'm going into a previously unexplored bay or inlet, I try to do so more-or-less at right angles, rather than nudging in round the headland, because that gives you more time for a good look round and keeps you clear of any shallow patches on the corners.

4. CHECK WEATHER FORECASTS

Have you ever gone to sea without first checking the weather forecast? Plenty of people do. On a fine, sunny morning at home it's easy to be seduced into thinking that it will be an equally fine, sunny day at sea. But just take 5 minutes to check the Inshore waters Forecast online at:
www.metoffice.gov.uk/weather/ specialist-forecasts/coast-and-sea/ inshore-waters-forecast

Or the shipping forecast at:
www.metoffice.gov.uk/weather/ specialist-forecasts/coast-and-sea/ shipping-forecast

There is an exhaustive list of sources of weather forecasts for the UK and Western Europe in Chapter 6 of the *Reed's Almanac*.

Elsewhere, like sailing across the Mediterranean, it's sometimes more difficult to find a reliable forecast, and you have to rely on local VHF radio broadcasts from the Coastguard. These, and other sources of weather forecasts, will be listed in the local *Sailing Directions*.

UK Met Office forecasts are excellent, and highly reliable. A huge amount of effort goes into making them as accurate as possible, particularly over the first 24 hours – and you can trust them. Elsewhere, the quality of the forecasts may be less reliable, but they're better than nothing, and you should always try to catch one before setting out.

And try to avoid the f-word. Fog is best seen from the shore. If you have no choice, and you find yourself at sea in fog, then take your time. Slow down and navigate carefully. Restricted visibility complicates everything at sea. It obscures navigation marks and it increases the risk of collision.

5. GIVE YOUR CREW JOBS TO DO

Your crew want to feel useful. And what's more, people who are prone to seasickness often feel a lot happier, and less queasy, when they're doing something that keeps their minds occupied – and I'm not talking about frying bacon in the galley. On anything but the shortest trips, divide your crew into watches so that everyone can play an active part in the passage.

Someone should always be keeping a proper lookout, regularly scanning the horizon, ahead and astern. That's easy enough in fine weather, but in heavy weather of reduced visibility it is more difficult, and more important too. In fog, they should be briefed to listen out for sound signals as well.

And finally, the best skippers take 5 minutes at the start of the trip, and before big evolutions like anchoring or entering harbour, to give the crew a quick briefing. That way, everyone knows what you are planning to do, how you're planning to do it, what the conditions will be like, and what they have to do. And that way too, they can pull your leg if you mess it up.

Give your crew things to do – they want to feel useful

12
A FEW TRICKS OF THE TRADE

Some odds and ends that I picked up along the way.

Like any acquired skill, navigation comes with a few handy shortcuts: different ways of solving problems that just seem to make sense. I've listed a few of these here which I found lurking around at the back of my mind. Don't be alarmed that this chapter starts with some mental arithmetic. It's not that complicated and these techniques are actually quite fun to put into practice.

Very little of this chapter is precise. These tips are all about making workable approximations, and getting close enough to the solution, without necessarily going to all the effort of finding the exact answer.

THE 6-MINUTE RULE

Suppose, like *Snowgoose*, our old yacht, you have the sails down, and you're cruising under power at 7 knots How long would it take you to cover 2.5nm?

At first sight, a question like that would have us all reaching for the calculator, but there's a quite neat trick that we all learnt as submarine captains for working out speed-time-distance equations in your head. It's called the 6-minute rule, and it involves breaking the speed down into the distance that you travel in 6 minutes – that is to say one tenth of an hour:

**You're travelling at 7kts
In 1/10th of an hour – 6 minutes
– you will travel 0.7nm
In 1min you will travel a
little over 0.1nm**

**If, in 6 minutes you travel 0.7nm
In 18 minutes: 3 x 0.7 = 2.1nm**

**2.5nm = 2.1nm + 0.4nm
Or 18mins + 4mins**

**So, you will cover 2.5nm in about
22mins[56]**

---

[56] It comes to 21.42mins on my calculator – but that's the great thing about mental arithmetic: it doesn't need to be pin-point accurate. 'About' is good enough.

How long will it take you to cover 1nm at 7kts?

In your head... 6mins (0.7nm) + 3mins (0.3nm) = 9mins[57]

You spot a merchant ship on your beam, coming towards you in mid-Channel You estimate its speed to be 20kts Radar tells you that it's 8 miles away How soon will it reach you?

The 20kts ship will cover 2.0nm in 6 minutes

It's 8nm away, so it will take 4 x 6mins to reach you = 24mins

THE ONE-IN-60 RULE

The 6-minute rule is useful, but my favourite bit of mental arithmetic is the 1-in-60 rule, because it has a lot of practical applications that you can use at sea. Again, it gives you an approximate answer – if you need precision you should use a calculator.

This rule boils down to a very simple quirk of everyday geometry.

If you draw a right-angled triangle with the longest side 60 units long – centimetres, miles or knots – the length of the shortest side is equal to the angle of the opposite corner, in degrees.

This applies from 1° to about 40°.

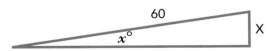

With the longest side 60 units long, the shortest side is equal to the angle of the opposite corner

So, if x = 10 units, the angle of the opposite corner is 10°.

Or, to put it another way:
The length of the shortest side = the length of the longest side x 1/60th of the angle

This gives you quite a nice table:

Angle (Degrees)	Ratio of shortest to longest side
1	1/60
2	1/30
5	1/12
6	1/10
10	1/6
12	1/5
15	1/4
20	1/3
30	1/2
40	2/3

So that if the angle is 5°, the shortest side is 1/12th of the longest side.

If the angle is 6°, and you are 12nm away, the shortest side would be 1.2nm in length.

And that's all there is to it. Take your time to get your head around it but, with a bit of practice, this becomes a really useful tool for working out courses to steer, distances off, and quite a lot more.

---

[57] 8mins 34secs on my calculator.

EXAMPLE 1. COURSE TO STEER

**You're on passage from the eastern
Solent to Cherbourg
You arrive at a point 10 miles due north
of Cherbourg
The tide is running westwards
at 2 knots
But you don't want to be swept down
to the west
If you maintain 6 knots through
the water
What course should you steer to get to
the harbour entrance?**

If you draw this out, on paper or in your mind, the longest side is not 60 units, but 6kts, and the shortest side is 2kts.

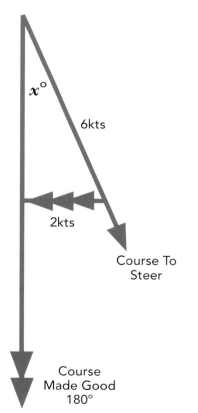

This is the diagram you would draw out to work out the course to steer

To expand 6kts to 60kts, you would have to multiply it by 10.
To keep the triangle in proportion, the shortest side would become 20kts.
The opposite angle is therefore 20°.

And there is your answer:
>**Steer 20° to the east of south
(that's to say a course of 160°),
and you will stay on track**

And the beauty of this is that it really does work!

EXAMPLE 2. DISTANCE OFF

**You're in your yacht and you can see
the Alderney lighthouse and
the right-hand edge of Cap de la Hague
to the south of you
You measure the distance between
them on the chart, and it's 8.4nm
The angle between them is 30°
How far away are they?**

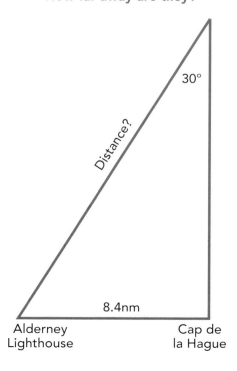

From the table, an angle of 30° means that the shortest side is half the length of the longest side. The distance off (the longest side) is 2 x 8.4nm:

2 x 8.4 nm away = 16.8nm

(Drawing this out on the chart, I make the distance 17nm.)

As I said at the start of this chapter, these rules are not about precision – they rely on sensible approximation. The triangle in this case may not be exactly a right-angled triangle, but if you are to the north of Cap de La Hague, it's not going to be too far off a right-angle, and by happy coincidence the geometry is remarkably tolerant of approximations like this – so don't be afraid to try this out for real and see how well it works.

A QUICK WAY TO CHECK BEARING MOVEMENT

At sea, there is just one criterion for whether something is going to hit you, and that's to check the bearing movement.

- If the bearing of a ship, a boat or a rock is steady, and the range is reducing, it will (in time) hit you
- If its bearing is moving steadily right, then the object will eventually pass to the right of you, and if its bearing is moving steadily left, it will eventually pass to the left of you

The 'proper' way of checking movement is by taking regular bearings with a compass. However, while this works well with a stable gyro compass repeater from the bridge of a big ship, it is sometimes more difficult to get a consistently accurate bearing from a hand-held magnetic compass in a small boat.

Quite a neat way round this is to watch the movement of the object against a distant object and judge the bearing movement from that. As long as the background is sufficiently far away – and stationary – you can assume that it is on a more-or-less steady bearing.

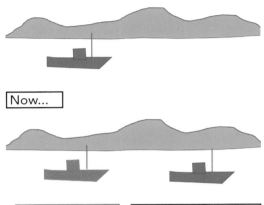

30 minutes ago you spot a ship...

Now...

| Bearing steady against the background: dangerous. | Bearing is moving steadily right against the background: looks OK. |

Monitor the bearing of a ship against a distant (and stationary) background

If an approaching ship is steady against the distant hillside, it is probably on a more-or-less steady bearing, and so it's dangerous. If something is moving steadily right or left against the hillside, it will probably miss you.

This is quite useful, but it does need to be used intelligently. For instance, you can use clouds as your background reference, but they can move quite fast across the sky – so they are not always reliable.

Also, when you're close to a big ship, it can happen that the bow is moving right while the stern is moving left – both at the same time. If so, it doesn't take the brains of an archbishop to realise that somewhere between the bow and the stern there's a part of the ship that's on a steady bearing, even though you have bearing movement at each end.

'Eyeballing' the bearing movement like this is a handy technique if you're trying to get through a narrow channel without hitting the buoys on either side. If you watch the movement of each of the closest channel buoys as you approach them, one of them should be moving right against the background, and the other should be moving left. If you're not seeing that, you probably need to change course to avoid the one that's on a steady bearing. It's also good for working your way through a fishing fleet, or a lot of sailing boats milling around off the entrance to Cowes.

This technique works well because it's intuitive. You naturally find yourself doing something similar when you walk across a crowded railway concourse, trying to avoid a collision with your fellow-commuters, or when crossing a busy road. I have to say, though, that it's not a substitute for the 'proper' way of checking for bearing movement with a compass, and the wise mariner will merely use it as a handy double check.

And one final word of warning: never be tempted to judge bearing movement against a fixed part of the boat's structure, like the shrouds, or one of the stanchions. The boat – or a ship, for that matter – is just not stable enough to do this reliably, and any random alteration in ships head (or your viewing position) may well lead you to the wrong conclusion.

THE 'YACHTSMAN'S EYE'

In a big ship, the crew rightly do things – like navigation – with rigorous formality.

Navigating a nuclear submarine, with an active nuclear reactor, round Drakes Island in Plymouth Sound and up into the dockyard at Devonport, is not something to take lightly, so every aspect of the port entry – preparation, briefing and navigation – is conducted with great thoroughness and precision. We fixed

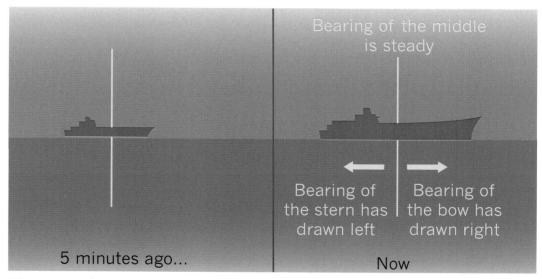

Bearing of the middle is steady

Bearing of the stern has drawn left

Bearing of the bow has drawn right

5 minutes ago...

Now

When you are close to a big ship, the bow might be moving to the right and the stern to the left – in which case there's a part of it which will hit you

our position every 3 minutes; we had a constant watch on the echo sounder; we made sure we stayed on track; there were meticulously plotted wheel-over bearings, and the clearing bearings were plotted well in advance.

Only by doing all this could we be sure that we were conducting this incredibly complex piece of navigation as safely and as professionally as possible.

In a yacht, you really don't need to go to those lengths to navigate safely – but you do need to develop a 'yachtsman's eye', which means spending time, particularly during pilotage legs, looking out at the water and the surrounding traffic; getting a feel for what's happening around you; sensing the weather, the tidal stream and your progress. Feeling how the boat is doing in these conditions – and reacting to the things that are happening around you.

Your eyes, your senses and your intelligence are priceless – every bit as valuable, in fact, as your radar set, or your chart plotter or the paper chart. Don't allow yourself to be seduced by your screens and your tablets. Keep your eyes outside the boat.

TRUST YOUR INTUITION

I don't really know where this comes from, but with experience I found myself developing a strangely accurate sixth sense that told me when things were starting to go wrong around me. Other captains and skippers have told me that the same thing has happened to them: you just seem to know when something is wrong, even when you're tucked up in your bunk. I have to say that the gentle voice of my intuition has never let me down.

Once, for no good reason, I woke up at 2am in my submarine with an uneasy feeling that I ought to go and have a quick look around the Control Room. Getting out of a cosy sleeping bag in the middle of the night in response to a subconscious whim is not an easy decision to make, but when I got up I discovered that the submarine, dived, had somehow worked its way into the middle of a fishing fleet and the Officer of the Watch was having a difficult time trying to find his way out. I couldn't say what exactly had woken me up, but I was glad to be there, and I was able to give him some badly-needed support as he worked his way out of a situation that he should never really have got into in the first place.

This 6th sense happens in yachts as well. I once woke up and struggled reluctantly into the cockpit only to find the boat dragging its anchor, and not far from colliding with another boat that had anchored behind us. Again, I've no idea what had prompted me to get out of bed, but I'm immensely glad that I did.

More consciously, when the boat changes course you can often feel the different movement of the boat through the swell, or a change in the wind's intensity. Sometimes, you can hear a different pitch in the murmur of conversation when the pressure ramps up on the bridge or the cockpit. And you can certainly feel a different purpose in the boat's movement when the wind freshens, and the boat starts to labour under her spread of sails. You should be aware of all this, even when you're getting some rest.

Sometimes of course you get up, look around, and find that all is well – in which case you have lost no more than about 10 minutes of sleep, and you can go straight back to your bed. But sometimes this intuition is priceless. Make sure that you listen to that little voice inside your head, even when you would rather not. If it tells you to go and have a quick look around, then go – it is generally worth the effort.

PART 2
DIFFERENT TYPES
OF NAVIGATION

The Rev John Morris and his family approaching
the anchorage at Houat under full sail in their
Westerly Sealord *Serendipity*

13
PILOTAGE

In open water, you navigate along your track with fixes, from which you plot forward Dead Reckoning positions and Estimated Positions. It's steady and predictable, and you normally have plenty of time to assess your progress and make any necessary corrections to your course and speed.

Pilotage is different. When you take your ship in and out of harbour, or through a narrow passage, the navigation becomes more fluid and immediate. You need to:

■ Find visual indicators that will tell you if you're drifting off track
■ Have a way of knowing that you're safe to alter course to avoid other vessels
■ Know when to wheel over to your next course

There's very little time to go back to the chart and pilot book to check the speed limit, or the minimum expected sounding, or the VHF frequency for harbour control: these all need to be in your notebook before you start. This all requires a fair amount of pre-planning, and the navigation itself is largely a virtuoso solo performance with the navigator centre-stage, controlling the position of the ship all the way in and out of harbour.

For that reason, unless you are really short-handed, I would advise against both steering and navigating at the same time, especially when negotiating a stretch of water that you're not familiar with.

Give yourself time and space to:

■ Watch what's going on
■ Keep an eye on the instruments
■ Avoid other shipping
■ Study the flow of the water

This is all much easier if you're not tied to the helm.

It's likely to be a lot busier on the water close inshore, so you need to have the flexibility to react to the unexpected, often dealing with a number of nearby vessels at once, while still keeping the boat on track and safe.

It takes a bit of practice to do this well, and quite a lot of concentration, so it's well worth giving each member of your crew a job in advance to take the weight off your shoulders.

PILOTAGE CHECKLIST

Planning

- ☐ Take 10 minutes of quiet time well in advance, just to study the chart
- ☐ Harbour regulations, including: speed limits, VHF channels to monitor, local *Notices to Mariners*, etc.
- ☐ Features of day marks, and characteristics of lights by night
- ☐ Height of Tide during the pilotage leg
- ☐ Any tidal gates, like lock opening times, etc.
- ☐ Tidal steam predictions
- ☐ Time to slip, speed required, estimate when you will enter and leave pilotage waters
- ☐ Weather forecast
- ☐ Time of sunrise, sunset, etc.
- ☐ Create your safe navigation corridor on the chart; identify how you will stay within it
- ☐ Identify wheel-over points

Equipment

- ☐ Binoculars
- ☐ Hand-held compass
- ☐ Chart and pilot book
- ☐ Navigation notebook
- ☐ Hand-held VHF, or remote handset for hard-wired radio
- ☐ Echo sounder read-out visible
- ☐ Have a spare pair of specs handy if you need them for pilotage
- ☐ Something heavy to weigh down the chart, and to keep the pilot book open at the right page

Making it Happen

- ☐ Clear all unnecessary clutter from the cockpit, and away from the chart table
- ☐ Brief crew on pilotage plan, times, jobs for individuals; at night, make sure that everyone has a hand-held torch and a light on their lifejacket
- ☐ Courtesy flag on starboard yardarm when visiting a foreign port
- ☐ Talk to the crew about the water conditions, tides, and the marks around you; if you're looking for a mark, or a light, tell them what to look out for
- ☐ Always try to be one step ahead of the game, so that you have identified the next buoys, the next leading lights or the next fixing points
- ☐ Decide when you want to stow ropes and fenders (or get them out) and raise or drop sails; don't forget that starting the motor requires you to show different navigation lights from when sailing
- ☐ Fix when needed to check your position, ideally asking one of your crew to do it for you; between fixes, check your progress against the chart plotter

PLANNING

1. TAKE A FEW MINUTES TO LOOK AT THE CHART

It's worth studying the chart with the relevant page of the *Almanac* and the *Sailing Directions*, open in front of you. If you have the internet available, check to see if the port has its own website – most do – because it will usually carry a lot of good and current information.

2. CHECK THE HARBOUR REGULATIONS

Most of the information that you need is available in the *Almanac* and the *Sailing Directions*, or on the harbour's own website like:

- Speed limits
- VHF channels to monitor
- *Local Notices to Mariners*
- Other important information shown in the *Almanac* or elsewhere

3. IDENTIFY FEATURES OF DAY MARKS & CHARACTERISTICS OF LIGHTS BY NIGHT IF RELEVANT

You need to familiarise yourself with the navigation marks that you will be looking for as you enter or leave the harbour – what to look out for and where they're likely to be.

4. UNDERSTAND THE CONSTRAINTS OF THE HEIGHT OF TIDE & THE TIDAL STREAM

The Height of Tide and the tidal stream will often dictate the best time of arrival or departure. First of all, decide when you want to arrive at the port, and check to see if there are any tidal constraints that may restict your time of arrival. This sometimes takes a bit of juggling:

- What time could you be at the entrance to the harbour? Is there any flexibility over this?
- What will the Height of Tide be at that point, or an hour earlier or later? Are there any Height-of-Tide constraints to safe navigation in the channel you will be using?
- Can you work with the predicted tidal streams?
- What time have you booked a table at the seafood restaurant?

On the whole this is a fairly straightforward process of ruling out the times that are not feasible and doing so early enough to allow you to shape the day's passage to fit in with these timings.

5. GET THE WEATHER FORECAST

I would never wish to be at sea without a current weather forecast, and it is useful to pick up a local forecast before entry and departure. This is not just a matter of academic interest: an accurate forecast is an essential tool in helping you to make the right decisions – and in a short-handed small boat with inexperienced crew it is absolutely vital that you make any weather-related decision in good time, before the weather forces a decision upon you.

The Coastguard VHF forecast channels and times are set out in the *Almanac*. I like to cut the relevant pages for the UK and France out of last year's *Almanac* and tape them to the bulkhead just by the VHF set so that I don't forget the times, and also to remind me to keep the right frequency up on Dual Watch.

6. WORK OUT TIME OF SUNRISE, SUNSET, ETC.

You may need to work out the times of sunset and sunrise. It is easy enough to download an app on your phone or tablet to do this. Failing that, your *Almanac* contains a table of sunrise and sunset times at particular latitudes throughout the year.

These tables are drawn up for the Greenwich Meridian, and you need to add 4 minutes for every degree of longitude westwards and subtract 4 minutes for every degree of longitude eastwards.

The times of sunrise and sunset do alter with latitude, but this is not as significant as for changes in longitude, so you can make the calculation on the basis of whole degrees and not bother to take account of any minutes.

7. CREATE A SAFE NAVIGATION CORRIDOR ON THE CHART & IDENTIFY HOW YOU WILL STAY SAFE WITHIN IT

This is probably the most important aspect of pilotage. Identify the areas where you will be safe, and where you won't. In a deep water harbour, and in a boat whose draft is less than 2m, I would be tempted to let the hydrographer do this bit of work for me and to say that I'll be safe as long as I remain in water deeper than 5m of Charted Depth – that's to say the white bit of the chart rather than the blue bits, the green bits or the yellow bits.

That's fine, except that you will probably pass over some rocks that are shallower than this if you stick to the transits. And that's fine too, as long as you can justify this to yourself by working out the total depth of water[58]. And for that, you will need to do your Secondary Port Height of Tide calculations for the time of entry.

The important thing is to trace a boundary on the chart within which you know that your boat will be safe – and this boundary then defines your safe navigation corridor.

ONCE YOU'VE DEFINED YOUR SAFE NAVIGATION CORRIDOR, HOW DO YOU STAY WITHIN IT?

The first thing to do is to identify the transits, or a headmark that you can follow to keep yourself on track:

- If you're using a **transit**, try to stick to

it like glue; it is by far the best indicator that you are on or off track. You may have to shift to one side occasionally to pass other shipping, but if this happens, make it a deliberate move, in an area where you know you have room to manoeuvre. Then, as soon as the other vessel has passed, come back onto your track.

- If you're using the **bearing** of a single headmark to stay on track, recognise the limitations of your hand-bearing compass and try to make your bearing as accurate as possible. Once you know you're on track, look for a natural transit: a house in line with a rock, or a couple of buildings in line, so that you have a visual indication of whether or not you start to drift away.

Keep watching the headmarks to make sure that you're not moving off to one side or another.

If you're worried about straying across the edges of a safe corridor, you should consider using clearing bearings, or a clearing range on radar, or clearing soundings.

Clearing bearings are limiting bearings of a head or stern mark that tell you when you're standing into danger.

Suppose you are heading into a narrowing estuary on a course of 095°. You have a lighthouse ahead that you can see clearly (which may or may not be your headmark – in this case, it is).

You can quite easily keep yourself safe by saying that the bearing of the lighthouse should be no more than (NMT) 098°, and no less than (NLT) 087°. This works well as long as your compass is accurate enough to give you bearings of this precision.

---

[58] Recognising that the **total depth of water = Charted Depth + Height of Tide.**

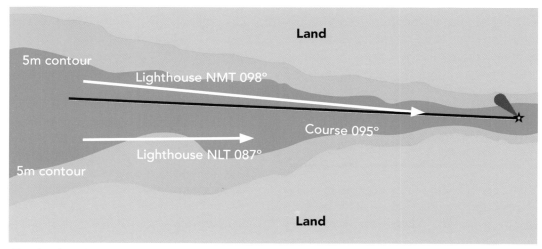

Clearing bearings

In this case, with the north shore running almost parallel to your course, you may be able to draw some **clearing range** to use with the radar. You need to identify a prominent headland and say that you want to stay within a defined corridor, passing more than 0.5nm from the headland, and less than 1.2nm. You can then draw the 2 boundary lines on your radar set and check to ensure you remain within them.

These lines are called '**parallel indices**'. It takes a bit of practice to get this right, and it's a technique better suited to a radar display than to a chart plotter, but it does work, and it will help you to stay safe.

And finally, you could use a **clearing sounding**. Assuming 2.5m Height of Tide, and working on your wish not to run into water with less than 5m of Charted Depth, you could say that you're going to be happy as long as the total depth of water, as shown on your echo sounder, is not less than (NLT) 7.5m.

All three of these clearing line techniques work well, and you should use

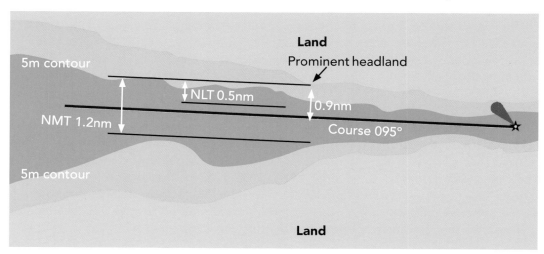

Parallel index

them as appropriate for any pilotage work. The other, simpler, way to stay safe is to hop from buoy to buoy. This is useful in restricted visibility or when a headmark may not be readily visible.

Buoys are secured in place by a couple of big anchors, but even so they can sometimes be blown out of position. You should, however, be able to spot this quite easily.

Provided there are no special navigation complexities, and as long as there are enough buoys and beacons on your way in, I would advocate using a headmark or transit, and checking this with reference to the passing buoys. And I would always calculate the minimum expected soundings for each leg.

USING A HEADMARK

Most of the time you won't have convenient transits marking your way into or out of a port, and you will have to rely on headmarks. That is to say you are running in on the lighthouse, on a course of 095°M. As long as it bears 095° you're on track. But if it suddenly increases to 097°, you are to the north of your planned track, and

need to steer right. Equally, if it drops to 090°, you need to steer left.

The corrective actions are obviously reversed on the way out, if you're using the bearing of 095° as a sternmark.

If you don't have a convenient charted headmark, you can usually invent one: the left or right-hand edges of land, a rock, the top of an island or a church might serve. Failing all that, you may have to revert to buoy-hopping.

WHEEL-OVERS

When planning a bit of pilotage, you should look at every planned alteration of course and work out how you will know that you have arrived at the wheel-over. The best marks for a wheel-over are those that are more-or-less on the bearing of your next course – or its reciprocal.

Ideally, in a yacht which turns on a sixpence, you would watch the bearing of your next headmark and alter course when it tells you that you're on the new track. However, if your next headmark is obscured by rain, or if it's ambiguous, you have little choice but to use the navigation points in your vicinity.

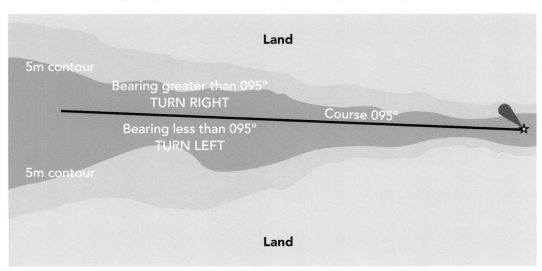

Using a headmark

MAKING IT HAPPEN

1. CLEAR THE CLUTTER

You don't need a whole lot of clutter in the cockpit while you're doing pilotage. The checklist at the start of the chapter shows the things that I like to have with me in the cockpit – it's not much, and this is a good time to take everything else below, before you get into the excitement of berthing. The chart will blow overboard in an instant if you don't weigh it down, and both the hand-held VHF and the binoculars will happily fall onto the deck given half a chance, so you need a handy but secure place to keep them.

2. BRIEF THE CREW

Brief the crew on your pilotage plan, times and any jobs that you want individuals to look after.

You need everyone to understand what you're planning to do, where you're going, how long it will take, and the bits that you will want their help with. If you have enough crew onboard, have someone on the helm, someone else keeping a lookout (for other vessels, fishing floats, navigation marks, etc.), and ideally someone to work the VHF and speak to the marina so that you know what berth to go to, and which side you will be tying up. The sooner you know this, the sooner you can get the deck organised. You will also want to have one or two people ready to get out the fenders and ropes (or to stow them when leaving port), but only do this in sheltered waters with the deck relatively steady.

People will be moving about the boat more than normal, and concentrating on things other than their own safety, so give everyone a lifejacket to wear[59] (brief them on how to inflate it), and at night everyone should have both a light on their lifejacket and a small pocket torch like a mag light for their own use.

3. COURTESY FLAG ON STARBOARD YARDARM WHEN VISITING A FOREIGN PORT

Hoist a courtesy flag on the starboard yardarm when in the territorial waters of another country (that is to say 12 miles from the coast). If necessary, transfer your club burgee to the port yardarm. The reason for this is that the starboard yardarm is held to be 'senior' to the port yardarm…. (Don't ask me… that's just how it is!)

4. TALK TO THE CREW AS YOU GO

Talk to the crew about the water conditions, tides, and the marks around you. If you're looking for a mark, or a light, tell them what to look out for. Use your crew well and make them feel valued. If nothing else, the more eyes you have looking out for navigation marks and other shipping, the sooner you will see them and the easier it will be to make the right decisions. The best navigators that I have been to sea with have maintained a gentle background commentary while they have been doing the pilotage so that everyone on the bridge has been fully informed of where we are, and what's coming up next.

Always try to be one step ahead of the game, so that you have identified the next buoys, the next leading lights or the next

---

[59] It would be more sensible still to insist that everyone wears a lifejacket as a matter of course, whenever they're on the upper deck at sea.

fixing points well before you actually need to use them.

5. DECIDE WHEN TO SAFELY GET OUT (OR STOW) ROPES & FENDERS, & WHEN TO RAISE OR STOW YOUR SAILS

This isn't something to rush. If possible, identify a calm, sheltered spot in advance where you can safely get people on deck. And then slow right down and point into the wind or the swell while your crew are working in an exposed position, raising or dropping sails, and fixing the mooring lines.

Don't forget that at night, when you start propelling under power – with or without a sail raised – you will need to show different navigation lights from when you are just sailing.

6. FIX YOUR POSITION WHEN NECESSARY

Putting a fix on the chart is the best way of confirming your position. In a warship, we would have one person whose sole job during pilotage was to plot 3-minute or 6-minute fixes on the chart. It's very unlikely that you would need to fix with this sort of intensity in a small boat, but you should be ready to fix if and when you need to:

- To confirm your position
- If you suddenly become less certain of where you are
- If the marks just aren't making sense
- In poor visibility

I would also use fixes to stay on track when approaching the coastline across a strong tidal stream, which could push you off course in a matter of minutes. Rapid, accurate fixing will quickly tell you how well you are doing.

If you're not actively fixing during pilotage, you should tick off the buoys and other navigation marks as you pass them, using them to confirm your position.

And finally, we all get confused from time to time. There's absolutely no shame in saying that you need a few minutes to sort things out, and taking the way off the ship or the boat while you do so.

The water gets busier during pilotage

SOME TIPS FOR SMALL BOAT PILOTAGE

1. WATCH WHERE OTHER YACHTS ARE GOING

This is a double-edged sword because you don't want to follow some hugely incompetent fellow-yachtsman right up onto a mudbank, but equally there is a certain wisdom in crowds, and if you find yourself following a solitary track with a stream of small boats proceeding happily on a different track a mile to port, the least that you can do is to ask yourself why they're over there, where they might be going, and whether you should swallow your pride and join them.

2. FOLLOW THE BUOYS

It was rightly drummed into me as a naval officer that buoys are unreliable navigation marks. But to be honest they are not all going to drag their moorings, and there's nothing wrong in following a line of buoys, or a line of beacons or perches out of a harbour – as long as you don't put too much reliance on the absolute position of a single mark.

3. USE THE ECHO SOUNDER INTELLIGENTLY

Try to understand what the echo sounder is telling you. Depending on where you are, the sounding, and particularly any trend of reducing or increasing soundings, may well tell you whether you are to port or starboard of your track, or how far you are from your destination. Just about every time that I've run aground in big ships or small boats, the one piece of equipment that could have saved me, had I bothered to look at it, was the humble echo sounder.

4. NEVER STOP CHECKING FOR TIDAL STREAM, SWELL & BROKEN WATER

In a small boat close inshore, the tidal stream can often be running at a rate that is close to your maximum boat speed. Take every opportunity to check the actual movement of the water around you:

- Watch for swirls on the surface that might try to throw off your ship's head
- Watch the tidal stream on any buoy or fishing float that you pass
- Watch for the small periodic appearance of breaking water that might indicate a rock that's awash or hiding just below the surface

Keep an eye out too for any areas of heightened swell, particularly standing waves that might indicate a shallow patch, or a bar at the mouth of a river. I once saw a massive standing wave at the mouth of the Gironde in western France – and it looked horrendous, a bit like one of those old Japanese paintings of a tsunami wave. Broken water might indicate a race or an area of seriously disturbed water.

And there's a port in southwest France called Cap Breton where, with precious little warning from the pilot book, I found myself helming a 38ft yacht in through the harbour entrance on the shoulders of a big, Hawaii-style surfing wave that had been thrown up by the rapidly shelving bottom. This wave is, I subsequently learnt, a particular feature of this port when the swell is rolling in from the Atlantic. My entry was closely studied by about a dozen French anglers who no doubt congregate there and award style points to hapless British sailors blasting up the channel, with minimal control, at about 20 knots.

14

BLIND PILOTAGE

BLIND PILOTAGE CHECKLIST
(elements different to Pilotage checklist in bold)

Planning

- ☐ Take 10 minutes of quiet time, well in advance, just to look at the chart
- ☐ Harbour regulations, including speed limits, VHF channels to monitor, local *Notices to Mariners*, etc.; **check local ferry operating times**
- ☐ Identifying features of day marks, and characteristics of lights; **identify any marks that make a sound in reduced visibility**
- ☐ Height of Tide during the pilotage leg
- ☐ Any tidal gates, like lock opening times, etc.
- ☐ Tidal steam predictions
- ☐ Time to slip, speed required, estimate when you will enter and leave pilotage waters
- ☐ Weather forecast
- ☐ Time of sunrise, sunset, etc.
- ☐ Create your safe navigation corridor on the chart; identify how you will stay within it
- ☐ **For each course, work out the predicted tidal stream, and both the course to steer and speed made good, so that you track from one mark to the next; work out how long each leg will take and the minimum expected sounding on each leg**
- ☐ **When you've finished, and if you have time, walk yourself through the entire navigation sequence from start to finish: how you will navigate, what the tidal stream will be doing, how you will react to other shipping, and what wheel-overs you will use**

Equipment

- ☐ Binoculars
- ☐ Hand-held compass
- ☐ Chart and pilot book
- ☐ Navigation notebook
- ☐ Hand-held VHF, or remote handset for hard-wired radio **for monitoring the Harbour Control channel**
- ☐ Echo sounder read-out visible
- ☐ **Foghorn**

☐ **A watch (for timing the interval between sound signals)**
☐ **In fog, I absolutely insist on the crew wearing lifejackets**

Making it Happen

☐ Clear all unnecessary clutter out of the cockpit, and away from the chart table
☐ Brief crew on pilotage plan, times, jobs for individuals; at night, make sure that everyone has a hand-held torch and a light on their lifejacket; **make one person responsible for operating the foghorn – one long blast every 2 minutes**
☐ **Switch on nav lights & check them**
☐ Courtesy flag on starboard yardarm when visiting a foreign port
☐ **Drop your sails before you start the difficult stages of navigation; identify a safe, quiet place to stow ropes and fenders (or get them out), and raise or drop sails**
☐ **Post a lookout – ideally 2 (one port, one starboard) – in the bow to watch and to listen out for sound signals**
☐ **If possible, have one other member of your crew watching for other vessels on radar**
☐ **Talk to the crew about your progress, and the marks around you; if you're looking for a mark or a light, ask them to look with you; always try to be one step ahead of the game, so that you have identified the next buoys, the next leading lights or the next fixing points**
☐ **Choose a safe speed for the state of visibility and the traffic density**
☐ **Note the time when you pass each mark and calculate ETA at the next one**
☐ **Regularly check your progress on the chart plotter, as a fail-safe**

If a yachtsman were to ask for my advice on blind pilotage – that is to say pilotage in limited visibility – I would quite simply say don't do it – unless you absolutely have to. And even then, choose a port or an anchorage that makes this quite specialised form of navigation as straightforward as possible.

Pilotage in restricted visibility is not easy, because you are using your electronics – and principally your radar – for both navigation and collision avoidance. There's a lot that can go wrong, from misidentifying marks to a collision with small vessels that are painting only intermittently on radar. Even experienced professional navigators feel apprehensive about it, and they have a bigger team and better equipment than you or I would ever have on our yachts. If you decide to enter or leave harbour blind – be careful; it's anything but simple.

CLASSICAL BLIND PILOTAGE

The classical form of blind pilotage is to measure how far off a prominent radar landmark your track will take you – in this diagram 0.9nm. You then draw a line on the radar screen (this is called a parallel index), displaced from the centre by 0.9nm and running parallel to your 095° track. And you adjust your course as appropriate to drive the landmark down this line.

In the meantime, you track all the other contacts on radar, picking out navigation buoys and other shipping, and take appropriate action to avoid colliding with any of them.

Your clearing ranges are important here: you would be standing into danger if the parallel index reduces below 0.5nm, or increases above 1.2nm, so you need to keep an eye on that as well.

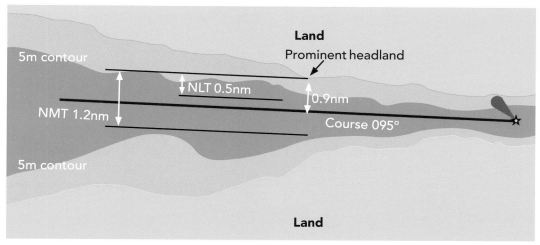

Parallel indices for blind pilotage

As you approach the next planned alteration of course, you pick up the next prominent radar mark on your display, draw the parallel index for that next leg, and alter course in time to drive yourself down the new line.

This system works well in a big ship with a well-trained team, but in all honesty it's quite difficult to pull off in a small boat, not least because the parallel indices are not easy to draw and monitor on a chart plotter's radar display. It also puts a huge burden on the shoulders of the navigator, who is responsible for both navigation and collision avoidance – often in busy, restricted waters.

Try this by all means if you feel confident in your ability to pull it off, but it's anything but simple.

BLIND PILOTAGE IN A SMALLER BOAT

In a small boat, I would advocate a simpler method of getting from A to B in fog: taking small steps and leapfrogging from one navigation mark or buoy to the next. This gives you the greatest number of opportunities to make a visual check on your position, and it leaves the radar set or chart plotter available for someone exclusively to keep an eye on collision avoidance. I would go about it like this:

1. First of all, **prepare thoroughly**. This may be simpler than 'classical' blind pilotage, but it is still not easy: it takes a great deal of mental effort and you won't have time to double-check your calculations once you're under way. Calculate and make a note of your Height of Tide and tidal streams in as much detail as possible. If you can, check the ferry and merchant ship sailing times so that you don't have to share a narrow channel with a big merchant ship.

2. **Draw a track, or a succession of tracks**, that take you safely from mark to mark. Use buoys, beacons, Spit Sand Fort – anything as long as it's in deep open water, and by going there you don't risk running aground.

3. **Choose a cautious speed** for the pilotage that allows you the time to react to anything suddenly coming into

view. It should be slow enough to give you adequate thinking time, and fast enough to prevent you being thrown all over the place by the wind or the tidal stream.

4. Then, for each leg, carefully work out the **course to steer**, the **speed made good** and the time that it will take you **to get from one mark to the next**. Also work out the minimum expected sounding on each leg. Make a table in your notebook, and record all this information for reference later.

5. **Make a note of any navigation marks that make sound signals** in reduced visibility.

6. **Allocate essential tasks to your crew:**
   - Collision avoidance on radar
   - Foghorn operator
   - Lookout, ideally 2: one on the port side, and one on the starboard side (they should be briefed to keep a listening watch too)
   - Helm
   - And somebody (probably you) to do the navigation, and check progress on the chart plotter
   - All your crew should wear lifejackets in fog, if they aren't already

7. Then, you **set off**. Switch on your navigation lights and start making sound signals. Note the time and brief your crew at the start of each leg: "*This leg will take 5 minutes at 6 knots and we are expecting to find a green No 5 buoy at the end of that time. Other shipping will be following the channel on our port side.*"

8. **Monitor your progress on the chart plotter**, if you have one. Also, check off each navigation mark as you pass it, recording the time when you pass. Each time you pass a mark, work out the ETA at the next one, and brief the crew.

9. And finally, if at any stage a mark doesn't turn up as expected, or if you get confused and lose track of where you are, **just stop**; point into the tidal stream and try to remain stationary over the ground while you get a good fix, and sort everything out. It is much, much better to admit that you are confused than to plug on, run aground and risk hurting someone.

By moving from one mark to the next you will accomplish 2 important things – you will be able to validate your position more often than if you had stayed in the middle of the fairway. And you will also be staying to one side of the main shipping channel, out of the way of the professional mariners.

Try to monitor the port control channel on VHF so that you know what other shipping is in the channel. In the last resort you can use it to call up a big ship that is threatening to trample you, and let them know you're there.

'THE RIDDLE OF THE SANDS' TECHNIQUE

I like this. It is quite a particular form of bottom contour navigation that has an elegance all of its own.

Only twice in my life have I had the opportunity to use **'The Riddle of the Sands' Technique'**[60] in anger, conducting an entire pilotage leg, in fog, using only a compass and an echo sounder. I'm including it for completeness, but with a big health warning; it sounds simple, but it's incredibly easy to get confused and run aground. When it works, however, it's a

---

[60] Named after my favourite sailing book – ever: *The Riddle of the Sands*, written by Erskine Childers, where he describes a just breath-taking episode of blind pilotage in fog.

bit like pulling a rabbit out of a previously empty top hat – and you can feel justifiably proud of a 'proper' piece of navigation.

It was a late summer Sunday morning, and we had spent the night at a buoy in the Beaulieu River at Needs Orr Point. I had planned to be back in Lymington at 10am to drop our guests off in time for them to get the train back to London. However, when I poked my head through the hatch at 0700, the river was looking beautiful, but it was covered in a blanket of thick fog with visibility hovering around 100 metres. I could just see the closest beacon through the murk. The tide was starting to ebb, so I knew that if I went aground, we would probably be there for quite a long time.

The right answer, of course, was to stay put, have a lazy breakfast and to go when the visibility had improved a bit. The

channel at the mouth of the Beaulieu River is only 100 metres wide in places, which makes it pretty marginal for using GPS and the chart plotter as your principal means of navigation.

But for years I had wanted to try 'feeling' my way out of a harbour with the echo sounder, and all the members of my crew were happy to go for it… So, I did a few calculations, briefed the crew and we set off.

The Height of Tide was 2m, so the expected depth of water in the channel would be 6m, increasing to 8 or 9m as we rounded the bend at Lepe.

If the total depth of water dropped below 2m – call it 2.5m to give myself a bit of leeway – we would go aground. The line of the channel is 074°T (075°M) with a small kink to the north in the middle, and a

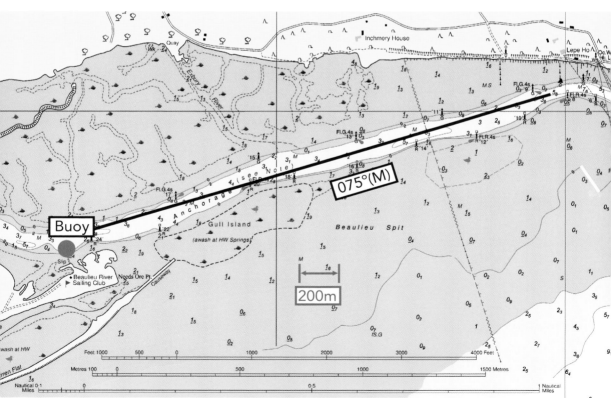

The Beaulieu River and our route out

bend at the end of the reach, leading you south, across the bar and into the Solent. We slipped the mooring buoy and, moving slowly but with enough speed to maintain steerage way, we passed the first beacon about 20m to starboard, which put us pretty much in the middle of the channel.

I wanted to 'bounce' off the south side of the channel[61], so I knew that if I steered about 10° to starboard of my track (085°M) the sounding would start to reduce.

When the sounding reduced to about 3m, or whatever felt like an appropriate margin of error, I turned 20° to port (065°M) and headed back out to the centre of the channel, until the sounding reached about 6m. Then 20° to starboard and watch the sounding reduce… and so on.

With this see-sawing motion, I found that I had pretty good control over our position, and I just needed to count down the beacons as they appeared out of the mist and slid eerily down the starboard side. As you can see from the chart, the channel narrows and turns west at No 8 beacon, deepening and bearing round to the right, so I worked my way round with it, 'bouncing' now between 9m depth of water and 5m. Every time we passed

a beacon I checked the flow of the tidal stream against the post.

After the turn to starboard came the bar, where the depth reduced rapidly to a minimum of 3m as we passed between Nos 1 and 2 beacons – which I was expecting, although for a long moment I found myself holding my breath willing the sounding to start increasing again! Once over the bar and past the final beacons, I came round to 145°M and made my way out into deeper water and then back to Lymington.

As if by magic, the moment we left the river, the fog lifted and it remained clear all the way back to the Lymington Yacht Haven, so we thankfully didn't have to employ the same technique to find our way back up the Lymington River.

I don't advocate doing this, particularly on a falling tide, but it is a tried-and-tested navigation technique that's as old as the hills and, if carefully executed, it can work very well. You do need very clear depth contours to allow you to execute your turns accurately – and it takes a great deal of concentration to get round the corners, so if you ever find yourself using this technique, do so with great care… and enjoy the moment; it's very special.

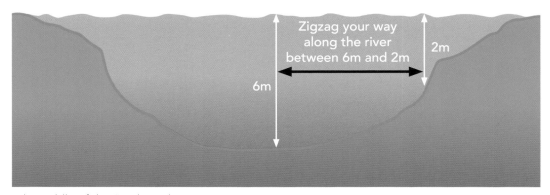

'The Riddle of the Sands' technique

---

[61] Metaphorically – not physically.

15
ANCHORING

ANCHORING CHECKLIST

Planning

☐ Spend as much time as you need to select a good spot to anchor. Time spent here may well save you a great deal of annoyance later. Make sure that there are no regulations prohibiting anchoring. Make a first guess at your perfect anchorage position (you may of course find that it has already been taken) and record it as a waypoint in your GPS.

☐ Work out what time you plan to anchor.

☐ Work out the Height of Tide throughout your planned stay at the anchorage. You are interested in 3 things: the Height of Tide when you drop the anchor, and the minimum and maximum heights of tide during your stay.

☐ Calculate the tidal stream for the time of anchoring, and check that the maximum rate of flow is acceptable during your stay.

☐ Make sure you hear an accurate weather forecast.

☐ Time of sunrise, sunset, etc.

☐ Plot a track to your anchorage; I like to make the planned anchoring position a GPS waypoint and track my way there using a hand-held GPS, or the chart plotter.

☐ Make sure you can find the anchor ball and check the anchor light is working.

A successful anchorage relies on getting both the navigation and the seamanship right. I don't intend to discuss the seamanship aspects of anchoring in this book, but I think it's important to talk a little about the navigation, because sound navigation is the bedrock on which a safe anchorage is laid and, if you get it right, anchoring becomes an absolute pleasure.

So, just to tantalise you – if you haven't already been there – I thought I would start with a small chartlet of one of the most wonderful anchorages that I have ever visited. This is the bay of Treac'h er

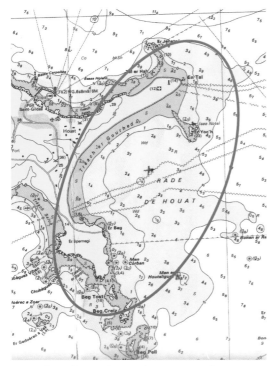

Treac'h er Goured – my favourite anchorage

Goured on the eastern side of the island of Houat, close to Quiberon in south Brittany. It has a gently shelving sandy bottom, good shelter, very little tidal stream and no passing traffic. The anchorage is about a mile from north to south, so you don't feel crowded, even though it's a popular spot for French boats in the summer months. There are, of course, a few underwater features to avoid, like a couple of rocky patches, shown as shallower soundings in the middle of the bay, and 3 submarine cables that annoyingly cut right across the bay. But, in general, this is a beautiful, relaxed anchorage at which to spend the night.

When you're looking for a spot to anchor, this is the sort of place that you should be looking for: good holding, sufficient depth of water, minimal tidal stream, sheltered from the predominant wind, and big enough to be able to anchor

without worrying about entangling your cable with others. And, if you want it, easy access to the shore.

I have included a worked example of pre-anchoring calculations in Chapter 19. For now, I will restrict myself to the issues that you need to think about in preparing to anchor.

PLANNING

1. SPEND AS MUCH TIME AS YOU LIKE SELECTING THE RIGHT SPOT TO ANCHOR

This is the most important part of anchoring and, if you look for it, you will get a lot of help from the pilot books and the chart. You want to find a spot where the holding is good: that is to say a sandy or muddy bottom. Avoid any chance that you might be anchoring on rocks.

Also, the bottom should be flat, or flat-ish. One incredibly hot day in Croatia when we were all longing to go for a swim, I anchored right at the top of a steep, gravelly slope. We all jumped into the water without properly checking that the anchor was holding… only it wasn't holding, and all I can say is that I've never had to swim so fast to catch up with an anchored boat. This was an entirely preventable incident, caused by my impatience. I had persuaded myself that this wholly unsuitable place was a safe anchorage, when it clearly wasn't. I should have known better.

Ideally, the anchorage that you select should also be sheltered from the wind, out of the main flow of the tidal stream and away from any significant traffic. Also, you need to carefully check the chart so that you avoid dropping the anchor on underwater cables, spoil ground or any form of underwater obstructions – like oyster beds.

Lastly, check that there are no local bylaws prohibiting anchorage. Prohibited anchorages should be marked on the chart and they should also appear in the pilot book.

Once you've selected the bay, or the area where you want to anchor, put it as a waypoint in your GPS. You can then use that waypoint to approach your anchorage and use it to count your crew down to anchoring.

THE GOOD ANCHORAGE GUIDE

A good anchorage should have:
- Good holding, ideally on sand or mud or coarse gravel
- Shelter from the wind and the swell
- Enough water to remain afloat at Low Water
- Flat seabed
- Away from passing shipping
- Clear of underwater obstructions
- Easy landing spot – if you want to go ashore
- Big enough not to feel cramped
- Minimal tidal stream, and out of the main flow of the river
- A good restaurant overlooking the bay

2. WORK OUT WHAT TIME YOU WANT TO ANCHOR

It normally doesn't matter much when you anchor. You can generally anchor at any state of the tide, and with any tidal stream, provided that there is enough water for you to make your approach safely. But you need to fix a time, because the rest of your planning will hang on this.

3. WORK OUT THE HEIGHT OF TIDE THROUGHOUT YOUR PLANNED STAY AT THE ANCHORAGE

I create a table in my notebook to do this. There are, in fact, only three parameters that you're interested in:
- The Height of Tide when you anchor
- The maximum Height of Tide during your stay
- The minimum Height of Tide during your stay

THE HEIGHT OF TIDE WHEN YOU ARE ANCHORING

This allows you to calculate the total depth of water at the spot where you want to anchor. If you watch your echo sounder as you approach the anchorage, you can drop the anchor when the sounder reaches this figure, knowing that the maximum and minimum depths that you have calculated will be correct.

THE MAXIMUM HEIGHT OF TIDE DURING YOUR STAY

This dictates how much cable you veer. In calm conditions, the generally accepted rule is that you need 4 times as much cable as the maximum depth of water during your stay. In calm weather and a sheltered anchorage, you may be able to get away with a multiple of 3, but in any sort of blow, or on poor holding ground, or with a strong tidal stream, you should not hesitate to increase the amount of cable that you veer to a multiple of 4, or 5, or even 6.

To make the multiple of 4 work, I mark off the chain in 4 metre lengths using aerosol car spray in a variety of wildly exotic colours. Aerosol car paint has proved to be surprisingly resilient on the anchor chain, and the colours give this otherwise rather drab part of the boat a small flavour of the Caribbean. The beauty of this is that it becomes so simple to veer the right length of cable. If I calculate that the maximum depth of water during my stay is 6 metres, I veer 6 lengths of 4 metres… and then 1 further 4-metre length for luck.

THE MINIMUM DEPTH OF WATER DURING YOUR STAY

Knowing this helps you avoid the embarrassment of going aground at Low Water.

4. CALCULATE THE TIDAL STREAM WHEN ANCHORING & THE MAXIMUM PREDICTED TIDAL STREAM DURING YOUR STAY

The maximum tidal stream that you can tolerate at anchor depends on how good your ground tackle is – and how willing you are to sit up all night on an anchor watch. Unless forced to do so, I would hesitate to anchor in a place where the predicted tidal stream exceeded 3 knots, and I wouldn't feel comfortable much above 2 knots.

5. MAKE SURE YOU HEAR AN ACCURATE WEATHER FORECAST

This is particularly important in the evening, before you turn in. If the wind is set to blow up overnight, you might want to set an anchor watch to make sure that you're not dragging.

6. WHAT TIME IS SUNSET & SUNRISE?

Apart from the obvious need to turn on anchor lights at sunset, and off again at sunrise, it's useful to know this in case you have to leave the anchorage suddenly for any reason. Equally, it's handy to know the state of the moon, for the same reasons. When anchoring in marginal weather, I usually make a note of the safe course to steer out of the anchorage and leave it on the chart table in case we have to leave the anchorage in a hurry in the dark. This is particularly reassuring when anchored in a spot where there are a number of unlit rocks around the boat.

7. MAKE SURE YOU CAN FIND THE ANCHOR BALL & CHECK THE ANCHOR LIGHT IS WORKING

You should show an anchor ball if you are anchored, except if you are tucked well inside an anchorage with vessels all round you. And you should show an anchor light at night. But remember to turn it off in the day to conserve your battery. A small laminated note on the chart table is quite helpful as a reminder to switch the light off at breakfast time.

8. SET AN ANCHORAGE WAYPOINT IN GPS

Almost as soon as you have anchored, secured the cable, and turned off the engine, I would recommend putting an anchorage waypoint into GPS and running a permanent display of range and bearing to that waypoint. It's not pin-point accurate, and the reading will change as the tide turns, but it should give you a pretty good idea of whether or not if you're dragging.

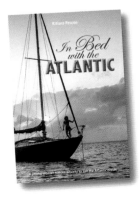

A perfect anchorage in the Caribbean as described in Kitiara Pascoe's book, In Bed with the Atlantic

16
COASTAL NAVIGATION

Coastal navigation – that is to say navigation in the proximity of the coast, and along the coastline – has always been a particular pleasure for me. Some of the most enjoyable passages that I have made have been along and around the coast of Brittany, or the West Country, with unparalleled views of the coastline from a few miles offshore.

The tidal streams almost always follow the line of the coast, so if you get the timing of your passage right you have the additional pleasure of zipping along with all the force of nature behind you. Conversely, if you mistime the tides, or if you're on a long passage, there will inevitably be times when the tide is dead against you, and you think that you are going nowhere (which does take some of the fun out of it).

The trick of coastal navigation is to make it easy for yourself by planning to pass close enough to the coast to enjoy the scenery, but far enough away to stay comfortably clear of any dangers. Unlike pilotage, which is full-on, coastal navigation is gentler, less intensive and more relaxing. So, get yourself well organised in advance,

and then settle down to enjoy sailing through a beautiful stretch of water – wherever you are.

The closer inshore that you go, the more you have to work at keeping the boat safe. Within a few miles of the coast you find more casual boats out enjoying themselves, many more fishing buoys, and often more floating debris. You also need to alter course more often to follow the shape of the coastline. In addition, as you pass along the coast, you inevitably encounter tough stretches of water from time to time: places like the Portland Race, the Raz de Sein or the Alderney Race, where the water conditions can be horrendous. You either have to avoid these obstacles altogether by going round the outside, or you must negotiate the tidal gates to pass through at slack water (which requires careful and deliberate planning).

I generally like to stay about 5nm offshore. On the north coast of Brittany, the French maritime authorities have helpfully laid a line of northerly cardinal marks a couple of miles offshore to guide passing traffic away from a treacherous stretch of

COASTAL NAVIGATION CHECKLIST

Planning

- ☐ Use medium scale navigation charts for coastal navigation
- ☐ Make sure you have an accurate weather forecast before you set out, and that you receive regular forecasts on VHF during the passage
- ☐ Calculate the time of sunrise, sunset, etc.
- ☐ Plan the time of departure and arrival at your next port to get the most out of the favourable tidal stream
- ☐ Work out the Height of Tide in advance for your departure and arrival
- ☐ Calculate the expected tidal streams for the hours that you will be under way
- ☐ Plan your track to be far enough offshore to provide a comfortable separation from dangers; by night, move further offshore
- ☐ Avoid places where you might expect overfalls or races (or else plan carefully to pass through the tidal gates at slack water)
- ☐ Store all the planned waypoints, and your point of arrival, into the GPS
- ☐ Before you slip, make sure you have enough water, fuel and food for the passage

Equipment

- ☐ Binoculars
- ☐ Hand-held compass
- ☐ Chart and pilot book
- ☐ Navigation notebook
- ☐ Hand-held GPS, or access to the chart plotter
- ☐ VHF monitoring Channel 16, ideally set to Dual Watch the local Coastguard weather forecast frequency
- ☐ Echo sounder read-out visible from the steering position

Making it Happen

- ☐ Brief the crew on the day's passage
- ☐ Try to get everyone up and leave on time, in order to make the best of the tidal stream
- ☐ Once you are clear of pilotage waters, settle into a loose watch-keeping system
- ☐ Close to the shore, keep a good lookout for ships, small boats, buoys and rubbish in the water
- ☐ Once you are clear of immediate dangers, fix your position on the chart every hour, reducing the fixing interval if you get closer to dangers
- ☐ Fill in the logbook hourly
- ☐ Use your GPS to monitor the ETA at your next waypoint, and at your destination
- ☐ Monitor the Coastguard frequency for routine weather updates
- ☐ Prepare for entry into your destination in good time, working out the pilotage plan before you get into restricted waters
- ☐ If possible, call up the Harbour Master before arrival to discuss your berth

coastline. Hopping along from one buoy to the next makes for pretty stress-free navigation, and provides you with regular waypoints, and at each one you get a visible demonstration of the tidal stream as it flows round the buoy.

When planning a coastal passage, I try to divide it into stretches that I can complete in daylight, and with a favourable tidal stream. That means limiting yourself to 6, or possibly 7-hour legs before heading into a port for the night. Even so, you can still make good 40-50nm of distance every day – and you will have the addition benefit of a new port or a new anchorage every night.

There is absolutely no problem with coastal navigation at night if you want to cover more ground. If so, you will need a more formal watch-keeping system, and I would plan the passage further offshore during the hours of darkness to make it less stressful for the watch keepers. You also need to be aware of the places of likely shipping concentrations, and make sure that the watch keepers who will be negotiating these stretches are confident in their ability to do so, particularly if you're planning to be asleep at that time.

PLANNING

1. USE MEDIUM SCALE CHARTS FOR COASTAL NAVIGATION

For coastal passages, use a chart which shows a good length of the coastline, but still has enough detail for you to navigate safely. The UKHO prints coastal navigation charts at a scale of 1:50,000, which are ideal. You could use anything up to about 1:150,000, although this would give you substantially less coastal detail.

2. PLAN THE TIME OF DEPARTURE & ARRIVAL TO GET THE MOST OUT OF THE FAVOURABLE TIDAL STREAM

Unless the timings are really terrible, I usually aim to set out in the last hour of the adverse stream, or at slack water, even if that means an early morning departure. And I then try to make a good enough speed to get us to the destination with a following tide.

3. CALCULATE THE EXPECTED TIDAL STREAMS FOR THE HOURS THAT YOU WILL BE UNDER WAY

The easiest way that I have found to do this is to just go through the *Tidal Stream Atlas*, noting the margin of each page with the time that it applies. You can then refer back to this at any stage during the passage.

4. PLAN YOUR TRACK TO BE FAR ENOUGH OFFSHORE TO PROVIDE A COMFORTABLE SEPARATION FROM DANGERS

In general, you will probably be safe enough running down the coast about 5nm offshore by day, but you need to judge the safe distance once you've opened up the charts and seen how the coast lies. If possible, I would avoid passing closer than about 2 miles to any charted dangers. If you do have to pass closer than that, make sure that you plan that part of the passage with greater care.

By night, give yourself a greater offing.

5. PUT THE DESTINATION INTO GPS AS A WAYPOINT SO THAT YOU HAVE A CONSTANT READOUT OF THE DISTANCE TO GO

Your GPS will give you an ETA at your destination, and I've always found this sort of dynamic ETA incredibly useful in helping me decide how much I need to push along to get there.

You can very often find a useful point-of-arrival waypoint in the *Almanac*, under the 'Navigation' entry for any given port. This is normally shown as a fine red crossed circle on the chartlet. These waypoints are a useful check when entering the point of arrival into your GPS.

6. BEFORE YOU SLIP, MAKE SURE YOU HAVE ENOUGH WATER, FUEL & FOOD FOR THE PASSAGE

This is basic good seamanship. Why would you do otherwise? I always aim to set out with full water tanks, even for a one-day passage; it takes very little time to top the water tanks off before you go, and you just never know when you will need it. Always be aware of your fuel state, topping up the tanks frequently. It is much better to do that, even though it entails a few minutes delay at the fuel berth, than to endure the embarrassment and potential dangers of running out mid-trip.

Coastal navigation in Desolation Sound, British Columbia

MAKING IT HAPPEN

1. BRIEF THE CREW ON THE DAY'S PASSAGE

This is a good thing to do the night before, once you have settled in after the previous day's passage. Get out a glass of wine and the chart (in that order, I would suggest) and just talk everyone through where you are going, the times of departure and arrival, the expected weather conditions – and what time you want them out of their bunks the next morning.

2. TRY TO LEAVE ON TIME, IN ORDER TO MAKE THE BEST OF THE TIDAL STREAM

This is quite a good discipline in a boat. Set a realistic time to leave your berth and stick to it. The tides won't wait for you and sometimes even a quarter of an hour's delay can make quite a difference to the water conditions.

3. ONCE CLEAR OF PILOTAGE WATERS, SETTLE INTO A LOOSE WATCH-KEEPING SYSTEM

For an unthreatening coastal passage, I would suggest that you organise yourself and your crew into a loose rota of 2 hours on, 2 hours off in order to give people time for a doze, or to read their books without compromising the boat's operations.

Whenever you're underway, there should always be someone who is responsible for keeping a lookout (astern as well as ahead). This is especially important in coastal waters, where there are often small boats, fishing buoys, bits of flotsam and other obstructions in the water. Even a rope cutter on your propeller shaft won't protect you from the worst tangles of discarded fishing netting.

4. ONCE CLEAR OF THE IMMEDIATE DANGERS, FIX YOUR POSITION EVERY HOUR, REDUCING THE FIXING INTERVAL IF YOU GET CLOSE TO DANGERS AGAIN

You need to decide how often you want to put a fix on the chart, but this should be a routine event that is performed at regular intervals. The purpose of the fix is to reassure you that you are safe from dangers, and it also gives you the opportunity to put a DR and an EP on the chart (I would suggest looking forward across 2 fixing intervals) to make sure that you are not running into danger. On a coastal passage, when you are clear of any imminent dangers, I would suggest hourly fixing, reducing the interval between fixes as you approach any potential dangers. Tie it in with putting the hourly entry into the ship's log; it's quite useful to get an alarm if you're likely to forget.

5. PREPARE FOR ENTRY INTO YOUR DESTINATION IN GOOD TIME, WORKING OUT THE PILOTAGE PLAN BEFORE YOU GET INTO RESTRICTED WATERS

With a bit of practice, it doesn't take long to put together an entry plan for most ports. It's far better to get the planning done early, before you arrive in pilotage waters, where you will inevitably find yourself with a great deal more to think about

All it takes is a quiet 10 minutes at the chart table, working out the heights of tide, the tidal streams, the opening times of the marina sills, the VHF channel to call up the Harbour Master, and to draw up the track into the port and any necessary clearing bearings. Then you're ahead of the game, and ready to go.

17
OFFSHORE NAVIGATION

Offshore navigation is the long game of maritime passage-making, when you can expect to be out of sight of land for a day, a week or even very much longer. It's not my intention in this book to write about long ocean passages, which have a rhythm all of their own; for now I will consider shorter offshore passages, like crossing the English Channel, the Bay of Biscay or the North Sea which may last 12, 24 or possibly 36 hours, but which don't involve ocean navigation techniques.

A number of things change as you move offshore:

■ VHF chatter gets quieter, and eventually fades away altogether
■ You move through, and eventually away from, the shipping lanes
■ You may often change the national jurisdiction of the water space
■ As the water becomes deeper you get into a longer, more comfortable oceanic swell and the tidal streams can often become less prominent (depending on where you are)
■ Your track becomes a succession of long, sometimes very long, straight lines with

no navigation hazards along the way

However:

■ Help is less immediate, so you need to be self-sufficient on board, and you must have enough vital supplies for the passage, especially water, fuel and food; you need to think about how you will do first aid on board
■ Ports of refuge are further away, with longer transit times to get there
■ And it starts to feel lonelier, but also rather more liberating, as all the random shipping, yachts and landmarks fall astern

PLANNING

1. USE APPROPRIATELY SCALED CHARTS FOR THE PASSAGE

On an offshore passage you will want charts in a variety of scales, depending on their purpose.

For instance, the passage that I have worked through later in this book, from Lymington to Guernsey, involves:

OFFSHORE NAVIGATION CHECKLIST

Planning

☐ Use appropriately scaled charts

☐ Make sure you hear an accurate weather forecast before you set out, and, where possible, at regular intervals on passage

☐ Calculate the time of sunrise, sunset, etc.

☐ Plan a time of departure that best suits your purposes

☐ To help you plan, work out the Height of Tide for both departure and, if possible, arrival before you set off

☐ Calculate the expected tidal streams for the hours that you will be under way in tidal waters

☐ Plan your track so far as possible to stay well clear of the shipping lanes and comfortably well-removed from dangers

☐ Store all the planned waypoints, and your point of arrival, into the GPS

☐ Before you slip, make sure you have enough water, fuel and food for the passage, together with any important equipment, and give your boat a pre-flight check: rigging, navigation lights, engine oil, lifejackets, liferaft, etc.

☐ Inform the Coastguard, and a reliable friend, of your plan and your ETA – and remember to let them know when you get there; you might also consider using a tracking device, like the HM Coastguard and RYA's SafeTrx App

Equipment

☐ Binoculars

☐ Hand-held compass

☐ Chart and pilot book

☐ Navigation notebook

☐ Hand-held GPS, or access to the chart plotter

☐ VHF monitoring Channel 16, ideally set to Dual Watch the local coastgaurd weather forecast fequency

☐ Echo sounder read-out visible

Making it Happen

☐ Brief the crew on the passage plan before you set out

☐ Once you are clear of pilotage waters, settle into a comfortable routine for the passage

☐ As the waters become less busy, it is just as important to keep a good lookout

☐ Fix your position on the chart regularly, possibly every hour when you are clear of the coast, and every watch on a long offshore passage

☐ Use your GPS to monitor the ETA at your next waypoints and at your destination

☐ Make a point of filling in the logbook hourly, and recording any unusual events in it

☐ Monitor the Coastguard frequency for routine weather updates

☐ At the other end of the passage, prepare early for the entry into your destination port

- A super-large scale chart of Lymington: 1:5,000
- Large scale charts of the Solent and the approaches to Guernsey: 1:25,000
- Coastal navigation charts: 1:50,000
- And cross-Channel charts: 1:150,000

Longer distance passages would probably require charts drawn to an even smaller scale.

The important thing when using paper charts is to ensure that you have the right level of detail for your purposes. Clearly, if you are only navigating with a chart plotter you can switch scales as you see fit.

2. PLAN A TIME OF DEPARTURE THAT BEST SUITS YOUR PURPOSE

Offshore passages are by their nature rather less time-constrained than coastal passages, so it's more likely that you will be able to choose a departure time to suit your crew, rather than one that is designed to meet tidal criteria.

That said, in my worked example of a passage from Lymington to St Peter Port (Chapters 19-23), the timing does matter because the passage is dominated by 2 tidal gates, one at the Needles and one at the Casquets. You have to set out at the right time, and maintain a specific speed, to make those gates with a favourable tidal stream.

On other passages when timing is less critical, you can please yourself and set out at a time that makes sense in the context of the whole passage: to arrive in daylight, for instance; or to cross the shipping lanes after breakfast; or just to leave before dawn because sunrise is the best time of the day to be at sea.

3. PLAN YOUR TRACK TO BE WELL CLEAR OF THE SHIPPING LANES & COMFORTABLY WELL-REMOVED FROM DANGERS

At the end of the day, seafaring is quite a solitary form of travel. In a small boat on a big ocean you are actually rather safer keeping it that way, avoiding the shipping lanes as much as possible. The further you are from land, the less likely that the bridge team of a large merchant ship will be looking out for a solitary yacht, so the burden of responsibility falls more heavily on your shoulders to avoid getting too close.

Equally, if you don't need to go close to big rocks and other dangers – don't. Leave them alone and get on with your passage.

Planning a short offshore passage is relatively simple; you use small scale charts, and the navigation plan normally consists of a few straight lines. The tidal gates, if there are any, are generally at either end.

You need to be aware of:

- When and how you are going to cross the shipping lanes
- When you might find yourself in limited VHF cover in case of emergency
- How reliable your weather forecast will be during the course of the passage, and how often you will be able to update it
- When you leave and re-enter a nation's territorial waters

When planning a longer passage in tidal waters, you should decide how closely you will stick to the charted track. There are 2 options:

- **Remain on track**: This inevitably requires you to alter course to prevent the tidal stream from pushing you off track, and it will result in a slower, but more tightly-constrained passage.
- **Remain on course**: If you do this you will accept some divergence from your track as a result of the tidal stream. On passages of about 12 hours or so (like a Channel crossing in a sailing boat – see opposite) you may find that the tidal stream pushes you one way and then brings you back onto your track. This usually results in a faster passage.

Both of these are valid options. Your choice will depend on how much divergence you expect from the tidal stream during the passage, and how close to your endpoint you are likely to finish if you stick to your charted course.

When deciding how to plan this, I find it quite useful (if a bit fiddly) to go through the *Tidal Stream Atlas* page by page, and make a note of how far and in what direction the water movement will set me every hour of the passage. If you add up the list of hourly sets, it should tell you how far left or right of your destination you can expect to be set, and where roughly you will end up. If, for instance, the predictions show that you will end up 5 miles to the east of your destination, you might consider setting a course from the outset that would, in still water, take you 5 miles to the west – and allow the tidal stream to do the rest.

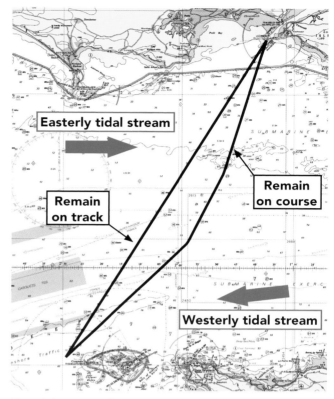

Remaining on track or remaining on course

4. BEFORE YOU SLIP, MAKE SURE YOU HAVE ENOUGH WATER, FUEL & FOOD FOR THE PASSAGE

There is nothing in the world so useful as a comprehensive checklist, and ideally one that you, personally, have compiled. Don't leave storing ship to your memory, because as sure as eggs you'll forget something, and on a long trip even the absence of AA batteries could be significant. Of all the supplies, the 'Big Four' – water, fuel, food and cooking gas – are the most important by far, but you only have to clear out a boat before putting her up for sale to realise the sheer number and variety of individual 'things' that are needed to run even a modest-sized yacht, and keep her well maintained.

Check that you have all important equipment onboard and give your boat a pre-flight check before you set out. Work around the whole boat just to make sure that everything is in good shape, and well secured. Check the rigging, the navigation lights (including the coloured filters which can often get so crazed that they become almost opaque), engine oil, lifejackets, liferaft, etc.

5. INFORM THE COASTGUARD, & A RELIABLE FRIEND, OF YOUR PLAN & YOUR ETA – AND REMEMBER TO LET THEM KNOW WHEN YOU ARRIVE

This is important. It will ensure that people sit up and pay attention if you're overdue, which is the first, vital step in launching a rescue operation. But don't forget to inform them when you arrive too; I can't imagine how embarrassing it would be to sit in a bar in north-west Spain reading a newspaper article about a Coastguard search for your boat, just because you forgot to let anyone know that you're safe.

The HMCG / RYA SafeTrx App may be useful here.

MAKING IT HAPPEN

1. BRIEF THE CREW ON THE PASSAGE PLAN BEFORE YOU SET OUT

In many ways, it is not just a question of briefing the crew; you also need to understand how robust they are. Are they happy to sail at night? Are they terrified of big waves? Or are they just happy to go with it? There is no point pushing people to the point where a sea trip becomes an ordeal. Make it fun, and stay within their comfort zone, even if it means that you are not able to be as ambitious as you might wish.

2. ONCE CLEAR OF PILOTAGE WATERS, SETTLE INTO A COMFORTABLE ROUTINE FOR THE PASSAGE

As far as a watch-keeping routine is concerned, I would suggest 2 hours on watch by day and 3 by night, but you can vary this to suit the number of crew you have onboard, and their competence. What matters is that you establish a daily routine for:

- Regular watch changes
- Mealtimes
- Sleep

You also need an established navigation routine of:

- Regular fixing, with a DR and an EP; as a rule, I fix hourly when away from the coast, moving to one GPS fix per watch on a long offshore passage
- Filling in the log hourly (including recording the position)
- Listening to VHF weather forecast

3. AS THE WATERS BECOME LESS BUSY, IT IS JUST AS IMPORTANT TO KEEP A GOOD LOOKOUT

The most important thing on an offshore passage is to keep a good lookout. In a submarine at periscope depth, we used to keep a 3-minute all-round look on the periscope. This was based on wanting to avoid anything small and fast that was aiming at us. Scanning the horizon once every 3 minutes in good visibility would give us enough time to spot it, assess it and, if necessary, get out of its way. This is not a bad discipline for yachtsmen. In poor visibility you need to increase the frequency of your 'all-round look'.

I know that it's not easy keeping a good lookout on a sunny day when you're deep in conversation – but you have to do it. It is all too easy to get distracted, and suddenly 15 minutes have gone past without a good scan of the horizon… and that's dangerous.

If keeping a regular lookout is difficult, it seems to be doubly difficult to keep a good lookout astern. But ships can – and do – creep up on you from any direction, not just ahead. In particular, I have become very wary of 'fastcat' ferries, which have an unnerving way of suddenly appearing without any warning at all, giving you almost no time to get out of their way.

I came across one just north of the Alderney Race, doing close to 40 knots in visibility that was rather less than a mile. I saw it first on AIS, closing our position at high speed as I did my best to get off track. A few minutes later we could hear the deep growl of its engines, and the predicted CPA was still only about half a mile. And then it roared past, noisy and unseen… and silence returned. It made me realise how little time you have to do anything meaningful to avoid a collision with something moving that fast, especially in poor visibility, and how important it was to spot it early.

4. MAKE A POINT OF FILLING IN THE LOGBOOK HOURLY & RECORDING ANY UNUSUAL EVENTS

There are a number of good reasons to fill in the logbook every hour, some of which date back among mariners for centuries:

- Firstly, at sea, it helps to have ways to mark the passage of time. An hourly routine of fixing and log-filling is exactly that. In the Navy we would also have little rituals that were always observed, like reporting sunset to the Captain each night, serving fish and chips for supper on Fridays, and roast beef for Sunday lunch. In the featureless landscape of the sea, these rituals were important ways of marking the progress of the voyage.
- Secondly, an hourly entry in the logbook provides a regular check on your position, your progress and any nearby or anticipated dangers.
- The logbook also gives you an important reference in the event that you lose the ability to fix your position. The last recorded position suddenly becomes your most accurate reference point from which to find your way home, which is

quite a valuable piece of information to know.

- It's a place to record the interesting things that happen during the voyage, and so it becomes a useful reference document for your boat.
- And finally, if you're ever challenged by the authorities (this has happened to me, more than once), it's good to be able to point to a diligently-completed logbook to at least provide some evidence of where you have been. This is particularly important when sailing across national borders.

5. CROSSING SHIPPING LANES

On most of my sailing holidays I have set out with an offshore passage across the English Channel, which inevitably means crossing the flow of shipping. These are some of the busiest shipping lanes in the world, which make it a complex place to sail in a small boat with an inexperienced crew. Even so, if you're careful you can always find a way across. It's a bit like crossing a busy road: big ships seem to come along in herds, and very often there's a gap before the next few come down at you. It is much easier to cross between the herds, rather than trying to weave your way between 6 big ships sailing in close formation.

The right way to go about crossing the shipping lanes (which are the areas of mandatory one-way flow that have been established within the Traffic Separation Schemes[62]) is to steer a course at 90° to the traffic flow, even if this means that the tidal stream pushes you well off course. This is sensible, because a 90° course will get you across the lanes as quickly as possible and, as long as it's safe navigationally to do so,

---

[62] The full IMO definition of a Traffic Lane is: '*An area within defined limits in which one-way traffic is established. Natural obstacles including those forming separation zones, may constitute a boundary.*'

I would recommend exactly that, especially if you're trying to cross the Straits of Dover themselves.

In a big ship navigating a Separation Scheme you often feel a bit like a caged bear with very little latitude to diverge from the standard track. In the Straits of Dover particularly, it's quite common to have other vessels flanking you, and your manoeuvring options for collision avoidance are at best limited. You really don't need a small yacht getting in your way and insisting that you manoeuvre to avoid them. The less time that small vessels like yours and mine spend in these schemes the happier everyone will be.

The COLREGs (Rule 10c) are specific about this:

"A vessel shall, so far as practicable, avoid crossing traffic lanes but if obliged to do so shall cross on a heading as nearly as practicable at right angles to the general direction of flow."

The areas where a mandatory direction of traffic flow have been established are shown on the chart with a solid arrow. Those with a recommended direction of flow with a pecked arrow.

Rule 10e builds on this with:

"A vessel, other than a crossing vessel or a vessel joining or leaving a lane shall not normally enter a separation zone..."

A separation zone is one of those magenta areas which mark the boundaries of the separation lanes on the chart. The track that I am planning for my cross-Channel passage (see Chapter 21) clips the southeastern corner of the separation zone, so I will need to make sure that I take a small detour to the south as I get there.

This is all well and good in theory, and it keeps me on the right side of Maritime Law. However, the shipping is unlikely to be any less dense 5nm to the east of the Separation Scheme than it is in the middle of the scheme.

I would not advocate steering a course at right angles to the traffic flow right across the southern half of the English Channel. You would probably end up in Dieppe. But even so I would cross the lanes as quickly as I could. Any leisure sailor coming into these busy waters needs to be vigilant, and to do as much as he or she can to avoid impeding the flow of traffic, recognising that at the end of the day normal rules of collision avoidance apply both in the Separation Schemes and outside them.

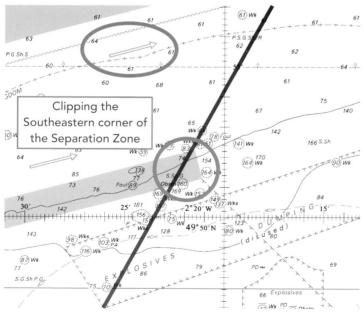

My proposed course clips the southeastern corner of the separation zone

PART 3
IN PRACTICE

For the next few chapters, I will run through the planning and the calculations for a passage from Lymington to St Peter Port in Guernsey.

The boat we are using is a well-found 38ft (13m) sailing boat with a draught of 1.7 metres. It has a good, reliable engine capable of a sustained passage speed of 7 knots. The boat is equipped with all normal navigation equipment, including a Raytheon chart plotter with radar and AIS transceiver, and the appropriate English Channel navigation charts.

I will be taking 2 other people with me, both moderately experienced sailors, but neither of them too keen on taking long night watches, or heavy weather sailing.

We are planning to make the passage on Saturday 20 June 2020, or as soon after as convenient.

This passage incorporates a bit of everything: pilotage, anchoring, coastal and offshore navigation.

The yacht making the passage, my old yacht, Snowgoose

18

PASSAGE PLANNING

In this chapter, I will start with the pre-departure passage planning, which is an essential part of any trip.

I have never considered passage planning a chore. In fact, it's a real pleasure; a chance to sit down quietly with books and charts, working out where we are going, and how we're going to get there. You almost live your voyage in advance, knowing that the more thorough your plan, the more enjoyable everyone onboard will find the passage.

Your aim in this early stage of passage planning is fairly simple: to work out where you will be, and when. And also to look at the outline plan of the passage and make sure that it is viable. Once you know that it will work, you can move onto the more detailed planning.

THE COMPETENCE & EXPERIENCE OF YOUR CREW

I have said it before in this book, but I will say it one more time because it's so important: in planning a trip like this, your first concern has to be the welfare of your crew. I've met so many people who have been put off sailing by one single trip with a gung-ho skipper who took them to sea well outside their comfort zones – and in some cases well outside the skipper's level of competency as well.

Sadly, no matter how beautiful the picture looks on the wall of the Beneteau dealership (opposite), the sea is not always as well-behaved as this. When it finds you wanting it is cold and wholly unforgiving, so it's vital that we all understand our limits at sea and stay within them.

Some skippers feel it's a sign of weakness if they allow an unfavourable weather forecast to delay their sailing time. I would call it a sign of strength. And in any case, it's both unfair and unnecessary to push your crew into situations where they feel unhappy, or where they question your competence or decision-making.

Your passage planning, the choice of route and the decisions that you make relating to acceptable weather should directly reflect your own competence, as well as that of your crew, and take account of their experience and resilience as well.

The sea is not always this well-behaved (© Beneteau / Gilles Martin-Raget)

HOW REALISTIC IS THE CHOICE OF DESTINATION?

Your choice of destination is crucial, and before deciding on a destination you need to ask yourself a few questions:

- Are you, your crew and your boat OK for a night passage, or will you restrict yourself solely to day passages (which, frankly, are a lot more enjoyable)?
- Are you happy leaving or entering harbour in the dark? It can be quite disorientating until you are used to it, and it's not for everyone – especially people who are colour blind.
- Are you OK to start this holiday with a fairly long day, from dawn to about supper time, without a break? A 13-hour passage from Lymington to St Peter Port, right out of the starting gate is quite a big ask of your crew, before they have got used to living on the boat – but it does get you across the Channel quickly.

- How many miles can your boat comfortably cover in a day?
- And finally, are you happy to anchor overnight, or would you prefer to overnight in a marina berth?

These questions, and others like them, should form an early part of your passage planning. There are no right or wrong answers; all that matters is that you have a realistic destination that works for you and your crew.

In this case, I have a crew onboard who are not just experienced yachtsmen, but who also know the boat well, and they're keen to get across the Channel. The weather forecast is fair, so we have decided that we will go directly for St Peter Port. If not, the alternative would be to either hop along the coast to Studland, which is a safe and sheltered anchorage, to give the crew an opportunity to settle in – or else cross the Channel and stop sooner – at Cherbourg, or Braye Harbour in Alderney, which would cut about 4 hours off the length of the passage.

CHARTS

The first job is to get the charts out. You will need large scale[63] charts for pilotage, medium scale charts for coastal navigation and smaller scale charts for the cross-Channel passage. Check that the charts are up to date using the QR code on the bottom left-hand corner and make any necessary corrections. This can be a time-consuming and detailed job, but it also gives you an opportunity to pore over the charts and look at them in more detail.

You should also look for local *Notices to Mariners* at each end of your passage. Guernsey, for instance, has a really impressive site at: http://www.harbours.

gg/Guernsey-Navigation-Warnings-Notices. This site tells you all you need to know about navigating round their waters, including the 4-day weather forecast, the expected movement of big ships and, if you want it, the tide tables. Many other ports have similar, and equally valuable, websites.

Local Notices to Mariners on the Guernsey Harbours website (© Guernsey Harbours)

On this passage, I plan to use the following charts:

5600.4	1:5,000	Plan of Lymington River
5600.7	1:25,000	Yarmouth to Beaulieu River
5600.18	1:7,500	Plan of Keyhaven
5600.5	1:25,000	Needles Channel
2035	1:25,000	Western Approaches to the Solent
2454	1:150,000	Start Point to the Needles
2669	1:150,000	Channel Islands and the Adjacent Coast of France
5604.3	1:150,000	Cherbourg to Guernsey
5604.9	1:50,000	Guernsey, Herm and Sark
5604.10	1:25,000	Approaches to St Peter Port
5604.11	1:6,000	St Peter Port

I would naturally carry other charts on board in case I had to divert to Alderney, Cherbourg or to a West Country port. These would be part of a wider folio of charts, built up over time, to suit my cruising needs.

---

[63] A lot of people are confused by large scale and small scale charts.
I remember it with a simple mnemonic: **'LARGE SCALE - SMALL AREA; SMALL SCALE - LARGE AREA.'**

TIMING THE PASSAGE

Measure out the distance from Lymington to St Peter Port. I have divided this passage into three bites, to make sure that we get the best run of tide around the Casquets:

- Firstly, a short hop from Lymington to Hurst Castle, where I propose to anchor overnight.
- Then, on the second day, it's 70nm from Hurst Castle to a waypoint 5nm west of the Casquets. There is very little to be gained by cutting any closer to the Casquets than this, and 5nm allows a comfortable margin of safety. 70nm at 7kts will take 10 hours.
- And finally, it's 17.4nm from that point to the mouth of the Little Russel, and 4.2nm from there into St Peter Port.

That's a total of 91.6nm on the second day – 13 hours of passage if we can make good 7kts.

If we decided to take it more slowly and, say, make good 5.5kts, it would take 16.5 hours. In this case, I would start thinking about setting off in the dark, or else overnighting in Alderney.

I have decided to avoid the passage to the east of Alderney – the Alderney Race – because I can see no point in doing that unless it is absolutely necessary. If I were going from Cherbourg to Guernsey or vice versa, I would probably cut through the Race, but in this case I would time the entire passage around hitting the Race at the right time to minimise turbulence. Equally, the Ortac Channel, which is the stretch of water to the east of the Casquets, is an ugly piece of water prone to overfalls, and is well avoided.

On this passage there are 2 'tidal gates' – at the Needles and the Casquets.

These are points where I will have to get the timing right in order to make the trip work: I need to time the passage so that the tidal stream is behind us as we hit each gate. A contrary tidal stream in either place would seriously slow us down and delay the passage.

The Casquets is by far the bigger and more significant of these 2 gates. The water is deep to the west and reasonably well-behaved, but even so the tidal stream flows strongly in each direction, and it's a great deal easier to get past with the tidal stream running in your favour.

The *Channel Islands Tidal Stream Atlas*[64] (overleaf) shows that the tidal stream starts to flow southwest around the Casquets, and down towards Guernsey from about HW Dover, and it continues in this direction for the next 5 hours. I would like to get on this bus and ride it all the way down to the Little Russel.

So, the latest time of arrival at the entrance to the Little Russel Channel is HW Dover +5.

The next thing to do is to check the Dover Tide Tables for 20 June 2020.

	Time	m
20	0518	1.3
	1023	6.1
SA	1738	1.3
	2234	6.2

HW Dover is at 1123 BST, 2/3 Springs.

We need to be at the Little Russel by HW Dover +5. That's 1620 BST.

---

[64] Or in this case the tidal stream diagram in the margins of *Chart 60: Alderney and the Casquets*.

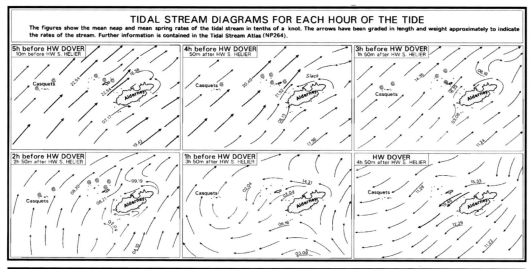

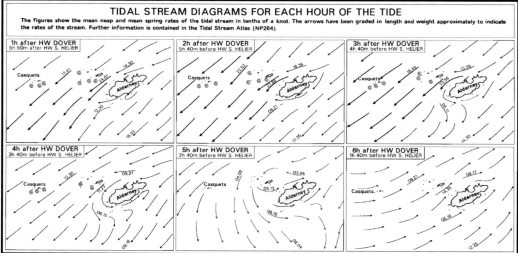

Chart 60: Alderney and the Casquets

The sun sets at St Peter Port at 2120 BST that evening[65], so we will have masses of daylight to get ourselves securely tucked up on arrival.

It's 17nm (2½ hours at 7 knots) from the Casquets to the mouth of the Little Russel, so it would be sensible to work on rounding the Casquets at or before HW Dover +2½ (1400 BST), when there's still be a strong southwesterly push around the corner. This should give us an exhilarating additional 2-3 knots of ground speed for the final couple of hours of our journey.

---

[65] I no longer use the *Almanac* to work out the time of sunrise and sunset, although it is easy enough to do so. Find a good website or app that you have confidence in and use that when you are planning a trip. I use an iPad app called: 'The Sun - Rise and Fall', which works well for me. I also use https://www.timeanddate.com, which has the times of sunrise, sunset, moon rise and moon set as well as civil and nautical twilight times.

Working back at 7 knots, we should therefore aim to pass Hurst Castle no later 10 hours earlier (70nm at 7kts). That has us leaving Hurst Castle no later than 0400 BST (HW Portsmouth +4½ hours). Is that viable?

- Sunrise at Lymington that day is at 0452 BST. Morning Civil Twilight[66] is at 0406 BST, so there should be just about enough light to see clearly by 0400. If the crew are OK setting out an hour earlier than this – at 0300 BST, which is before twilight – we would be less squeezed by time all the way across the Channel, but that would entail passing through the Needles Channel in the dark.

- Now take a look at the *Solent Tidal Stream Atlas*. HW Portsmouth is at 2335 BST on the evening of 19 June, so at 0435 (HW Portsmouth +5) the tidal stream through the Needles Channel is just about slack, before starting to flood into the Solent at 0535 BST. The adverse tidal stream would make leaving through the Needles Channel quite a struggle for the next 6 hours, so it is worth getting up early to make sure we have cleared the channel by about 5am.

Although this would be quite a long day, and it would probably require us to motor for most of the passage to maintain 7 knots of speed over the ground (SOG), a passage of this length is entirely viable and it has the merit of getting you across the Channel in one jump.

Others will take a different view, but I personally take little pleasure from a Channel crossing. For me the holiday starts when I get to the other side, so I like to cross the Channel quickly and efficiently. That means that I'm happy to motor as much as necessary while I'm mid-Channel to keep my speed up. A bit of additional speed and the extra manoeuvrability of the engine also make it easier to avoid the traffic in the shipping lanes.

The only other thing to consider (and I'll plan for in this passage) is that if we're going to pass Hurst Castle at 0400 BST, it would be a lot more convenient to anchor there the night before. It will save an hour and a half of passage, and a night-time departure from Lymington. It's quite easy to tuck in and anchor close to the shore, clear of the main tidal stream and well sheltered from the west by the shingle

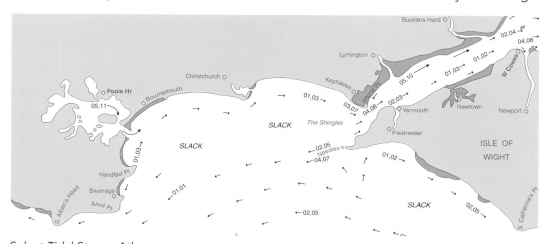

Solent Tidal Stream Atlas

[66] Civil Twilight is the point at which there is deemed to be enough light *'for ordinary outdoor occupations'*.

bank. A night at a sheltered anchorage like this is a special and very peaceful way to start your holiday.

So, all things considered, it looks like it's viable to leave Hurst Castle at 0400 BST and make our way directly across the Channel, round the Casquets and down to St Peter Port. Provided the weather forecast is benign, we can go ahead and plan this passage in more detail.

I will therefore note down the outline timings in my notebook. This is a really important aide-memoire for the passage so that I can make sure that we're keeping up with the schedule.

Weigh anchor Hurst Castle	No later than 0400 BST
Morning Civil Twilight	0406
Sunrise	0452
Clear of Needles Channel	0445
5nm west of Casquets	No later than 1400
Enter Little Russel Channel	1620
St Peter Port	1730

SAFE HAVENS

This is also a good time to check the chart for convenient safe havens in case we are delayed or choose to shorten the day. The 2 best stopping places on this passage are the anchorage at Studland Bay, close to Poole Harbour on the north side of the English Channel, and Braye Harbour in Alderney on the south.

SAILING DIRECTIONS & TIDAL STREAM ATLASES

Always try to read the *Sailing Directions* before leaving or entering a port, even if you have been there a few times before. In this case I would look up Lymington, the Needles Channel and St Peter Port in *Reed's Almanac*, and also in the *Shell Channel Pilot*.

Now that we have the timings, it's a good time to note the time on each page of the *Tidal Stream Atlases* for the Solent, the Channel and the Channel Islands, so that we can easily refer to the book during the passage. Annoyingly, while the *Tidal Stream Atlases* for the Channel and the Channel Islands are both referenced to HW Dover, the Solent is referenced to HW Portsmouth.

WEATHER FORECAST

The night before departure, I will also pick up the latest forecast. You can get any number of forecasts online, some more reliable than others, but the UK forecasting sites that I really like are:

For the general forecast:
www.metoffice.gov.uk/weather/forecast/gby1q7guf

For the shipping forecast:
www.metoffice.gov.uk/weather/specialist-forecasts/coast-and-sea/shipping-forecast

For the Inshore Waters forecast:
www.metoffice.gov.uk/weather/specialist-forecasts/coast-and-sea/inshore-waters-forecast

For the Jersey Met Office forecast:
www.gov.je/weather/pages/guernsey-forecast.aspx

If you have a grasp of French, however slight, listen out for the French Coastguard CROSS Forecasts. On this stretch of the coast the forecasts are regularly transmitted on VHF at times that are shown in your *Reed's Almanac* from the station at Joburg close to Cherbourg (Channel 80) and Corsen on the Pointe de Bretagne (Channel 79). They are accurate, regular and worth listening to, and normally spoken in slow and very precise French.

I have also recently been using an excellent Norwegian Weather app which seems to be as accurate as anything else online. It's called YR.no and you can get it from the App Store.

THE BIG FOUR: FUEL, WATER, FOOD & COOKING GAS

Top yourself up before you go! This doesn't really sit here in the navigation section, except to say that I'm always astonished by the number of people who have to call out a lifeboat each year because they run out of fuel. It's basic good seamanship to make sure that you are properly provisioned for the voyage ahead, whether it's a day out on the Solent or a longer trip across oceans. Once you are out there, it's quite a long way to the nearest supermarket.

CREW BRIEFING

Always brief your crew before you set out. They're coming with you, and they deserve to be told what you are planning, what role they will play in it, how long they can expect the passage to last, and the expected weather. You should also give your crew a full safety briefing before a passage, even if they have heard it all before, because when things start going wrong, they do so quite quickly. I like to use a pre-planned template for crew briefing so that I cover everything and don't leave any vital gaps.

Make sure that your crew are happy with what you are proposing. If anyone is prone to seasickness and can't face a Channel crossing, it's perfectly easy for them to cross the Channel by ferry, and for you to collect them in Guernsey, or St Malo – or even, if they take the car across with them, to meet you every evening in a new port just as you open a bottle of wine in the cockpit. Sailing should be fun – for everybody.

It's standard practice to refuel a lifeboat everytime she returns to port

19
LYMINGTON TO HURST CASTLE

1800 BST 19 June 2020

One of the really good things about navigation is that no two elements are ever the same, and pilotage (the process of getting off your berth and out of the harbour into open water and returning from the open sea into harbour) is often the most interesting and challenging part of the whole trip.

At the start of this trip there are two pilotage legs:

■ From Lymington to our anchorage at Hurst Castle

■ From Hurst Castle through the Needles Channel to open water (Chapter 20)

The first leg, from Lymington to Hurst Castle is not far – no more than an hour or so – so we should have no trouble getting ourselves out of the marina, clear of the river and anchored, all in full daylight. Sunset in Lymington on 19 June 2020 occurs at 2122 BST[67].

PLANNING TO LEAVE LYMINGTON (FRIDAY 19 JUNE 2020)

To allow time after anchoring for a glass of wine before supper, I have decided to leave the Lymington Yacht Haven at 1800 BST and plan to anchor at about 1930.

HIGH & LOW TIDE TIMES AT LYMINGTON

The first thing to do is to work out the high and low tide times at Lymington on 19 June. Using *Reed's Nautical Almanac*, this is a straightforward Secondary Port calculation with one simple twist: that Lymington is one of the Solent ports with its own Height of Tide graph, referenced to Low Water.

As ever, you start as always by looking up the port in the *Almanac*. Lymington is a

---

[67] www.timeanddate.com/sun

Secondary Port, and the Standard Port is Portsmouth.

Times (GMT)				Heights (metres)			
High Water		Low Water		MHWS	MHWN	MLWN	MLWS
0000	0600	0500	1100	4.7	3.8	1.9	0.8
1200	1800	1700	2300				

Differences LYMINGTON

–0110	+0005	–0020	–0020	–1.6	–1.2	–0.4	–0.1

Secondary Port corrections for Lymington from Standard Port Portsmouth (in GMT)

Look up Portsmouth in the *Tide Tables* and note down:
- The time of High and Low Water at Portsmouth (adjusting for BST)
- The corresponding Height of Tide

19 F	Time	m
	0303	1.4
	1020	4.2
	1519	1.4
	2235	4.4

On 19 June 2020:
- Low Water is at 1519 GMT (1619 BST), with a height of 1.4m
- High Water at Portsmouth is at 2235 GMT (2335 BST), with a height of 4.4m

20 SA	Time	m
	0343	1.2
	1100	4.3
	1601	1.3
	2311	4.5

And on 20 June:
- Low Water is at 0343 GMT (0443 BST), with a height of 1.2m

So, the tidal range in the evening of 19 June is 4.4 – 1.4m = 3.0m
   From the Portsmouth Height of Tide graph, you can read off:
- The mean Spring Range is 3.9m
- The mean Neap Range is 1.9m

So, this tide is a whisker over ¹/₂ Springs.
   Now you just need to work out the time and height corrections for Lymington... which requires a small bit of interpolation. Slightly confusingly, this is best done in GMT, because the time corrections in the Secondary Port tables are laid out in GMT. You can correct to BST later in the process.

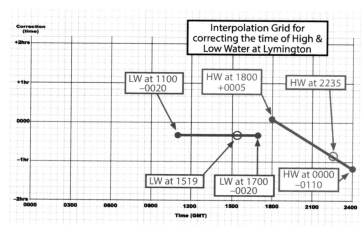

You can use an interpolation grid

- LW Portsmouth is at 1519 GMT. The correction is –20mins (you don't need an interpolation grid for his one!)
- HW Portsmouth is at 2235. GMT. This is 3/4 of the way between 1800 and 0000 GMT, so the correction is 3/4 of the way between +5 and –70 mins. I make that about –51mins
- The next morning, LW is at 0343 GMT, and the correction is again –20mins

- At 1/2 Springs the height correction for HW is half-way between –1.2 and –1.6: –1.4m
- The LW correction is half-way between –0.1 and –0.4: –0.25 (call it –0.3)

You can now draw up a table in your navigation notebook, shifting effortlessly from GMT to BST in the process:

19, 20 June 2020	Friday 19 afternoon LW (BST)	Friday 19 afternoon LW (m)	Friday 19 night HW (BST)	Friday 19 night HW (m)	Sat 20 morning LW (BST)	Sat 20 morning LW (m)
PORTSMOUTH	1619	1.4	2335	4.4	0443	1.2
Correction	–0020	–0.3	–0051	–1.4	–0020	–0.3
LYMINGTON	1559	1.1	2244	3.0	0423	0.9

Next, you will need to find the page in the *Tide Tables* or *Almanac* titled 'Special Tidal Curves from Christchurch to Selsey Bill', where you will find the specific curves for the Solent Secondary Ports. The one we're looking for is: Lymington and Yarmouth.

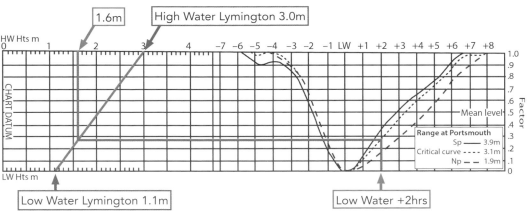

The tidal curve for Lymington

There are 3 curves for the Height of Tide – each corresponding to a particular tidal range at Portsmouth. Use the curve closest to the Portsmouth range on that day (3.0m): that is to say the 'Critical curve',

shown with the shorter dashes.

On the left-hand side of the diagram draw a diagonal line joining the heights of HW and LW Lymington that you have just calculated: 3.0m and 1.1m.

Then you can go ahead and read off the Heights of Tide at each hour in relation to the time of Low Water. As an example, I have drawn in the red line for LW +2hrs (1759 BST), when the Height of Tide is 1.6m.

If you do this every hour that you are on the water in the vicinity of Lymington, you can create a table of Height of Tide in your notebook. It should look something like this:

Time (BST)	Time in relation to HW Lymington	Height of Tide (m)
2244	HW	3.0
2159	LW +6	2.7
2059	LW +5	2.4
1959	LW +4	2.3
1859	LW +3	1.9
1759	LW +2	1.6
1659	LW +1	1.3
1559	LW	1.1

This Height of Tide table is an essential piece of your pilotage or anchorage planning:
- At 1800 BST, when you leave the marina, the Height of Tide will be 1.6m
- At 1900, you will have 1.9m
- At 1930, when you anchor, the Height of Tide will be 2.1m

While we're at anchor, the Height of Tide will rise to 3.0m, and then fall to 0.9m at 0423 BST, which is just about the time when we are planning to weigh anchor and set out.

In this calculation I have demonstrated the full Solent Secondary Port calculation, which is slightly different from the 'normal' calculation of Secondary Ports that I demonstrated in Chapter 4.

You may find it simpler just to work out the tides at Lymington – or any other Solent port – as a normal Secondary Port, referred to the curve of its designated Standard Port (in this case Portsmouth). It may not be quite as accurate, but it's quicker. I have sometimes done it that way – and it's quite accurate enough for my purposes in a small yacht.

But, as luck would have it, there's an even simpler way of working out the tides at Lymington. While *Reed's Nautical Almanac* treats Lymington as a Solent Secondary Port, the *Admiralty Tide Tables* have made Lymington a Standard Port, along with Poole, Cowes, Southampton, Warsash, Portsmouth and Chichester. So, if you're a Solent sailor, with a boat based in one of these harbours, you can save yourself a great deal of hard work by investing in Volume 1A of the *Admiralty Tide Tables* and working out the Height of Tide as a Standard Port.

It's interesting to compare our Secondary Port calculations against the Standard Port Tide Tables for Lymington:

Times BST Heights (m)	19 June LW Time	19 June LW Height	19 June HW Time	19 June HW Height	20 June LW Time	20 June LW Height
Secondary Port calculations	1559	1.1	2244	3.0	0423	0.9
Standard Port tables	1556	1.2	2348	3.0	0422	1.0
Difference	−0003	+0.1	+0104	0	−0001	+0.1

The results are almost identical, with the exception of the time of High Water. This is a measure of the ambiguity caused by the 3-hour High Water stand at Lymington.

MINIMUM DEPTH OF WATER

Before we leave Lymington, we should check – as in all pilotage – what the minimum depth of water will be on each course. Our boat has a draught of 1.7m.

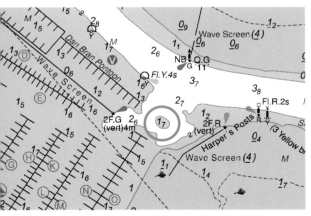

Chart of Lymington River

Leaving the marina, there is a patch of water that you may pass over with a Charted Depth of 1.7m. You will be passing this at 1800 BST when the Height of Tide is 1.6m.

The total depth of water =
Charted Depth + Height of Tide

The total depth of water =
1.7 + 1.6 = 3.3m
**And the under-keel clearance = 3.3 – 1.7
= 1.6m (which is safe)**

The river itself is deeper than 2m below Chart Datum; no doubt it's kept that way for the Yarmouth car ferry service that operates in the river. I'm going to use this 2m contour as the boundary of my safe navigation corridor when leaving the river, and so I need the echo sounder to alert me if we cross this line.

On the 2.0m contour, the total depth of water = 2.0 + 1.6 = 3.6m.

And at this point the under-keel clearance would be: 3.6 – 1.7 = 1.9m.

So, even if I have to squeeze to one side to avoid a ferry, I know that as long as the sounder is showing more than 3.6m total depth of water we're doing OK.

TIDAL STREAM PREDICTIONS (FRIDAY EVENING)

From the entrance to the Lymington River down to Hurst Castle is just 2.5nm, so in all we will be underway for less than 90 mins, leaving Lymington at 1800 BST, and anchoring by 1930.

High Water at Lymington is at 2244 BST, so while we are in the Lymington River, we can expect a flood stream to be flowing into the river, against us. Out in the Solent it will be similar, with an east-going flood stream on our bow.

- Look at the *Solent Tidal Stream Atlas*, referenced to HW Portsmouth (2335 BST)
- At 1835 (HW Portsmouth –5hrs), there is a strong flood coming in from the Needles Channel at 2.9kts (1/2 Springs), but there is also a small counter-eddy in a westerly direction closer inshore

None of that should concern us: it's all manageable. We have a lot of time in hand before sunset, and we don't have very far to go.

DEPTH OF WATER & CHOICE OF ANCHORAGE POSITION

Looking at the chart of the Hurst Point Anchorage, the bottom is pretty flat with a general depth of about 1.7m, and a deeper channel running north/south, a small 2.4m pool and then to the west a gentle slope up to the beach.

The bottom type is charted as 'M' (for 'Mud') – this is normally a good holding ground. And you can see too that the main contours of the seabed running roughly 020°/200° where the tidal stream out of the Solent, past Hurst Point, has dug a trench for itself.

In the shallower, muddy waters to the north of Hurst Point the tidal stream will

191835

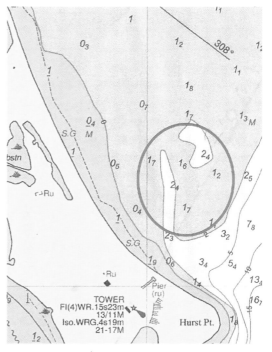

Hurst Point anchorage

be running very much less strongly than in the channel itself. This anchorage has good holding, slight tidal streams; it is sheltered from the west and out of the way of passing traffic. At first sight, this looks like a reasonable anchorage, except in a strong easterly or southwesterly wind, when I wouldn't touch it with a bargepole! But before deciding to spend the night there, I need to know three other things:

- The depth of water when we drop the anchor
- The maximum depth of water during our time at anchorage
- The minimum depth of water during our time at anchorage

Helpfully, I've already worked these depths out – we're close enough to Lymington to safely use those figures.

1. The Height of Tide when we anchor (1930 BST) is: 2.1m
2. The maximum Height of Tide during our stay is at HW (2244 BST): 3.0m
3. The minimum depth of water during our stay is LW (0423 BST):   0.9m

On this basis:

1. I'm planning to drop the anchor in the deeper part of this anchorage, where the Charted Depth is between 1.7-2.0m. The Height of Tide when we anchor will be 2.1m: we'll be looking to anchor in a spot where the echo sounder displays a total depth of water of 3.8-4.1m.
2. The maximum Height of Tide during our stay is 3.0m, so the maximum depth of water will be 4.7-5.0m. The safe length of anchor cable to veer is 4 times the depth of water, so we should plan to let out 20m of cable on the waterline… or more if I start worrying about our exposure to strong tidal streams or an overnight wind.
3. At Low Water we probably want 1.0m under the keel (total depth of water 2.7m). If the Height of Tide at Low Water is 0.9m, I am looking for a Charted Depth of not less than 1.8m. However, given the bottom topography, I would be prepared to stretch this to not less than 1.7m, which gives me a fairly extensive stretch of water to choose from.

The tightest thing about this anchorage is the plan to leave at 0400 in the morning, when we'll have just 0.9m of water under the keel. There's a small channel filtering out to the south, so we should be OK with this as long as there is not too much of a swell when we leave.

Alternatively, we could leave one hour earlier at 0300 BST, when we will have a little bit more Height of Tide. This would also give more time in hand at the other end of the passage.

LYMINGTON YACHT HAVEN TO HURST CASTLE ANCHORAGE (EVENING OF 19 JUNE 2020)

The Lymington River, like many Solent rivers, is a bit of a gift for navigators, because the main channel is lined with moorings. If we stay between the moorings there's a good chance that we will also stay inside the channel.

Leaving the marina behind, we come into a right-hand bend in the river, where we stay between the lines of moored buoys, before picking up the twin transits and the beacons that mark the next reach, heading 188°M. There is one pair of transit marks to the north, and a separated transit to the south – set up to allow 2 ferries to safely pass each other on this stretch of water. These are conspicuous marks, and

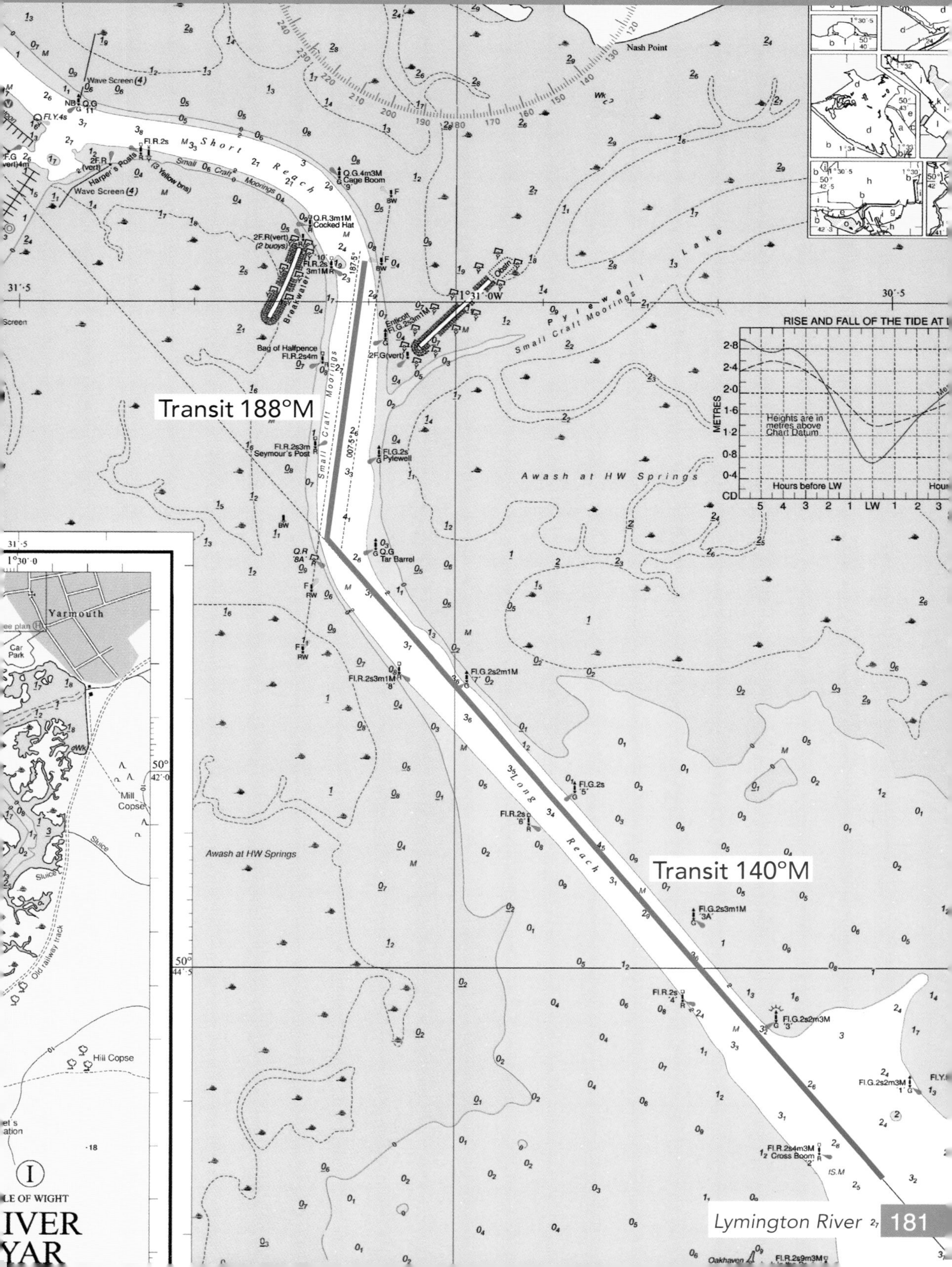

Transit 188°M

Transit 140°M

RISE AND FALL OF THE TIDE AT L

METRES

Heights are in
metres above
Chart Datum

Hours before LW

CD

Awash at HW Springs

Awash at HW Springs

Nash Point

Short Reach

Small Craft Moorings

Small Craft Moorings

Pylewell Lake

Long Reach

Yarmouth

Car Park

Mill Copse

Hill Copse

Old railway track

ISLE OF WIGHT

RIVER YAR

it's quite easy to stay between them. With a Height of Tide of 1.7m, I'm not greatly fussed by the 2m shoal at the start of this reach.

Transits are by far the easiest option for pilotage because there are no compass errors to worry about, and we get a clear and immediate read-out if you are drifting off track. I would always recommend using a transit where one is available, and I would always look for a natural transit, even if none is charted. However:

- Always check the bearing of a transit before you use it. In this case, it's drawn on the chart as 187°T which, with 1° of westerly variation, converts into 188°M.
- Even after a lifetime of navigating, I still need a few moments to work out which way to turn if the front marker slips to the right, or the left, of the rear marker:
  - If you're heading towards a transit and the front marker moves to the right of the rear marker, you need to steer to the right
  - If you're heading away from the transit and the front marker moves to the right of the rear marker, you need to steer left

Finally, we come to the Long Reach marked by a lit stern transit in the town, and a conspicuous line of beacons, also lit, on each side of the channel. We stay between the lines of beacons, guided by the transit, but ready to move to the starboard side of the channel if there is other shipping coming in. And all the time I would be keeping an eye on the echo sounder to make sure we're still safe. The line of this transit is 140°M.

Once clear of the Lymington River, we turn right and, to stay out of the worst of the tidal stream, I would plan to follow the 4-5m Charted Depth contour line (5.7-6.7m total depth of water at 1830 BST), steering

about 234°M, and heading just to the north of Hurst Castle. There are no obstructions on the way.

If the sounding starts dropping, I would turn left a bit, towards deeper water. The depth will fluctuate but if we keep the sounding greater than 5m, we'll be safe until we get to a point to the north east of Hurst Point when we can turn west and feel our way into the anchorage on the echo sounder, dropping the anchor about 200m off the beach in about 3.9m of water.

I would be tempted to put a GPS waypoint on my desired anchorage position – something like 50° 42'.61N. 001° 32'.93W. Using a waypoint is a simple way of finding your way into an anchorage.

I have always found this to be a reliable, sheltered anchorage, and we should be able to spend an easy night snugged up here without undue concern.

At some point on the run down to Hurst Point I would brief my crew on the anchorage, including the amount of cable to veer (20m on the waterline) and any other details.

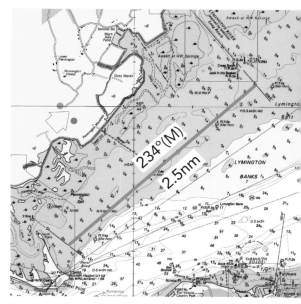

Passage to Hurst Castle

20
HURST CASTLE TO THE NEEDLES

0400 BST 20 June 2020

This is a short piece of pilotage, out through a long, narrow channel in the morning twilight. The channel is, however, well-marked both by day and by night and, so long as we stay clear of the Shingles Bank, we are free of dangers.

Probably the toughest thing on this leg will be the challenge of getting the crew up when the alarm goes off some time before 0400. If possible, I would have done all the preparations the night before, so that both I and the boat are ready for the off with minimum delay this morning. Given reasonable weather, however, there is nothing better than a summer sunrise under way, ideally with a toasted bacon sandwich and a good cup of coffee in your hand.

In the Chapter 19 we worked out that Low Water at Lymington is at 0423 BST, when the Height of Tide will be 0.9m. We should be able to feel our way out of this anchorage safely, however, by heading slowly down to the south, and staying in the deeper water before veering round to port, following the line of the coast about

100m to seaward. By watching the echo sounder closely, I would hope to be able to stay in deeper water.

Once out of the shallows, we skirt round Hurst Point, giving it a reasonable clearance, and I've drawn a track down the starboard side of the channel on a heading of 225°M. The channel is well marked by buoys, and I would keep a chart in the cockpit right down this leg (weighted down against the wind), so that I can tick off each buoy as we pass it, just buoy-hopping down the channel, and watching to see how the tidal stream is flowing on each one when we go by.

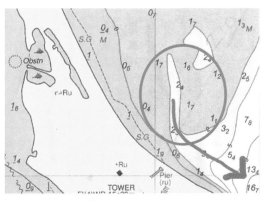

Leaving the anchorage

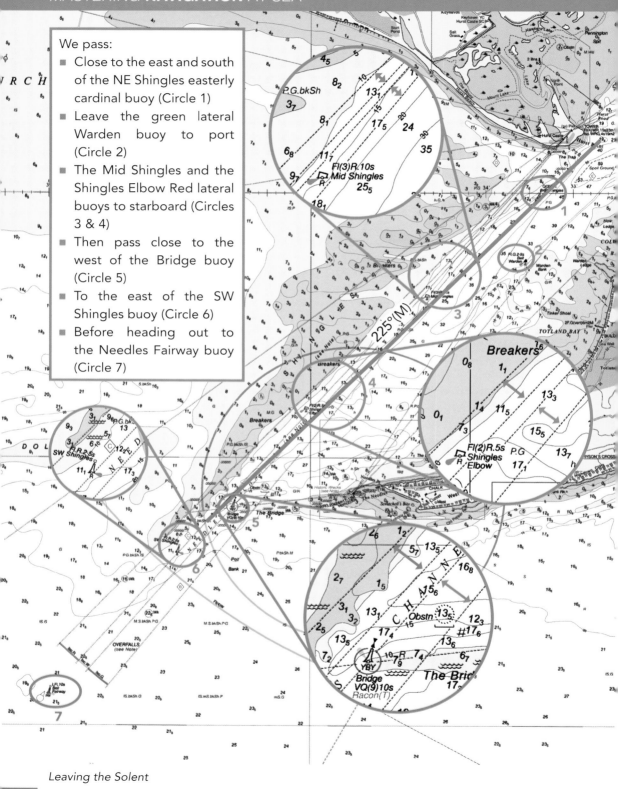

We pass:

- Close to the east and south of the NE Shingles easterly cardinal buoy (Circle 1)
- Leave the green lateral Warden buoy to port (Circle 2)
- The Mid Shingles and the Shingles Elbow Red lateral buoys to starboard (Circles 3 & 4)
- Then pass close to the west of the Bridge buoy (Circle 5)
- To the east of the SW Shingles buoy (Circle 6)
- Before heading out to the Needles Fairway buoy (Circle 7)

Leaving the Solent

There are 2 sectored lights overlooking this channel: the Needles Lighthouse, and the Hurst Point Lighthouse. Neither is perfect for keeping us on track but, as we move down the channel, we pass through the green sector of the Hurst Point light, and into the white sector. These sectors are really narrow; we could pass through them incredibly fast if we don't keep an eye on them but, other than the buoys, they are probably the best indicator we have that we're safe. The critical thing is to keep watching this back mark over the shoulder, and to check that somewhere just south of Mid Shingles buoy, we DO start moving into the green sector, and then into the white sector, but that we DON'T get into the red sector, which covers the Shingles Bank. The light is Isophase every 4 seconds: that is to say, shining for 2 seconds and dark for 2 seconds. If I found it turning red, I would quickly turn to port, back into the white sector.

I want to stay in deep water, greater than 10m all the way down the Needles Channel. There will be just about 1m Height of Tide, as I calculated for the anchorage, so we need to keep a beady eye on the echo sounder, which will fluctuate, but really should not fall below 11m total depth of water the whole way out.

Of course it's possible to cut across the Bridge, which is the shallow reef between the Needles and the Bridge buoy, but there can be overfalls there and, since we're heading in a roughly southwesterly direction across the Channel, there's no need to do so.

That said, as we start to get into more open water, we should be prepared for the direction and strength of both the wind and the tidal stream to change, and we need to be ready to deal with that. A passage through the Needles Channel is not a good time to be finishing off an exciting novel!

TIDAL STREAM PREDICTIONS (SATURDAY MORNING)

With an 0400 departure, I would have worked out the tidal streams for the Needles Channel the night before. I try to annotate the time in the top margin[68] of the *Tidal Stream Atlas* and put a small cross over my anticipated position at that time.

HW Portsmouth is the tidal reference for much of the Solent, and on the night of 19 June, HW Portsmouth is at 2335 BST, with a height of 4.4m. The next Low Water, the following morning, has a height of 1.2m – so this morning's tidal range is 3.2m: about 2/3 Springs.

	Time	m
19	0303	1.4
	1020	4.2
F	1519	1.4
	2235	4.4
	Time	**m**
20	0343	1.2
	1100	4.3
SA	1601	1.3
	2311	4.5

The *Tidal Stream Atlas* for 0435 BST (HW Portsmouth +5) shows weak and confused streams in the Needles Channel, right out from Hurst Castle to the Needles.

---

[68] The convention that we used in the Royal Navy of a 6-figure 'date-time group' works well here. The first 2 digits specify the date, 20th June, and the last 4 digits the time. It saves me from getting confused when I forget to rub out my previous workings.

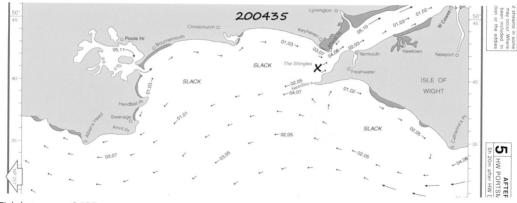

Tidal streams 0435

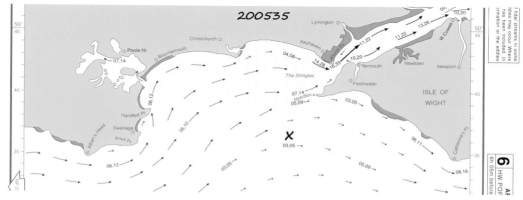

Tidal streams 0535

We should be passing the Needles Fairway Buoy shortly after 0435 BST (HW Portsmouth +5), in which case Tidal Diamond C (Circle 6 in previous chart) shows that we're right at the turn of the tide, with the start of a gentle easterly set at about 0.6kts.

As we start to clear the Needles Channel and head out into exposed waters, the boat and its crew need to be ready to encounter a heavier swell and stronger wind. Everything should be secure below, with the hatches shut and clipped; there should be no further need for anyone to venture out on the foredeck, and the crew should have been warned to prepare for slightly less benign conditions.

From here on, the tidal stream will slowly pick up, starting to run eastwards over the next 5 hours, before it turns and flows back to the west. But it starts slowly: one hour after passing the Fairway buoy, at 0535, the tidal stream is still only pushing us weakly to the east.

	Tidal Streams referred to														
	A 50°42'·93 N 1 38 ·58 W			B 50°39'·03 N 1 37 ·48 W			C 50°39'·41 N 1 37 ·38 W			D 50°42'·23 N 1 33 ·88 W			E 50°42 1 32	
−6	093	0·9	0·4	064	1·4	0·7	070	2·3	1·1	121	3·2	1·6	049	3·7
−5	100	1·0	0·5	076	2·2	1·1	086	3·1	1·5	114	3·2	1·6	053	3·9
−4	090	0·8	0·4	082	2·5	1·2	083	2·9	1·4	109	3·2	1·6	055	3·5
−3	089	0·7	0·4	083	2·3	1·1	081	2·4	1·2	108	3·0	1·5	057	3·5
−2	089	0·5	0·2	074	1·6	0·8	080	1·9	1·0	106	2·3	1·1	064	2·5
−1	260	0·4	0·2	074	0·7	0·3	082	0·9	0·4	282	0·9	0·4	263	0·2
0	277	0·8	0·4	268	0·9	0·5	278	1·2	0·6	291	3·2	1·6	235	2·8
+1	281	1·0	0·5	264	2·2	1·1	270	2·3	1·1	295	3·3	1·6	233	4·0
+2	270	0·9	0·5	258	2·2	1·1	267	2·6	1·3	294	3·3	1·6	232	4·4
+3	262	0·8	0·4	245	2·2	1·1	250	2·5	1·7	292	3·5	1·7	234	4·4
+4	263	0·4	0·2	241	1·9	0·9	251	3·0	1·5	289	2·2	1·1	238	2·2
+5	074	0·3	0·1	258	0·7	0·4	257	0·8	0·4	102	0·7	0·3	052	0·8
+6	090	0·8	0·4	048	0·9	0·5	062	1·3	0·6	119	2·8	1·4	047	3·3

The tables show we're right on the turn of the tide

21
THE NEEDLES TO THE CASQUETS

0500-1500 BST 20 June 2020

This leg of the passage, from the Needles Fairway Buoy to the Casquets, constitutes the lion's share of your passage, 65 miles in length, crossing the English Channel and some pretty busy shipping lanes. The predominant tidal stream is east / west, and it gets stronger in the vicinity of the French Coast and the Channel Islands. Otherwise, there are few obstructions, and this is an opportunity to settle into a pleasant cruising routine for 10 hours or so.

Chart 2454 'Start Point to the Needles' is a good choice for this passage. At 1:150,000, it is a good scale for an offshore passage and helpfully it covers this entire leg, which I have drawn as a single straight line directly from the Needles Fairway Buoy to a point about 5nm west of the Casquets. The direction of this track is 212°M.

CALCULATING THE EFFECT OF VARIATION

Variation is marked on *Chart 2454* as:

2° 30'W 2008 (8'E)

That is to say: in 2008, the direction of Magnetic North was 2° 30' to the west of True North, but it is reducing at a rate of 8' each year.

So, by 2020, 12 years later, the variation should have reduced by 8 x 12 minutes = 96' (1° 36'). With a very small amount of rounding up, you can safely use a variation of 1° W (2°30' – 1°36' = 0°56').

Going back to the two mnemonics for variation in Chapter 3:

'C - A - D - E - T'

And

'Cadbury's Dairy Milk Very Tasty'

You can work out the course to steer with a small table (with 'CADET' reversed) (see overleaf).

If you have a Deviation Card for your steering compass, then you should use it in this table. If not, and this is the norm for a small, plastic-hulled boat, use 0° for deviation.

As you clear the Needles Fairway Buoy,

TRUE	Variation	MAGNETIC	Deviation	COMPASS
211	1°W	212	0	212

you should be quite safe to turn a few degrees to port onto your next course of 212°M.

MAKING ALLOWANCE FOR THE TIDAL STREAMS

Whenever you are on a track that crosses the tidal stream you have to decide whether to stay on track or stay on course.

- **If you decide to remain on track**, you will inevitably have to steer off to counteract the tidal stream. If you do, a proportion of your forward speed will be taken up dealing with the tidal stream, and this will slow down your progress towards your destination. Staying on track gives you more precise control over your position and your end-point; it's useful in places where your freedom of movement is constrained – when you want to stay clear of shoal water or overfalls, for instance, or when you're working your way towards a waypoint in a strong tidal stream.

- **If you decide to remain on course**, that is to say you steer 212°(M) all the way across the Channel, you will make a

Needles to the Casquets

faster speed towards your destination, but you will find yourself swept off track, possibly by a quite substantial distance (see p161), and you need to make sure that this is going to be safe – and that you know where you are going to end up.

The night before setting out, I would have checked the effect of remaining on course across the Channel, adding up the hourly tidal stream predictions for the whole crossing, to see how far off track we would most likely end up.

For this, I have written the time on each page of the *Tidal Stream Atlas* and added a small pencil cross showing where I expect to be at that time. The *English Channel Tidal Stream Atlas* is referenced to HW Dover, which on the morning of 20 June 2020 occurs at 1123 BST. And we've already established that this is approximately ²/₃ Springs.

It is then just a question of noting

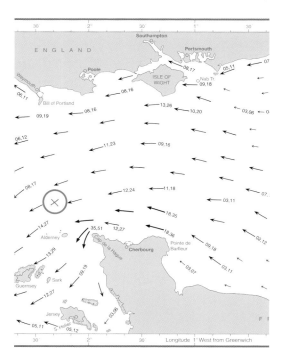

Marked up Tidal Stream Atlas for 1223

down each hourly set, with its direction (east or west). This requires a little eyeball interpolation, but it's not difficult to do. Although the tidal streams are measured in knots, they each equate to miles over a period of 1 hour.

If we pass the Needles Fairway Buoy at 0500 BST and arrive off the Casquets at 1400, the hourly set looks like this:
0.5E - 1.4E - 2.5E - 3.0E - 2.0E - 0.5E - 0.2W - 2.5W - 3.5W - 4.0W

By some strange alchemy, the total set comes out as 9.9nm East and 10.2nm West… so we should end up just about on track when we get to the Casquets, albeit having left a bit of a sinuous wake behind us across the Channel. And just as importantly, the maximum divergence from our track (the Cross-Track Error) will be 9.9nm to the east, at about 1100 BST, before the westerly set comes along to bring us back onto track. That will look a bit shocking on the chart, and I will certainly start to fret about being too far off track, but it's safe navigationally and if we hold the faith (and if our calculations are correct) nature will eventually drop us off at the right spot. When it works, it feels like a little bit of magic!

The track across the Channel is pretty straightforward, but on this passage our timings are quite tight, so we do need to keep an eye on progress during the crossing. It's worth keeping a summary of the passage plan in the notebook (Chapter 18) so we can refer to it on the way across.

The Casquets is our second tidal gate, and it's important to be there on time to catch the southwesterly tidal stream down to Guernsey. So, to help get the timing right at the Casquets, I have marked off the distance to that waypoint at 10nm intervals along the track. I will also put that waypoint into the GPS during this leg of the passage so that I have a constant read-out of bearing and distance. When working out the speed required to get to the Casquets at 1400, don't forget to factor in the fact that we'll enjoy a strong favourable tidal stream for the final couple of hours before we get there.

Weigh anchor Hurst Castle	No later than 0400 BST
Morning Civil Twilight	0406
Sunrise	0452
Clear of Needles Channel	0445
5nm west of Casquets	No later than 1400
Enter Little Russel Channel	1620
St Peter Port	1730

PLANNING YOUR ROUTE ACROSS THE SHIPPING LANES

When the COLREGs talk about crossing a shipping lane, they are referring to the lanes of mandatory one-way traffic in Traffic Separation Schemes. If you plan to cross these shipping lanes in any vessel, including a small sailing boat, you need to do so on a heading that is at right angles to the main traffic flow. But the density of heavy shipping continues unabated beyond the Separation Schemes, and in a small boat, we need to tread carefully whenever we're crossing the main shipping flow, here in the English Channel, or elsewhere. The chart helpfully shows the position and the recommended direction of the main traffic flows outside the Separation Schemes as a series of pecked magenta arrows.

On this passage, we will enter the main shipping flow when we get to a point about 30nm north east of the Casquets and stay with it for the next 21nm. As we established in Chapter 17, there is no obligation to turn onto a track at right angles to the traffic unless we find ourselves crossing a Separation Scheme.

You should nevertheless expect to find a great deal of heavy metal lumbering up and down this part of the Channel, and it's not good for our health, or for our boat insurance premiums, to get in its way. The traffic density is neither as compressed here, nor as dense as it is in the Straits of Dover, but it's likely that the Bridge Team on a large merchant ship in these more open waters will not be as sharp as they have to be in the Straits.

So this is a good time to stay alert, particularly if the visibility is not so good.

The planned track does clip the south-eastern corner of the Separation Zone (see p164), which is something that's frowned on by the COLREGs. If, when we get there, we find ourselves in a position where we're likely to intrude on a Separation Scheme, I would just make a short detour to avoid it and pass round the southern boundary. As luck would have it, the tidal stream will have set us to the east of the planned track, so the chances are that, on this crossing, we'll remain clear of the Separation Scheme as we pass its southeastern corner.

HURD DEEP

There is quite a nice little navigation indicator to watch out for as we approach the Casquets. From about 10nm to 5nm out from the Casquets, our track passes over the Hurd Deep (see p188) which should show up with a rapid increasing in sounding from about 60m to 100m, and back again. If we keep an eye in the echo sounder, this should give us a fairly clear confirmation of our position – or at least our latitude – as we approach the waypoint.

22

THE CASQUETS
TO THE LITTLE RUSSEL

1400-1630 BST 20 June 2020

As we pass the Casquets, I have switched to *Chart 2669 'Channel Islands and the Adjacent Coast of France'* which is another small scale chart at 1:150,000, but which will take us down safely to the point where we change again to the first pilotage chart, at the northern entrance to the Little Russel.

A straight track of 174°T (175°M) will take us down to the entrance to the Little Russel without difficulty. By this stage, we should be moving quite fast southwards towards the island of Guernsey with a strong tidal stream on our port quarter.

If we keep to the passage plan, and round the Casquets at 1400 (HW Dover +2½), we will find the tidal stream flowing at about 225° – 2.1kts at 1420 BST, then coming round to a more southerly direction and slackening to about 1.5 knots as we leave the main flow of the English Channel.

We're starting to move into more restricted coastal waters, so now it becomes important to stay on track – rather than staying on course. That means that we should start fixing more often,

probably about every 15 minutes, and we should be prepared to alter course if we start coming off track.

In fact, recognising the strength of the southwesterly flow as we turn south at the Casquets (we may well be seeing this on

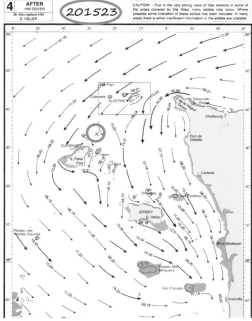

Tidal stream at 1523

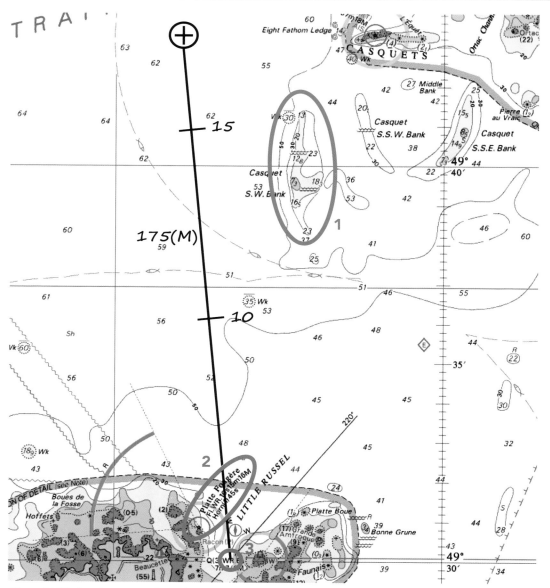

Chart 2669 showing route from the Casquets to the Little Russel

fishing floats in the water) we could usefully start off by steering about 15° to the east of our planned track (say 160°M), in order to compensate for the tidal stream.

There is one navigational danger on this route, before we get to the shoals that lie off the north coast of Guernsey, and it's potentially quite a nasty one. That is the Casquets SW Bank (Circle 1). With a minimum Charted Depth of 7.3m, we're not going to go aground on this bank, but in the severe tidal streams that flow through these waters, this bank will undoubtedly throw up heavy overfalls, particularly at Spring Tides and in heavy weather. The Bank is 3 miles off our track, and up-tide too so, although we'll keep an eye on it as we pass, it shouldn't trouble us as long as we're careful.

This leg is 17nm long, and at 7kts we can expect to finish it in 2½ hours, so we will enter the Little Russel at about 1630 BST, just as the tidal stream is starting to turn to the north.

STAYING ON TRACK

We can check that we're on track in one of two ways. In fact, given the strength of the tidal stream, I would recommend doing both.

The first is to **fix regularly** – probably every 15 minutes. I would plot the fix on the chart, and then steer to compensate for any divergence from the track. We need to be confident of our position here, as we approach the rocks lying off the north of Guernsey. It is, moreover, an area where we can expect to see a greater concentration of shipping: yachts, fishing boats and ferries, not to mention fishing floats… all of which adds to the watch-keeping load as we try to identify the navigation marks in the Little Russel.

It's important too to plot a DR and an EP with every fix on the chart so that we can project our position forward in full recognition of the effect that the tidal stream is having on the boat.

The second way of staying on track is to use a **headmark**. This is the point where we start moving back into pilotage territory, even before we enter the Russel itself. Our headmark can be a visual headmark, or a GPS waypoint.

VISUAL HEADMARK

The point at which we will see a visual headmark depends on the conditions: visibility, the direction of the sun, the Height of Tide, and the time of day. If we can see that far, our planned track takes us down to the mouth of the Little Russel (175°M), and has us heading straight for

the right-hand edge of the small island of Jethou, which is low-lying and not easy to see at the best of times.

In practice, we probably won't be able to pick this up, but we could use the very much more conspicuous mark of the Platte Fougere Light beacon (Circle 2), recognising that at about 2 miles distance, we'll need to veer to the east and follow a track into the Little Russel.

GPS WAYPOINT

Alternatively (and to be honest, this is my favourite option, and one that I have often employed on this leg), I would put a mid-water waypoint into the GPS at the next turning point. The GPS will then give us a constant read-out of range and bearing to the waypoint. We can use this to all intents and purposes as a headmark and run down the 175°M bearing line until we reach the next leg.

As luck would have it, there is quite a neat waypoint at 49° 30'.0N 002° 28'.0W (Circle 3), which brings us right onto the 220°T (221°M) transit line down to the mouth of the harbour entrance. I would put that position into the GPS as a waypoint and use it as my mid-water headmark as we approach the Little Russel from the north.

- When the waypoint bears 175°M, we're on track
- If the bearing starts increasing, to 176° or 177°, we are to port of track, and need to adjust our course to starboard to bring the bearing back
- If it starts to decrease (which is more likely with this tidal stream), we are to starboard of track, and need to turn to port to bring the bearing back again

This is an accurate and very sensitive method for approaching landfalls when you want to remain exactly on track.

As we approach this waypoint, I would

be working hard to identify the navigation marks in the Little Russel so that, when we turn in, I'll know which to keep to starboard and which to port. For complex passages like this, there are often diagrams or photographs of the principal navigation marks on the chart, as well as in the pilot book and the *Almanac*.

I would also be watching every fishing float we pass for the first indication that the tidal stream is starting to turn against us, which should happen at about 1620 BST; this observed tidal stream will also allow us to make appropriate compensations in our heading, in order to remain on track.

HARBOUR ENTRY INFORMATION

The *Almanac* (Section 9.19.11) carries some very useful information about port entry communications. This is worth reading on the way down to the Russel.

WHAT FREQUENCIES WOULD I MONITOR?

- Notwithstanding DSC, I would still listen out on Channel 16 at all times at sea, including as you approach your destination
- As we come into the Little Russel from the north, I would be increasingly interested in ferry and big ship movements, together with anything that the harbour office has to say to nearby shipping, so I would dual monitor Channel 16 and Channel 12, the Port Control frequency, recognising that they really don't want us to transmit on this frequency unless it is 'absolutely necessary'
- Later, as we get into the harbour, we can, if necessary, establish communications

with the Marina Control on Channel 80 and work out where they want us to berth, although here in St Peter Port, during the summer months, this is often done from a tender in the harbour entrance

ONBOARD ADMINISTRATION

If it's calm enough, and the situation is sufficiently well under control, I would use the second half of the leg from the Casquets to the Little Russel for final entry preparations. Things like:

- Make sure that the entry charts are to hand.
- I would re-read the pilot book, so that I can recognise the shapes and colours of the navigation marks as they appear.
- Make sure that I've calculated the Height of Tide for St Peter Port.
- Crew briefed.
- Cockpit stowed away for entering harbour, with novels, cushions, cameras and the debris of lunch all packed down below.
- Decide when to drop the sails and get out ropes and fenders.
- Do we need to be flying a courtesy flag? This flies on the starboard yardarm – displacing the yacht club burgee to the port yardarm. If so, try to get it up before you enter the port. Also (and I've never yet seen this happen), the Almanac suggests that yachts visiting Guernsey must fly a Q[69] flag until customs clearance has been obtained. This might happen more widely on the continent in the future, post Brexit. So, just to be safe, I would make sure that I have a Flag Q onboard.

---

[69] Flag 'Q' is a square yellow flag that is flown to indicate that customs clearance has yet to be given. In practice, it is not very often used, but it's useful to have one in your flag locker, just in case. It is flown on the port yard arm; the courtesy flag of the country that you're visiting being on the starboard yard arm.

23

THE LITTLE RUSSEL INTO ST PETER PORT

1630-1730 BST 20 June 2020

This leg is pure pilotage, from start to finish.

There's a fair number of people who find the whole business of entering harbour quite stressful. I can understand that: there's a lot to think about but, at the same time, most of it is quite predictable, and, as ever, the secret of doing it well is to put in the preparation beforehand. In a nutshell:

- I would have prepared the charts and drawn the tracks into the harbour; I will have worked out how to remain on track on each leg
- We should know how the water will flow as we approach the harbour, and how those flows will change (often quite significantly) with both time and position
- Heights of Tide calculated, with the minimum safe sounding on each leg
- Worked out what the various navigation marks will look like, so that I can identify them at a distance and mentally plot our course, leaving some to port and others to starboard
- I would expect to know the speed limits

- Crew briefed in advance
- I would be listening out on VHF for any big shipping movements that might affect us

Other than that, it's a walk in the park…. Actually, if you've got your head around all this (and it's not as difficult as it looks), it WILL be a walk in the park, and you can quietly, if a little smugly, feel properly in control of your boat as you nuzzle into the safety of a sheltered harbour after a long passage.

The Little Russel can be quite demanding, although I've never found it to be a particularly difficult challenge by day or by night; on the contrary, it is an interesting and unusual harbour approach, and there's no need for a yachtsman to shy away from it. I would, however, have to think seriously before entering the Little Russel in poor visibility. It would be easier and safer, if a lot longer, to go right round the outside of Herm, through the Big Russel and either anchor off Sark, or feel your way into St Peter Port – depending on the strength and direction of the wind and the tidal stream.

THE APPROACH TRACK

Passing the Platte Fougere Light (Circle 1), I would move to a larger scale chart, *Chart 5604.10* from the *UKHO Channel Islands Small Craft Folio*[70], and use this chart to manage my alteration of course into the Little Russel. This chart, which is scaled at 1:25,000, is ideal for this part of the passage, and it has the added advantage of being small enough to sit easily with you in the cockpit without getting in the way.

From the waypoint at the top of the Little Russel (49° 30'.0N 002° 28'.0W – Circle 2), I would run straight down the lit transit on 221°M, towards the harbour entrance. This passes to the north of the Roustel beacon (Circle 3), leaving the Platte beacon (Circle 4) to starboard, and Brehon (Circle 5) to port. It passes over 2 patches with a Charted Depth of 2.3m and 2.5m (Circle 6) and extends right down to the harbour entrance.

This is an easy transit to follow, with 2 strong headmark lights by night, and by day the breakwater lighthouse (Circle 7) in transit with Belvedere House (Circle 8) on top of the cliffs, behind.

It is, however, quite a narrow channel, and the tidal stream will probably throw us around a bit, so once we've established ourselves on the transit, I would be working hard to ensure that we stay there.

TIDAL STREAMS

There's a lot of water constantly in motion round here, and I wouldn't even think of moving around the Channel Islands by boat without working out the Height of Tide and the strength of the tidal streams in advance. There are of course two main sources of data on tidal streams: the Tidal Diamonds, and the *Tidal Stream Atlas*.

St Peter Port Harbour – we're nearly there (© Aurora GSY / shutterstock.com)

---

[70] As I write, the UKHO is considering ending its supply of Small Craft Folios. If they do, the information will, however, still be available through other sources: digital or printed, Admiralty or Imray.

TIDAL DIAMOND

On the chart, Tidal Diamond C (Circle 9 – actually diamond B on *Chart 5604.10*) is situated right in the middle of the Little Russel Channel, and referenced to HW St Helier. St Helier is a Standard Port, so there is no need to mess around with Secondary Port calculations – but don't forget to add an hour to convert the times to British Summer Time.

TIDAL STREAMS

...ation at position B only reflects the Tidal Streams in the ...ose experienced between Saint Peter Port pier heads or i

Tidal Streams referred to HW at SAINT HELIE

Hours		Geographical Position		49°28'·64 N 2 29 ·78 W			49°26'·44 N 2 26 ·38 W		E
Before High Water	6	Directions of streams (degrees)	Rates at spring tides (knots)	Rates at neap tides (knots)	213	5·1 2·2	212	5·4 2·2	21
	5				213	4·1 1·8	214	5·0 2·1	21
	4				213	2·7 1·2	213	3·1 1·3	21
	3				213	1·2 0·5	353	0·2 0·1	11
	2				033	1·2 0·5	049	3·9 1·6	04
	1				033	3·9 1·7	045	4·8 2·0	03
High Water					033	5·2 2·2	040	4·9 2·0	03
After High Water	1				033	4·9 2·1	034	4·0 1·6	03
	2				033	3·3 1·4	040	2·2 0·9	02
	3				033	1·5 0·5	022	0·9 0·4	01
	4				213	1·3 0·5	234	0·7 0·3	22
	5				213	4·0 1·7	213	2·4 1·0	21
	6				213	5·2 2·2	214	5·0 2·1	21

Tide tables for diamond C

From the *Tide Tables*, you get the following for the times of High and Low Water at St Helier:

Tide Times St Helier Afternoon June 2020		
Time (BST)	Height (m)	Tidal Range
1313 (LW)	2.3	7.8m which equates to appoximately ²⁄₃ Springs
1852 (HW)	10.1	

Assuming that you arrive at the top of the Little Russel at any time from 1600 BST onwards, you can make another small table for the predicted tidal stream at diamond C:

Little Russel Diamond C Tidal Stream Prediction			
Time (BST)	Time in Relation to HW St Helier	Tidal Stream Direction	Tidal Stream Rate (kts)
1552	HW – 3	213	0.9
1652	HW – 2	033	0.9
1752	HW – 1	033	3.1
1852	HW	033	4.2

The tide will be turning to the northeast at 1600, and then strengthening considerably as it picks up power. There is a lot to be said for getting to the top of the Little Russel early, if possible. It will get increasingly uncomfortable from about 1700 onwards.

TIDAL STREAM ATLAS

The *Tidal Stream Atlas* tells a similar story. The page titled '4 hours after HW Dover' also carries the legend: '3h 40m before HW St Helier' – in other words: 1512 BST. For ease of reference, I have once again written the 'date-time group' in the margin, signifying 1512 on the 20th of the month. Interestingly, this is exactly the same page of the tidal stream atlas that we used in Chapter 22 when I referenced it to HW Dover, and titled this page 1523 BST – the time difference is not significant.

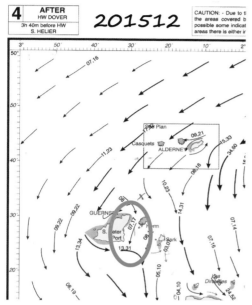

Tidal Stream Atlas at 1512

The diagram shows the strength of the tidal stream as: 07,17. This indicates that the Neap Rate is 0.7kts, and the Spring Rate is 1.7kts.

So, on 20 June ($^2/_3$ Springs) at 1512

BST, the rate will be about 1.4kts, flowing south through the Little Russel.

An hour later, at 1612, the rate[71] is 01,03 which is more-or-less slack water, and an hour after that, at 1712, it rises to 13,30 – giving us about 2.5 kts of contrary tidal stream: the start of the northeasterly set.

HEIGHT OF TIDE

Wherever the direct flow of the tide is blocked by an obstruction, you tend to get strong tidal streams and impressive tidal ranges. In this part of the world, the Cotentin Peninsula, which runs from the Mont St Michel northwards to Cherbourg, is a massive blockage to the flow of water, and this in turn amplifies the tidal effects in the Channel Islands, lying just to the west of the peninsula. These tides can at times be quite frightening and should not be underestimated by any mariner.

Calculating the Height of Tide at St Peter Port on the afternoon and evening of 20 June is not difficult. This too is a Standard Port, so it's just a case of reading the times and the heights directly out of the tables.

And from here it is relatively simple to calculate the predicted Height of Tide, using the St Peter Port Height of Tide graph from the *Tide Tables* or *Almanac*:

Tide Times St Peter Port Afternoon 20 June 2020		
Time (BST)	Height (m)	Tidal Range
1313 (LW)	2.1	
1903 (HW)	8.5	6.5, which equates to appoximately $^2/_3$ Springs
21 0124 (HW)	2.0	

---

[71] The information in this paragraph is taken from the next couple of pages in the *Tidal Stream Atlas*, which are not shown here.

Height of Tide St Peter Port Afternoon 20 June 2020		
Time (BST)	Time in Relation to HW St Peter Port	Height of Tide (m)
1903	HW	8.5
1803	HW –1	8.0
1703	HW –2	6.8
1603	HW –3	5.5
1503	HW –4	3.8
1403	HW –5	2.6

HEIGHT OF TIDE OVER THE SILL INTO THE VICTORIA MARINA

There are very good visitors' pontoons in the outer harbour, so we don't have to enter the marina at St Peter Port. But if we choose to go into the marina, we would need to calculate the Height of Tide over the marina's entrance sill, a sort of cofferdam that dries 4.2m above Chart Datum and keeps boats in the marina afloat at Low Water.

With a draught of 1.7m, I would like to enter the marina with at least 2m of water over the sill, so I would be looking for a Height of Tide of 4.2 + 2 metres, or 6.2m.

The simplest thing is to predict the time when this will occur with the Height of Tide graph that we used to draw up the table (opposite). Looking at the graph, this occurs 2 hours and 25 minutes before High Water – at 1638 BST.

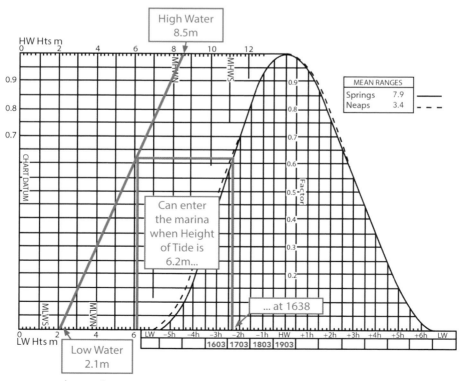

When to enter the marina

There's also a small table in *Reed's Nautical Almanac*, at Section 9.19.11 under Tidal Access, which usefully does this calculation for you as well.

There is also a tide gauge on each side of the marina entrance showing depth of water over the sill – so you can do your own last-minute idiot-check before committing yourself.

MINIMUM DEPTH OF WATER IN THE LITTLE RUSSEL

Passing through the Little Russel at about 1630, you will have 6.1m of water above Chart Datum. If you stick to your track, the minimum Charted Depth you will pass over, or close to, is the Boue Agenor and Trois Grunes shoals (Circle 6) about a mile northeast of the harbour entrance, with a minimum Charted Depth of 2.3m – so the minimum expected depth of water is 6.1 + 2.3 = 8.4m.

Many of the rocky outcrops on each side of the channel appear to be steep-sided, which means that you will have very little warning from the echo sounder before hitting one, so I would be thinking of using Chart Datum as my limiting sounding line. I would therefore try to remain within the white section of the chart, avoiding anything that is blue or green, and work on the minimum safe depth of water being 6.5m (call it 7.0m). This gives you a pretty hefty (and comfortable) margin of safety.

THE TIGHTEST PARTS OF THE PASSAGE DOWN THE LITTLE RUSSEL

Where are the tightest parts of this passage and how will I stay safe as I pass through them? This is a good question to ask before any bit of pilotage, because there will always be stretches that are more complex and demanding than others.

These are very often where the channel is squeezed into a narrow space with more complex water flow, greater traffic density and frequent changes of course. It's useful to look for these 'squeezes' well in advance and think your way through them in your head.

On this leg, the squeeze starts at Roustel Beacon (Circle 3); it lasts for about a mile and ends when you pass Brehon (Circle 5). The channel here is only about 3-4 cables (600-800 yards) wide, the bottom is uneven, and you can expect the tidal stream to run faster, with surface turbulence caused by the rocky seabed.

In tight spaces like this, clearing bearings of the headmark with a hand-held magnetic compass will probably not be accurate enough to reliably keep you safe, so I would always look for natural transits to give me my clearing marks. In this case, there's a very strong main entry transit – between Cornet Castle (Circle 7) and Belvedere House (Circle 8) on the hilltop – which is ideal for keeping us on track.

If we're forced off the transit by other shipping, and particularly if this happens while we're passing through the tightest part of the Little Russel, we'll need to make sure that we don't diverge by much more than 100-150 metres from the transit. If I was pushed off the transit, I would go as far off track as I was comfortable with and then look for a natural transit ahead of the boat: perhaps between the end of the Castle Cornet and some other conspicuous point on the hilltop. I would then use this natural transit, and stay on it, until I was happy to come back onto the main track.

CHECK OUT THE NAVIGATION MARKS

There are many reference publications where we can check the appearance of these navigation marks in advance: The *Shell Channel Pilot, Reed's Nautical Almanac* and even the chart: *Admiralty Leisure Chart Folio 5604, chart 10.*

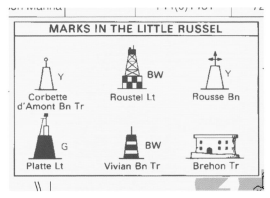

Marks in Little Russel on Chart 5604.10

The good thing is that there's little danger of confusing one mark for another: they're all very different, by day and by night. This is nicely illustrated by the chartlet (right) from the Guernsey Harbours website at: http://www.harbours.gg

COMMUNICATIONS

As you get closer to St Peter Port, I would want to make sure that we're monitoring the correct VHF frequencies. In this case, Guernsey VTS[72] on Channel 12 or 67, will keep us informed of any impending commercial or big ship movements, but this frequency is not to be used for 'berthing information or general enquiries'.

To find out where to berth, we could call St Peter Port Marinas on Channel 80, which is only available at certain times of the day, or else just wait until we get into the harbour where, in the summer months, there is often an incredibly helpful person from the port authority, afloat in a small boat, who will direct us to our berth.

Guernsey Approaches from the Harbour website (© Guernsey Harbours)

DESTINATION

As we approach the harbour entrance, we'll change chart to the harbour plan of *St Peter Port, Chart 5604*.11 which is drawn to a very large scale, at 1:6,000.

It's important to get the big distractions out of the way before you get to this point. Things like dropping the sails, getting out and securing ropes and fenders, etc. Small harbours with heavy shipping demand a great deal of concentration.

In St Peter Port, the harbour rightly segregates small leisure boats from the commercial traffic. To that end, you will

---

[72] VTS stands for 'Vessel Transit Service'; it's the harbour control frequency for commercial shipping.

find a small buoyed and lit channel on the southern side of the harbour which is exclusively set aside for you and me. This lane means that we won't obstruct the big ships on tight timescales that use the port, and it also avoids people feeling the need to shout at us.

In a harbour, it's important to obey the speed limits. It is 6kts from the Outer Pier Heads to a line south from New Jetty to Castle Pier, and 4kts to the west of this line.

I always start to suffer from FOMO[73] about half an hour before arriving at a destination – the growing certainty that the boat right ahead will take the last available place in the harbour, and that we'll be left with nowhere to go. So, quite irrationally, I start to go faster and faster,

trying desperately to overtake everyone in sight… until my wife tells me not to be such an idiot. All I can say to anyone else who finds themselves behaving like this is that my wife (as ever) is right: just relax, because it always seems to work out just fine, and there really is no need to exceed the speed limits.

Finally, as we enter the harbour, I would start worrying about coming alongside, checking out the wind and any movement of the water close to the berth – so that I can plan my approach. Do we need to make any special arrangements to get alongside, or will we be OK going straight in? As ever, the more I think it through, the more swanky it will look (and the safer it will be).

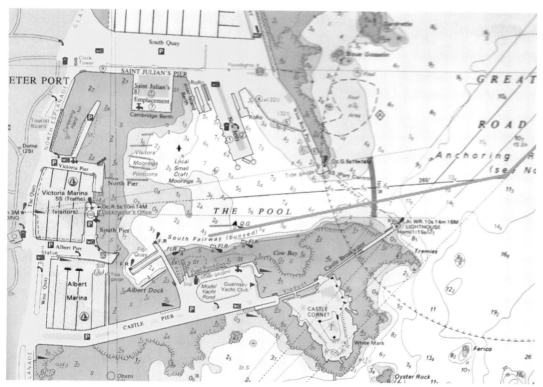

We now use the very large scale chart of St Peter Port (for reproduction reasons we are actually showing Chart 3140)

---

[73] FOMO: Fear Of Missing Out.

24
SOME CAUTIONARY TALES

The sea is a serious place, and it doesn't take kindly to people who don't take it seriously: they put themselves, and very often their families and friends, at unnecessary risk.

In the spirit of helping other people to learn from my own misfortunes, I have set out a few stories throughout the book (all of them true) that have had an impact on me over the years. I have added to the rogues' gallery with a few more cautionary tales in this chapter. Most of these relate to mistakes that I have made – and a few to others who have had unfortunate experiences on the water.

There is no shame in making mistakes; what matters is that we all learn from our mistakes, and those of others.

I guess that the common theme is that all of the incidents that I've set down here could all have been avoided with a little more forethought and better planning.

If you have a cautionary tale to tell, send it to me via my publisher at **fernhurst@fernhurstbooks.com** and I will include the most interesting in subsequent editions of this book.

1. LEAVE SOME MARGIN FOR ERROR

From time to time we're all guilty of cutting things too fine. Some years ago, I came within a whisker of embarrassing myself greatly at the entrance to the Victoria Marina in St Peter Port. We wanted to get into the marina on a falling tide, but we arrived at the harbour entrance later than expected. I had carefully calculated the Height of Tide, and I reckoned that we would get to the sill with precisely enough water to cross it, but with absolutely no margin for error at all.

When we got to the marina entrance, I decided to go for it and, of course, within seconds we started grinding the keel along the bottom as we approached the sill. It was only because Susie, my quick-thinking wife on the helm, went hard astern and backed out as rapidly as possible that we avoided going hard aground in a very public place, where we would have remained for the next 6 hours. It was a schoolboy error – the result of wishful thinking in the face of overwhelming evidence to the contrary –

and it was certainly not one of my golden sailing moments.

2. UNDERSTAND THAT PREDICTED WATER LEVELS ARE JUST THAT – PREDICTED

On my first sailing trip to the Channel Islands, when I was still a teenager, we took refuge from a westerly gale at Spring Tides in the small harbour of Gorey on the east coast of Jersey. It was a horrible night with a strong wind and belting rain. The height of the tide had been enhanced by the wind, and at High Water the waves were lapping over the top of the breakwater where we were berthed. The whole family spent an unhappy couple of hours standing on the pier, with the waves lapping at our feet, desperately fending the boat off and trying to stop it from damaging itself against the top of the wall. Eventually the tide and the wind subsided and we turned in – only to be woken a few hours later, in the early dawn twilight, by loud diesel engines and a lot of shouting as a small French sailing boat was towed into the harbour by the lifeboat, and secured to the harbour wall behind us. A very frightened young couple were sitting in the cockpit.

It turned out that they had anchored further up the coast as the wind freshened, but they didn't have enough cable on their anchor to accomodate for the tidal surge caused by the storm. To make matters worse, the anchor cable was shackled to the hull of the boat, and the shackle had corroded so that it couldn't be released, particularly with the cable under load. As the tide came in, the couple paid out all the cable they had, but it wasn't enough – and slowly their boat started to dip by the bow, being dragged under by the now taut anchor cable. They put out a Mayday call and were rescued by the lifeboat and

its big pair of bolt croppers, and they were towed in.

I learnt a lot from that episode:
- I saw at first-hand how a strong wind or a deep depression can significantly raise the water level beyond the predicted levels
- You need to have more anchor cable onboard than you ever think you will use
- The 'bitter end' of the cable should be lashed onto the boat with rope – so that it can be cut, and the cable released, in an emergency
- And this incident, more than anything else, showed me how dangerous these waters can be, and that you need to be careful if you want to navigate them safely

3. SOLO NIGHT PASSAGE FROM LYMINGTON TO GOSPORT

It was February and we needed to relocate our boat from Lymington to Gosport, a passage of about 20 miles east along the Solent. I was spending the night onboard the boat, on my own, and before I turned in I checked the tides and discovered that the east-going flood would start at about 2am, which would make for an easy night-time passage up to Gosport. The night was cold and clear with light airs. I woke up at 2am and, sure enough, the conditions looked fine to just nip across to Gosport.

Having checked the tides, and put on my lifejacket, I slipped the ropes and worked my way out of the Lymington Yacht Haven, down the Lymington River. It was an absolutely lovely night for a gentle passage under power. I remember the clarity of the shore lights, the shipping, the buoys and the stars. The water was calm, and we were making good about 10 knots with the tide behind us.

But as I approached Gilkicker Fort,

it all changed. A couple of miles west of Gosport, the shore lights dimmed and disappeared, and I suddenly realised that I had entered a fog bank. I switched on the radar, but the display was in the saloon, and the only way I could see it was to leave the wheel and go below.

I found my way into Portsmouth Harbour without too much difficulty, passing an unseen ferry in the fog at a range of about half a mile, and as I turned into Haslar Creek the visibility started to lift to reveal the clear night sky once again.

But once I was safely tucked up, reality caught up with me. In my enthusiasm to get away, I hadn't considered the possibility of fog, or what I would do if I hit fog – which was never going to be easy in that boat, single-handed at night. In fact, to tell the truth, I can't even remember listening to a weather forecast before setting out.

What did I learn from this?

- I should have listened to the forecast, and in the event that fog was forecast, I should not have left the marina
- There is no problem with a single-handed passage; even at night they can be performed safely, but they require more planning, not less – and you do need to ask yourself a few tough what-ifs before you set out

4. LOG TOWING OFF VANCOUVER

We have twice chartered a sailing boat from Nanaimo Yacht Charters on Vancouver Island: it's impossible not to love sailing in the wild, beautiful and sheltered waters of the Strait of Georgia between Vancouver and Vancouver Island. But there are dangers.

There is a massive logging industry around the coast of British Columbia, and these waters are used extensively to transport logs from the forests to the pulp mills on the mainland. As a result, there is the ever-present danger of striking a waterlogged piece of timber just below the surface, which can do considerable damage to your hull.

One morning, sailing northwards towards Desolation Sound, we saw a tug with a black diamond in the rigging, indicating a tow greater than 200m in length. We could see a tow cable from its stern arcing down into the water, but we couldn't see any vessel being towed. We were going to pass quite close, so I altered to starboard to pass a respectable distance astern. We were happily chatting away when Susie looked over the bow and asked *"What's that?"*

It turned out to be the tow: a long, semi-submerged raft of logs, about 200m ahead of us, starting some 400m astern of the tug and about half a mile in length. It was nearly invisible from any distance, and so far astern of the tug that we had almost stopped looking for the tow. If Susie hadn't been so vigilant, we would almost certainly have run into it. Happily, this isn't a mistake that any of us is likely to make twice.

What did I learn?

- Read the pilot book.... It was all there! Different sea areas have different hazards, and the more that you can learn from the pilot books, from locals and from your own observation before you set out, the better placed you will be.

If a tug is signalling that it's tow exceeds 200m, it probably does

- Don't make assumptions. I had assumed that because I couldn't see a tow, that there wasn't anything on the line astern of the tug. Tugs don't gratuitously trail a tow rope in the water with a black diamond in their rigging. There was a tow, and I should have known it.

5. HITTING THE BOTTOM OF A SCOTTISH LOCH

The thing about navigating a submarine is that you have the opportunity to go aground in places that other vessels can only dream of – like 120ft below the surface of a Scottish Loch. This was a long time ago in a diesel-powered submarine, and we were in a loch for the day using the silence of the waters to accurately map our sound signature. This involved running up and down the loch both at periscope depth, and some way below the surface, passing over underwater hydrophones that could hear and record the noises that we were making. It was a lovely still day, and there was one yacht out and about on the southern end of the noise range, happily pottering along in the sunshine.

At the start of the 5th run of the day, the Captain took a look through the periscope before we went deep, and gave me, the navigator, the range and bearing of the yacht. I plotted its position on the chart: they were right at the spot where we would return to periscope depth at the other end of the run. "*No problem*," said the Captain. "*At the end of this run, we'll stay deep to turn, and return to periscope depth after the 6th run.*"

So, at the southern end of the range we slowed down as much as possible, applied full starboard rudder and started turning… right up to the point where we hit the side of the loch. We surfaced in a hurry, much to the surprise of the yacht, and assessed the damage (which was slight). Happily, no-one had been hurt.

This was an interesting incident because it is always so tempting to extemporise and to do something a little out of the ordinary, often without thinking it through as carefully as one should, and without making a proper navigation plan. When we came to reconstruct this manoeuvre, we realised that the loch narrows so much as you get deeper that this was always going to be a risky manoeuvre, and the one instrument that could have kept us safe, the echo sounder, had been switched off as a result of the need for silence on the noise range.

We should never have attempted this turn. The Captain should not have attempted it, and I should have stopped him from doing so. We were all perhaps just a little bit naive.

- In a yacht, just as in a submarine, you should only embark on risky manoeuvres with adequate thought and preparation. It is almost always a mistake to do so on the spur of the moment.
- If a manoeuvre looks like it will be difficult, or if there is someone in your way, have the patience to wait and let things settle down before you go for it. The right thing to have done in this case would have been to stop and wait for the yacht to move away before we started the 5th run.
- Anyone onboard must be able to speak up if they think that something risky is going on. I didn't do this, and I should have done.

6. LOST, IN SIGHT OF THE ISLE OF WIGHT

Some years ago, I was navigator of a submarine, and we were on the surface, heading back into the Channel after a period of operations in the Atlantic. As we were approaching the south coast of the Isle of Wight, the electrical circuit linking the gyro compass to the many repeaters around the Control Room and the bridge failed, freezing the compass repeats in position. Since it was the middle of the night and we were on a steady course, just to the north of east, this failure didn't become immediately apparent. The log entries did in fact record a growing discrepancy between the gyro compass and the magnetic compass, but the watch keepers just put down to crankiness in the magnetic compass (a device which they never paid much attention to anyway).

We were navigating with Decca, and from about midnight onwards, the Decca fixes started diverging from the planned track, but not by enough for the watch keepers to call me out of my bunk. It was only at about 6am when I got up to take over on the bridge that my predecessor pointed over the starboard side, and told me excitedly that: "*The visibility is just AWESOME – you can see all the way to Cherbourg, as if it was just 10 miles away.*"

Well, the land was just 10 miles away on the starboard beam, but this wasn't Cherbourg – it was the Isle of Wight. Over the preceding 30 minutes, the submarine had turned in a full half-circle, and no-one had noticed. I really would not have believed that to be possible if I hadn't been there myself.

This episode taught me a really important lesson: very often there are small tell-tales that are the early indicators of something going wrong. You need to watch out for these, and react, or at least check, when things don't look right. If the watch keepers had picked up the discrepancy between the magnetic and gyro compasses a couple of hours earlier, this potentially very dangerous situation would have been sorted out long before it developed into something truly embarrassing.

7. A LAZY DAY IN MID-CHANNEL

It was one of those beautiful sailing days, with a gentle swell rolling up the Channel, blue skies flecked with contrails and a clear horizon. We were half-way across the Channel, from Studland Bay to St Vaast, with the mainsail and genoa up, and the engine adding a few knots on top of that. There was no other shipping that was likely to bother us. Susie was below in the saloon and the autopilot was taking the strain of keeping us on track.

I was alone in the cockpit and I'm ashamed to say that I started reading a novel. It was the sort of book that just draws you in, and the next thing I knew, 15 minutes had passed (I hadn't been keeping a good lookout) and ' saw a big Sunseeker motorboat speed about 100m away, heading n towards the Solent. Looking up, I c see anyone on the helm, or on the brid – or anywhere else for that matte close enough for us to roll around viol in her wake.

We had been a whisker away fron a collision by neglect. Two boats, each believing that they were alone on an empty sea but closing each other at a combined speed of 40 knots. Neither of us was keeping a lookout, and to be honest I couldn't say that the owner of the other boat even realised how close they had come to a big, ugly collision. It was quite an eye-opener.

I learnt, or should I say relearnt one of the vital, the age-old lessons of the sea: always, always, always keep a good lookout – even if you think you're miles for the closest ship. It's surprising how quickly people can creep up on you.